The MEN and
the MOUNTAIN

The MEN and the MOUNTAIN

FRÉMONT'S FOURTH EXPEDITION

by

WILLIAM BRANDON

WILLIAM MORROW & COMPANY
New York   b   1955

To Betty

Contents

Acknowledgments

I am indebted to many people for help in writing this book. My very grateful thanks to:

The Henry E. Huntington Library and Art Gallery, San Marino, California, for permission to use excerpts from the Kern Diaries and other manuscript material and letters and to reproduce a part of R. H. Kern's "Map of the Territory of New Mexico" from an excellent copy in the Library's collections; the Bancroft Library of the University of California, Berkeley, for permission to publish excerpts from manuscript material included in the Frémont Miscellany and from the manuscript of the Thomas S. Martin Narrative; and the Southwest Museum, Los Angeles, for permission to publish excerpts from papers and letters in its Frémont collection.

The entire staff of the Huntington Library, where I worked periodically for several years while pursuing the fourth expedition, for much kindness and assistance.

The Missouri Historical Society for considerable useful material.

Dr. Robert Glass Cleland and Dr. LeRoy R. Hafen for many instances of expert information and advice. Dr. Ralph P. Bieber, who furnished a number of otherwise unfindable newspaper items from his remarkable files.

Mark Ratliff, District Ranger, U.S. Forest Service, Del Norte, Colorado, with whom I rode on the trail of the expedition; Ambrose Burkhart, Senior Clerk, U.S. Forest Service;

Antonio J. N. Valdez, Del Norte; Harold Ford, Masonic Park, Colorado; Mr. and Mrs. Ira Goodman, Del Norte; and Stanley Walker, South Fork, Colorado; all of whom helped reveal the mountains and their past.

WILLIAM BRANDON

St.-Paul-de-Vence, France
Devonshire, England

Dramatis Personae

THE LEADER:
Ex-Lieutenant Colonel John Charles Frémont, age 35, explorer

THE GUIDE:
Old Bill Williams, age 61, mountain man

THE VETERANS:
Alexis Godey, a young man of the mountains
Henry King, a recent bridegroom
Edward M. (Ned) Kern, a young artist
Charles Preuss, German, topographer
Raphael Proue, French, an engagé
Charles Van Linneus Taplin, a young frontiersman
John Scott, a hunter
Thomas E. Breckenridge, a young Missourian
Thomas Salathiel Martin, a Tennessee backwoodsman
Lorenzo D. Vincenthaler, a courtier
Manuel, a Cosumne Indian
Joaquin, a Tulare Indian
Gregorio, a Tulare Indian
Carver, from Illinois
George Hubbard, from the Iowa border
Joseph L. Stepperfeldt, a gunsmith
Benjamin Beadle, of St. Louis County
Antoine Morin, an old engagé

Vincent (Sorrel) Tabeau, an engagé
Longe, an engagé
Josiah Ferguson, from Missouri
Billy Bacon, of St. Louis County

THE GREENHORNS:
Richard H. (Dick) Kern, an artist, brother of Ned
Dr. Benjamin J. Kern, brother of Ned, physician
Frederick Creutzfeldt, a botanist
Henry Rohrer, a millwright
Henry J. Wise, from St. Louis
Midshipman Elijah T. Andrews, of St. Louis
Amos Andrews, his father
Theodore McNabb, age 14, Godey's nephew
Julius Ducatel, son of a Baltimore doctor
Micajah McGehee, son of a Mississippi judge
Saunders Jackson, freed slave, Frémont's personal servant
Captain Andrew Cathcart, 11th Hussars, British sportsman

This is the story of John Charles Frémont's fourth expedition of exploration in western America. The fourth expedition attempted a winter crossing of the Rocky Mountains at the end of the year 1848, hunting a pass that could be used for a railroad route across the Continental Divide. It happened that the winter selected was one of the two hardest ever known in that high mountain country: so local tradition inherited from the Indians still reports. And it happened that the backbone of the fourth expedition was made up from that race known as the mountain men, consummate experts in the ancient warfare of man against nature.

The men of the fourth expedition fought the winter and the mountains for thirty-two days and were defeated, and for another thirty-two days fought to escape from the winter and the mountains after their defeat.

Part One
PREPARATION

1

Exploration is a solitary art. Whether it is undertaken in the laboratory or the library or in strange lands, the explorer leaves organized society behind him and goes essentially alone, an ambassador to the unknown. But clothed with this office he necessarily becomes the creature of his times, bearing their spirit as his portfolio, representing, in his isolation, the civilization of his epoch.

John Charles Frémont lived in the heart of the romantic age, and it suited him extremely well. The romanticist was engrossed with imagination and emotion and the free flight of the ego, and so was erratic as a matter of course, almost as a point of pride. He was incapable of the detachment and clarity of conception which distinguished the classicist before him, and would have been impatient with the wistful hunger for orderliness of the materialist of today, displaying itself in the painstaking perfection of mundane details of preparation.

Present-day explorers have been quoted as saying they do not have adventures (Vilhjalmar Stefansson: "Adventure is the result of incompetence on the part of someone"), adventures are what happen when you make a mistake in your preparation, and in this respect Robert Falcon Scott might be called the last of the great romanticists in exploration. Typically, though, Frémont once crossed the high Sierra in midwinter with no preparation whatever except the warning of an aged Indian that the crossing was impossible, that ahead there was only "snow upon snow, snow upon snow, rock upon rock, rock upon rock." That was on his second expedition, and that time he was successful, the party only losing half its horses and mules, two men who went temporarily insane from suffering and privation, and a little pet dog which was cooked up for dinner one evening by Godey, the young mountain man. X

Classic exploration in America reached its climax and conclusion with Lewis and Clark, and with their report of the beaver swarming in the streams of the western mountains the era of the mountain man, a character important to this story, officially opened. This is an arbitrary date but it will do.

The mountain man was a different model from his immediate forerunners, Daniel Boone or the French Canadian voyageurs. Due to the remoteness of his hunting grounds, he was the first inhabitant of America to find himself at ease with the familiar concept of great land distances that Europeans still remark as one of our national attributes. He was seldom a pioneer consciously clearing a way for others to follow—he was only hunting beaver. He was seldom an integrated unit of an organized company, with a big business character all the company's own harnessed to him, as in the case of the hired pork-eaters of the North West Company. He was not a family man in a covered wagon, a settler. He was, at his best, defiantly independent and individual, and he forthrightly referred to himself as free, a free trapper.

He lived on his own in a neolithic world far removed from the steel-age civilization that had bred him. He brought along only a few of its tools: traps, rifle, knife, awl, powder and lead. He traveled with small loosely organized groups of his own kind, a handful of men swallowed in an infinity of dark forests and strange winds. His joy was the sensual animal pleasure of life lived for its moments, one by one. He hunted with glowing eyes and spilled blood on pine needles unstirred for centuries.

He owned a mule or horse or two and an Indian girl. He dressed in skins she worked up for him, and she had warm water ready for his feet when he came in to his camp from wading the icy beaver streams. In the summer, when trading caravans came from St. Louis, he packed the spoils of his year's plunder to the great trappers' rendezvous in the mountains, bartered it for a whoop and a holler and a howling hangover, and set out on the next long hunt.

He floated on the rolling rivers in boats of skin or bark or rafts of logs. He probed out trails across the land that are railroads and highways today, and learned the way from the plains of Kansas to California and from the deserts of New Mexico and Utah to the fern-grown rain forests of Oregon.

Probably the mountain men surpassed the Indians in at least a number of the necessary skills of reading sign, hunting, living off a wild and ominous land, fighting and hiding and running like agile beasts, lying still and concealed in brush and rocks throughout a thirsty day if necessary, starving, stealing horses, going dirty, enduring sun and cold and cracking alkali. In some of these things they must have surpassed the Indians to survive, for the Indians were living at home, cushioned by the web of their established society, and the mountain men were interlopers with no support to back them up other than what they carried in their hands, so far in time and space from the established society from which they had sprung that they had all but forgotten its existence.

In their brief time, and it is noteworthy that it was without intention on their part—they were only hunting beaver—the mountain men created a vector of force that was an important factor in extending the sovereignty of the United States over the whole enormous western half of the continent. History, like virtue, often seems to flow most readily from hands that are not conscious of it.

By the late 1830's the fur trade was slacking off. The market for beaver was disappearing and the beaver was going with it, almost trapped out. In 1837 two families named Sloover and Pope, with wagons and two Mexicans, went to California from Taos by way of the Cochetopa Pass through the Rockies. These may have been the first American overland emigrators to the far West. In 1840 the first emigrants to Oregon passed by the trappers' rendezvous on Green River, the sixteenth rendezvous and the last one. They were a family of man and wife and five children, and the man of the family was Joel Walker, brother of Joseph Reddeford Walker, of mountain man aristocracy. They had wagons, which they later abandoned to be picked up by three mountain men who loaded their Indian families into them and likewise went to Oregon to settle, getting there with nothing left of the wagons but the wheels.

Jim Bridger and his partner "old Vaskiss" quit trapping and set up their trading post of Fort Bridger on the Oregon Trail in 1842, and at the southern heel of the central Rockies, on the Arkansas River within reach of the Taos trade, the part-Negro mountain man Jim Beckwourth and fifteen or twenty other trappers and their Indian wives built a little adobe village they called the Pueblo and began raising corn and potatoes.

The pageant of the mountain man was ended and in 1842, a reasonable date for his official exit, Frémont's first expedition was setting out westward with the mountain man nonpareil, Kit Carson, as guide, and Kit's sidekick, Lucien Maxwell, as hunter.

Between the time of Lewis and Clark and of Frémont the mountain man flourished. Without the mountain men, Kit Carson, Tom Fitzpatrick, Joe Walker, Alexis Godey, and Old Bill Williams, who guided Frémont, and the many others who served with him, the Frémont expeditions would have been far less successful, and consequently far less effective than they were in molding the shape of the new West.

Frémont realized his debt to the mountain men and made much of it. Carson and Dick Owens and Godey and Basil Lajeunesse, these last two St. Louis French, were his favorites. It is not too much to say that Carson was his hero. A romanticist always goes better with a hero in his sights, but it's a selection that does Frémont sound credit. To the end of his life Frémont was proud of having been associated with these men, having, still finer effulgence, been their leader, and the time of his association with them on his expeditions was for him the time, I paraphrase, of the blossoming of the rose that o'er his glad life its color threw and gave to his heart its springing hue and world of hope. He wrote a poem in his old age, when once going west by train, that says so, and adds a poignant word about the vanishment of the bloom along false roads to fame, when "the world's rude contact killed the rose no more its shining radiance shows." *

But in the time of the rose no schoolboy of the day, breathlessly reading Frémont's reports and standing by in spirit while a war party of the savage Arapaho swarms down from the hills, "two or three hundred, naked to the breechcloth . . . sweeping across the prairie," could have been more intoxicated by the sheer romance of the picture than was Frémont himself.

It was in the land they saw, when from the misty mountaintops: "Even to our great height the roar of cataracts came up, and we could see them leaping down in lines of snowy foam." They looked down on lakes and "rushing waters," and about them at "mountains of rocks naked and destitute," and into "dells and ravines of the most exquisite beauty, all kept green and fresh . . . and sown with brilliant flowers. . . ." They rode through "sage . . . glittering like silver, as the southern breeze turns up its leaves to the sun," and in California wound their way among "grand bouquets" of purple lupine growing

* See Notes: A Note on the Poem.

to twelve feet in height, "flowering groves, which filled the air with a light and delicate fragrance."

The air itself seized up the spirit and imagination. In the mountains it was spiced "with the odor of pines; and I realized this delightful morning the pleasure of breathing that mountain air which makes a constant theme of the hunter's praise." In silent forests the air turned into wandering fog, wreathing them in mystery; and on a May day in the desert the air was wild and rough and blue.

Movement and action were seen by an eye bright with feeling and emotion. There was a rumor of Indians and "Kit Carson, springing upon one of the hunting horses, crossed the river, and galloped off into the opposite prairies. . . . Mounted on a fine horse, without a saddle . . . Kit was one of the finest pictures of a horseman I have ever seen." Water is found after a dry jornada and "as fast as they arrived, men and horses rushed into the stream, where they bathed and drank together in common enjoyment."

Or buffalo appear, and the drawing is sketched with the passion and ecstasy of a Delacroix. "In the sight of such a mass of life, the traveller feels a strange emotion of grandeur . . . there was not one among us who did not feel his heart beat quicker. . . . It was the early part of the day, when the herds are feeding; and everywhere they were in motion. Here and there a huge old bull was rolling in the grass, and clouds of dust rose in the air from various parts of the bands, each the scene of some obstinate fight. Indians and buffalo make the poetry and life of the prairie, and our camp was full of their exhilaration." And the hunt is crescendo: "My horse . . . with his eyes flashing, and the foam flying from his mouth, sprang on after the cow like a tiger." After the hunt, "In place of the quiet monotony of the march, relieved only by the cracking of the whip, and an 'avance donc! enfant de garce!' shouts and songs resounded from every part of the line, and our evening camp was always the commencement of a feast. . . ."

There was the sentiment of knight-errantry so important to the era: "While we were at breakfast a buffalo calf broke through the camp, followed by a couple of wolves. In its fright it had probably mistaken us for a band of buffalo. The wolves were obliged to make a circuit around the camp, so that the calf got a little the start, and strained every nerve to reach a large herd at the foot of the hills, about two miles distant; but first one, and then another, and another wolf joined in the chase, until its pursuers amounted to twenty or thirty, and they ran him down before he could reach his friends. There were a few bulls near the place, and one of them attacked the wolves and tried to rescue him; but was driven off immediately, and the little animal fell an easy prey, half devoured before he was dead. We watched the chase with the interest always felt for the weak; and had there been a saddled horse at hand, he would have fared better." On another occasion they came upon eighteen or twenty buffalo all trying to down one lean old bull—"Of course, we took the side of the weaker party, and attacked the herd. . . ."

There was the sentiment of individual courage against great odds. Warning is given that the trail ahead is swarming with war parties of Gros Ventre and Sioux, and to go on may be suicide, and Frémont solemnly reads the roll, to inquire which of his men will not go on with him. Only one caitiff drops out. To the fierce old men of the threatening Cheyenne, Sioux, and Gros Ventre, Frémont said, "We have thrown away our bodies, and will not turn back."

Or another drawing is colored with the fashionable senti-ment of the exotic: "Our cavalcade made a strange and gro-tesque appearance . . . in this remote solitude . . . guided by a civilized Indian, attended by two wild ones from the Sierra . . . our mixture of American, French, German—all armed—four or five languages heard at once—above a hundred horses and mules, half wild—American, Spanish, and Indian dresses and equipment intermingled. . . . Scouts ahead and on the flanks; a front and rear division . . . and the whole stretching a quarter of a mile along our dreary path . . . looking more as if we belonged to Asia than to the United States of America."

Again and again in his reports Frémont stood aside to look on with the keenest sort of delight at the scene presented, so perfectly in keeping with the romantic preconceptions of the time as to what such a scene should be. We have no way of knowing how much of this (in the reports) was the subtle romancing of the youthful and even more imaginative Mrs. Frémont, who helped with their writing, but essentially the genre of such scenes was still and always Frémont's own, and beyond this, the enthusiastically accepted genre of the time. The great popularity of his reports was partly due, as is the popularity of any work of art, to putting before the readers' eyes what they already had in their minds.

There is always distortion in viewing Frémont out of such context, apart from all those implications of that romantic age which gave him substance. Precisely that extravagant romanticism which was taken for heroic stature in the day of Scott and Byron brings him to suspicion in our own time—the heedlessness, impetuosity, caprice and courage, the damn-the-consequences opportunism, the unashamed idealism naively combined with the shameless self-dramatization, the sudden strengths and mysterious weaknesses—all these smack of the charlatan to modern judgment, the more so when modern judgment thinks principally of Frémont the later politician, who was another man from Frémont the explorer, politics being anything but a solitary art. Modern judgment likes to find its springs in modern materialism and is affronted by a code of conduct that is literary in origin and so of course really impossible to practice, since people are more complicated than poems. The spectacle of a struggling attempt to live up to it must naturally be misunderstood by those honest workaday souls who could not conceive of finding their compulsion in a literary convention.

2

The fourth expedition had its source in the grandest of literary conventions, a fall from grace.

The renown of his earlier expeditions had bathed young Frémont in glory, a resplendent glory untouched by any breath of tarnish, and made of him a bright new national hero, the boy explorer of the far West, his name synonymous with romance and adventure. His third expedition brought him to a new high point of triumph when it took part in the conquest of California during the Mexican War.

But this selfsame triumph involved him in a snarling political dogfight that ended in his return to Washington under arrest, and trial at court-martial. Frémont was infuriated by the charges, humiliated by the trial, and stunned by the verdict. The court sentenced him to be cashiered from the Army, in which, as an officer of the Corps of Topographical Engineers, he had skyrocketed to his fame in exploration.

The hazardous fourth expedition, led by him as a private citizen, was his answer of typical melodramatic defiance to the fates that had cast him down.

The child Frémont had his beginnings cradled in the standard trappings of romanticism. He might have been born out of one of the early novels of George Sand. His father, a royalist French emigré, stole away Frémont's mother, a Virginia girl married to an old husband, and they galloped off into the sunset to live on love forever after. John Charles Frémont, their first child, was born in Savannah on January 21, 1813. A few years later the boy John Charles—Charley, to his friends of school and college days—was growing up in Charleston, South Carolina. His mother was by then a poor widow. From later recollections of his schoolmasters a picture emerges of a brilliant, impetuous, manly little chap, gleaming all over with promise, irresistibly attracting the patronage of influential people. He learned Greek and Latin with effortless velocity, he spoke French as a birthright, he read widely in the classics and studied the natural sciences, and revealed an exceptional talent for mathematics. He did not quite graduate from Charleston College, being expelled when within three months of graduation for chronic class-cutting. At the age of twenty he served as an instructor in a U.S. Navy sloop-of-war during an extended South American cruise, teaching mathematics to midshipmen. He was helped to the job by an influential Charleston citizen, Joel Poinsett, Secretary of the Navy. Following this he spent three years as a surveyor in the mountains and forests of Carolina and Tennessee and Georgia, employed by the Topographic Corps.

Commissioned a lieutenant in the Corps (the commission bore the signature of Joel Poinsett, now Secretary of War), and granted a belated B.A. by a relenting Charleston College, Frémont went west for the first time in 1838 as an assistant to Joseph Nicolas Nicollet, on a survey of the region of the upper Missouri and Mississippi. He worked with Nicollet for four years, part of the time in the Indian country that is now western Minnesota and the Dakotas, and part of the time in Washington transferring their observations and findings to maps and reports. Nicollet was his master in exploration, an example of the finest type of savant on horseback, enormously learned, thoroughgoing and painstaking far beyond the common practice of his day, one of the ablest scientists ever to concern himself with unveiling the magnificent geography of western America. Frémont learned from him to see with the varied eyes of geology, mapmaking, astronomy, and botany, and to amalgamate these lines of vision into an accurate and revealing view of country before known only from the often contradictory hearsay of trappers and Indian traders. From Nicollet, too (who killed himself with overwork as a matter of course), Frémont caught a wildfire enthusiasm, something of a sense of dedication, a habit of ardent application to the work in hand.

The young Lieutenant Frémont was lean and dark, fine-boned and not very tall, as handsome as a new dime, earnest and tough, sentimental, and, in a favorite word of the period, refined, with an engineer's square-cut mind and the soul of a cavalier.

He fell in love with a seventeen-year-old girl in a candy-striped dress; she was Jessie Anne Benton, the daughter of Senator Thomas Hart Benton, one of the most powerful men in Washington. Her father's favorite, she had grown up at his right hand in the inner circle of society and politics in Washington and St. Louis and Virginia, the home of her mother's aristocratic family. She was older than her years. By the age of sixteen she had collected three proposals of marriage. Jessie was brown-eyed and very beautiful to look upon, lighthearted, and possessed of a lively interest (which she never lost) in pretty dresses and parties and fashionable attitudes. In her notions of the proper life she cherished a set of poetic clichés that surpassed Frémont's own. In spite of this she brought a secret dowry of uncommon good sense and stability, and a quick and knowledgeable intellect.

She married Frémont adoring him (it was an elopement, naturally) and kept on adoring him for the rest of her life.

Senator Benton, being one of the leaders of the expansionist group in Congress devoted to the cause of turning the eyes of

America to the unopened and undeveloped West, now made his new son-in-law Frémont an important instrument of his policy. The expansionists held that it was the manifest destiny of the United States to build a great continental empire all the way to the Pacific. Benton had predicted, with inspired prophecy which seemed fantastic at the time, that within a century there would be a greater population beyond the Rockies than the entire population in his day of the Eastern States. To achieve this destiny it was desirable to advertise the West and at the same time learn what the West had to offer, learn officially, with government-countenanced surveys that would determine the navigability of trails and rivers, the fertility of valleys, sites for the location of forts; and thus encourage settlers to go forth and make conquest by covered wagon. A prime objective at the moment was Oregon, then held jointly with the British. A trickle of emigration to Oregon was already beginning. It was imperative that this be swollen into a flood of homemaking families that by laying hold of the land would strengthen the American claim to the territory.

So in the summer of 1842, within six months after his marriage, Lieutenant Frémont led his first expedition to the Rocky Mountains, with official instructions to explore the country between the Missouri River and the Rockies, and with extra added unofficial instructions from Senator Benton to aid the Oregon emigration by examining and mapping the famous South Pass in the Rockies, the gateway of the Oregon Trail. Kit Carson guided him, the little German mapmaker, Charles Preuss, went along as topographer, and the rest of the command of two dozen men was made up principally of Missouri French engagés, of whom Raphael Proue was typical, men of old acquaintance with the empty plains and the silent mountains and the willful ways of pack mules.

Jessie served as Frémont's amanuensis in preparing the report of the expedition after his return, and it developed that

Jessie could write. The report was packed with careful information on wood and water, trails and weather, and with vivid pictures of Indians and buffalo and the lonesome splendor of the country. Some of the information was geographically revolutionary merely because it was patiently and conscientiously gathered and assimilated—such as the revelation that the plains comprising the present states of Kansas and Nebraska were really rich and fertile and not the Great American Desert previous government surveys, hasty and ill-informed, had described.

The West was then growing like a beanstalk in the public fancy, and the report put the West in print so that avid readers could see the very grass blades underfoot along the way. The Senate ordered a thousand copies, and it was widely reprinted by private publishers and newspapers. The report made Frémont famous.

The second expedition left in the spring of the next year, 1843, and stayed out fourteen months. Its mission was to survey the entire Oregon Trail from South Pass west to the Columbia Valley and the Pacific, thereby connecting a survey of the interior of the country with the recent surveys made along the Pacific Coast by the Navy's Lieutenant Charles Wilkes.

This time Frémont set out with nearly forty men, most of them, again, French voyageurs like Proue. There were a few Delaware Indians, and a few Yankees gone western, such as Charles Taplin, of New York, Texas, and Missouri. Taplin was young but already experienced and dependable. In his report of this expedition Frémont speaks of a scouting foray handled by "Taplin, one of our best men." Preuss was again topographer. Kit Carson and the storied Tom Fitzpatrick, and late in the journey the equally famous captain of trappers, Joseph Reddeford Walker, were guides. Alexis Godey came out of the mountains to join the expedition when it reached the Rockies and go along as hunter.

The expedition crossed the country to Oregon, happened

onto a midwinter look at the Mexican dominion of California
(premeditated spying, perhaps), and returned across the West
by a southern route, the Old Spanish Trail, having accomplished much more than it had been expected to do. On this
expedition Frémont was at the top of his form as an explorer,
which was very good indeed, brilliantly exhibiting his virtuoso
powers of imagination and initiative, determination and daring
and luck.

His report, again written with Jessie's pen, authoritatively
described the far free reaches of Beulah Land in the Oregon
country and gave a sunlit glimpse of California that seized on
the people's dreams, saying of southern California—the one
part he hadn't yet seen, by the way—that it was a place "where
the country is so beautiful that it is considered a paradise, and
the name of its principal town (Puebla de los Angeles) would
make it angelic." The discussion in the report of the valley of
the Great Salt Lake influenced Brigham Young in deciding to
lead his Mormon migration there three years later. Gallant
scenes of derring-do, the remarkable winter crossing of the
high Sierra, rainbow waves of wild flowers rolling before the
wind, snowy peaks in "hue of rosy gold," brushes with raiding
Indians in the desert—one man, one of the French voyageurs,
was picked off and butchered—were thrown in for good measure. The Senate ordered 10,000 copies of the report, trade publishers brought out best-selling editions at home and abroad,
Frémont received a double-jump promotion through first lieutenant to captain, and he was the celebrity of the hour.

When the third expedition was formed the following spring,
to explore the central Rockies and examine routes through the
Sierra and the Cascades, he was literally mobbed by hundreds
of aspiring explorators filled with the spirit and raring to go
along. The feeling of the excited populace was neatly put in
writing by a bibulous traveling portrait painter—one Alfred S.
Waugh, known as Colonel Waugh for short—who was hustling

up from New Orleans with a younger partner, another artist, named Tisdale, to honor Frémont with the offer of their services.

"The desire of going into a region so remote and of seeing the red sons of the forest in all their native habits so occupied our thoughts that it became an all absorbing topic with us," Colonel Waugh stated in his journal, with simple candor.

Colonel Waugh owned a small hatchet which he very kindly allowed young Tisdale to wear in his belt, ready to serve as a tomahawk when they got among the red sons of the forest. Unfortunately, Frémont couldn't take them on, whereupon Tisdale threw his little hatchet away in a rage of disappointment, choking out, "There, I have no further use for that." Tisdale was "so full of seeing wild life and adventure," Colonel Waugh wrote, "of participating in the excitement of a buffalo hunt, in a word, of knowing something of existence beyond the bounds of civilization, that he would have done almost anything in order to gratify his taste in these particulars. . . ."

Captain Frémont did do Colonel Waugh the courtesy, as from one gentleman to another, of advancing him a small loan. "I have every reason to be thankful to Captain Frémont for the kind and courteous manner he treated me in supplying me with funds in the then exhausted state of my treasury. These funds I promised"—one hears a stout ahem—"to return to Col. Benton in Washington City." Perhaps the return of the funds slipped Colonel Waugh's mind later on in the pressing business of buying another drink, but he more than repaid the loan by leaving a portrait sketch of Frémont drawn straight from the heart of his captivated public.

"I was not a little disappointed with the manners and personal appearance of Captain F. I found him a pale intellectual-looking young man, modest and unassuming, seemingly more accustomed to the refinements and luxuries of life, than to the toils and dangers of the wilderness. I had pictured to myself a man of herculean frame, of a loud voice, and rough manners. What was my surprise to find him the reverse of all these— small in stature, and delicately formed—voice low and musical, and of manners bland and gentlemanly. I could scarcely be- lieve him to be the man who had gone through so much hard- ship in the previous expeditions. He had no outward indica- tions of the mountain traveller about him; all was quiet, well bred, and retiring. His conversation was modest, instructive, and unpretending, with a grace and suavity that irresistably won all who approached him. Yet in his eye, you saw some- thing which shewed contempt of danger, and proclaimed him a man to be obeyed under all circumstance . . . he alone wore the garb of an officer—undress frock coat. With his men he was kind and affable attending to their wants and studying their comfort. The Expedition being formed for scientific and not military purposes, it partook more of the character of the civilian than the soldier. . . . Among the company were many droll characters, mostly from the Western states, with a few canadian voyageurs, who had been out with the captain on a former expedition."

On this third expedition one of the Canadian voyageurs was, again, Raphael Proue. Another was Antoine Morin, a whiskered engagé grown old in the service of caravans and trading posts, and another the superlative scout Basil Lajeunesse, who had been an invaluable member of both previous expeditions and was to be killed by a Klamath ax on this trip. Other veterans were Charles Taplin, a group of Delawares, some of whom had been with the second expedition, and a couple of young California Indians who had returned from the Coast with the second expedition. The topographer Preuss did not go along this time; his place as artist was taken by twenty-one-year-old Ned Kern, of Philadelphia.

There were a few other green hands from the East, such as young Henry King from Georgetown, the suburb of Washington, D. C., where Jessie Anne Benton had gone to school. King, like Ned Kern, was to prove himself exceptionally able on this expedition, and win Frémont's complete confidence.

Many young men were hired in St. Louis: Tom Martin, Billy Bacon, Marion Wise, and several dozen others, backwoods boys of the restless border country from Missouri to Iowa Territory, who came recommended as "good riflemen and packers." Most of them were handy enough with a rifle, but it developed that all of them had cheated on their letters of recommendation in regard to the rest of it; none of them knew anything of the mystery of packing mules. By the time they reached the Rocky Mountains they had a good start on their education. Those who had not learned their lessons well enough were there culled out and sent back home and to take their places a few more men, of mountain experience, were added on, picked up around the trading posts of Bent's Fort and the Pueblo. The third expedition as finally shaken down and organized to head on west across the Rockies numbered more than sixty men and its general staff read like a page from the Almanach de Gotha of mountain men: Joe Walker, Alexis Godey, Kit Carson and his old companions of trapping times Dick Owens and Lucien Maxwell, and, to lead the way through a pass of the central Rockies, Old Bill Williams.

Huzzas followed Captain Frémont as he marched away. The Washington *Daily Union* summed them up:

"Captain Frémont has gone upon his third expedition, determined upon a complete military and scientific exploration of all the vast unknown region between the Rocky Mountains and the Pacific Ocean, and between the Oregon River and the Gulf of California. This expedition is expected to continue near two years, and its successful result is looked to with the highest degree of interest by all the friends of science in America and Europe.

"Perhaps no man of his age (thirty-two) in this country has

gone through such labor of body and mind as has Captain Frémont. Mathematics is his favorite study, botany his recreation, Greek and Latin came with his schooling, French and Spanish had been added, and German he is acquiring. From the age of twenty, the canopy of heaven has been his covering; the mountains, plains, the lakes and rivers from the Atlantic to the Pacific have been his home. The fruits of his researches are scarcely prepared for publication before he is off on new explorations. His life is a pattern and his success an encouragement to young men of America who aspire to honorable distinction by their own meritorious exertions.

"Captain Frémont is very youthful in appearance as well as in fact. Mr. Wilkins, Secretary of War, could hardly believe his ears when in the autumn of 1844 a modest-looking gentleman appeared before him and announced himself as Lieutenant Frémont just returned from the expedition to Oregon and California. To see the leader of such an expedition in the person of such a stripling was a surprise from which the Honorable Secretary could not recover himself until after repeated interrogations."

This was the young hero Frémont as a fond public saw him in the summer of 1845 when he sallied forth with his third expedition. Two years later, in the summer of 1847, he was brought back in disgrace, a prisoner under military arrest— "the mutineer in irons" as some reports erroneously had it, reflecting in their spontaneous exaggeration the jubilant malice with which the fond public leaps hobnailed on a fallen idol.

It came about in this way. The third expedition crossed the country to the West Coast, experiencing sundry adventures among which was a haughty row with the Mexican authorities in California, and by a lucky contingency, thoughtfully foreseen by the high brass of President Polk's Administration in Washington, was still lingering in the vicinity of California when the long-anticipated Mexican War finally broke out.

Frémont was thoroughly familiar with the political machinery creaking behind this setting of the stage for conquest. When in Washington he lived at Senator Benton's C Street residence, where Jessie acted as her father's hostess, entertaining friends ranging from Secretary of State James Buchanan and General Sam Houston to Samuel F. B. Morse; Frémont had conferred with President Polk and dined with a leader of the opposition, Daniel Webster; Senator Benton and Secretary of the Navy George Bancroft, a determined empire builder, had had much to do with outlining the desired route of the third expedition. Frémont was intimately aware of plan and design as viewed from the top policy level in Washington.

He knew that, in the words of George Bancroft, "a great object of the President was to obtain possession of California." In fact, the acquisition of California was to the President the most important object of the expected war with Mexico. Even those opposed to an outright war of conquest, as was Benton, were nervously anxious for California to be seized at the first whistle of hostilities, having excited themselves with fears that another strong power, namely Britain, might otherwise seize it first. It has since been supposed that this was a baseless fear, which, of course, made it no less real at the time.

And so the third expedition did a quick change in the field from a scientific exploring party to a military task force and participated with precipitate enthusiasm in the conquest of California.

A California Battalion of Volunteers was chiefly made up of the men of the third expedition and a healthy fifth column of American settlers in California. The Battalion was taken into the U.S. service by the newly arrived commander of the Navy's Pacific squadron, Commodore Robert F. Stockton. Stockton was impulsive, genial, political (he had been a guest of honor at a dinner at the Bentons' before he left the East), oratorical, bombastic, with a saving touch of buffoonery, an earnest loyalty, and a real yearning to be a good hero in the best tradition of pluck and hustle. He was known among the troops as Gassy Bob.

Stockton appointed Frémont major commanding the California Battalion. Frémont's promotions were now coming too fast for him to keep up with them; he hadn't yet had time to hear that a couple of months earlier the War Department back in Washington had promoted him to the lieutenant colonelcy of a newly formed regiment, the Mounted Rifles.

A few skirmishes were fought. The California Battalion was led by a Frémont in muddy moccasins and a blue wool shirt open at the neck (no longer undress frock coat) and a handkerchief bound round his head; a string-bean Kentuckian in his command affected a coonskin cap, with the tail in front. Sailors and volunteers were deployed here and there by land and sea. Stockton issued torrential pronunciamentos, alive with leaping hyperbole. The Mexican soldiery shrugged and stole away home and their generals went into hiding, and the California conquest was accomplished. Stockton said he had to seize the crown with his own hand and place it on his own head, for the Californians ran, and wouldn't stop to transfer it.

A letter came from Jessie relating congratulations received on Frémont's promotion to lieutenant colonel, and on the publication of the report of his second expedition. "So your merit has advanced you in eight years from an unknown second lieutenant, to the most talked of and admired lieutenant-colonel in the army. Almost all of the old officers called to congratulate me upon it. . . . Father says you are to accept the appointment as it was given, with the understanding that you were to be kept on scientific duty under the direction of the Senate. Mr. Webster says it would be too great a loss to the science of your country if you were stopped in your onward course. If I begin telling you the sincere compliments from people whose names are known in Europe as well as America I would need a day. . . . You are ranked with DeFoe. They say that as Robinson Crusoe is the most natural and interesting fiction of travel so Frémont's report is the most romantically truthful. I have a letter from the President of the Royal Geographical Society, Lord Chichester, who says he could not help preparing a paper on your travels to be read at their meeting—and more and more and many more of the same."

Jessie, now twenty-two and the mother of a three-year-old daughter, also wrote, "Editors have written to me for your biography and likeness, but I had no orders from you and then you know it would look odd to leave out your age, and you never told me how old you were yet. . . . How old are you? You might tell me now I am a colonel's wife—won't you, old papa?" Frémont was then within a couple of months of his thirty-fourth birthday.

Jessie also wrote, "I have some beautiful poetry to show you on our motto *le bon temps viendra.*"

And she wrote, "Dear, dear husband, you do not know how proud and grateful I am that you love me. We have found the fountain of perpetual youth for love, and I believe there are few others who can say so. I try very hard to be worthy of your love."

And by now the glorious news was gone to Washington revealing the explorer Frémont as something greater still, America's secret weapon in the far West, co-partner in the conquest of California. He was, it would seem, spinning in a very sea of sparkling honors.

During this period he made arrangements to purchase a handsome ranch site on the California coast, a place where he and Jessie could some time come and live while this province he had helped win grew great and waxed fat in its future of certain prosperity. Thomas Larkin, the United States consul at San Francisco, agreed to act as his agent in buying the place for him.

But in the meantime Commodore Stockton's new crown had been given a nasty shake. The southern Californians had risen in revolt, chased out Yankee garrisons here and there, and ungraciously refused to let Los Angeles be recaptured. Stockton was based in the south at San Diego and Frémont to the north, at Monterey, both preparing a full-scale drive on Los Angeles, when still another American conqueror appeared, marching across the desert from the East.

This was Brigadier General Stephen Watts Kearny, sent west with an army at the outbreak of the war to invade New Mexico and California. New Mexico had fallen without a battle. Hearing the glad news that California was also taken, General Kearny left his army in New Mexico and came on to California with only a token force of a hundred dragoons. At San Pascual, when only some forty miles from San Diego, he ran into a hot little battle with a troop of California vaqueros. Kearny made the mistake of charging these hell-for-leather horsemen, who turned the engagement into a pig-sticking party with their lances, left twenty-one of Kearny's men dead and dying and the general himself and a number of others wounded, captured a howitzer, and cut off the survivors from escape to San Diego. Gassy Bob sent out reinforcements which rescued Kearny and brought him in.

A month later Stockton recaptured Los Angeles; Frémont arrived from the north just in time to meet the defeated Californian commander and accept his surrender.

As soon as Los Angeles was reoccupied, Kearny turned on Stockton in a savage quarrel over the loot, that is, the place of supreme command in this new territory so important to the cod-cold eye of little President Polk. The basic conflict between Kearny and Stockton is best illustrated in an unfortunate conflict in orders issued by the War and Navy Departments in Washington. The War Department authorized Kearny to take and administer California, and the Navy De-

partment authorized its Pacific commander to take and administer California—although Stockton had not yet received
these orders. A trace of the well-known good-natured rivalry
between the services may have been evident even in Washington; one line of the Navy Department's orders read: "The
department confidently hopes that all Upper California will
be in our hands before the relief [Army] shall arrive."

Kearny, who had served in a subordinate capacity to Stockton without demur during the march against Los Angeles,
now displayed his War Department orders and announced
that he would assume the place at the head of the table, if
Stockton would kindly step out of the way. Stockton, outraged,
replied by summarily dismissing Kearny from any connection
whatever with his sailor and ragtag army, and, as far as he
was concerned, from any official position whatever in California.

Kearny, in great dudgeon, then tested his muscles with an
order to Frémont, countermanding a routine order from Stockton. His object was to force Frémont to choose between them,
and it is not inconceivable that if Kearny had won the support
of Frémont and his Volunteer Battalion he might have argued
the point of rank with Stockton on the spot with force.*

Frémont chose to side with Stockton, believing himself
more properly under Stockton's authority than Kearny's at the
moment, his battalion having been raised and taken into service under Stockton's authority and having operated under
Stockton's command for months before Kearny appeared on
the scene. He therefore disobeyed Kearny's test order and
obeyed Stockton instead.

This naturally infuriated Kearny still further. He immediately left Los Angeles and went to Monterey, where he waited
for clarification of authority, and more troops, to arrive from
the East.

* See Notes: A Note on the Trial.

General Kearny was grim and ferocious, the type of the old Army that produced iron men with wooden heads. Gassy Bob Stockton was a bouncing firecracker, with a sensitive honor that had involved him in a couple of duels in his midshipman days. He was a rich man, and at least as much a politician as a sailor; he had been offered the office of Secretary of the Navy in the Tyler Administration. Both were about the same age, in their early fifties. Frémont, established by Stockton as the governor of California (both Kearny and Stockton had promised him the governorship), took himself very seriously, and was serene in the certainty of his righteousness. Now that the die was cast he went all the way with Stockton and openly contended with Kearny in what was essentially a political struggle for power in this richest of plums, California.

When clarification arrived it gave Kearny clear-cut authority over the civil government in California.

Thus the conclusion was victory for General Kearny and there came now the rather pleasant business of revenge upon the fallen foe. Stockton, in the Navy, was out of reach, but Frémont was not. Kearny and his officers took him over a series of galling disciplinary jumps ("indignities, outrages, and illegalities," Frémont said) while they stripped him of his trophies, down to and including the astronomical instruments he had used in his explorations, and in the summer of 1847, accompanied by a forlorn remnant of nineteen men of his third expedition, he was marched behind Kearny back to Fort Leavenworth and there told to consider himself under arrest, and repair to Washington and report himself to the adjutant general. The charge was mutiny, later enlarged to include charges of disobedience to the command of his superior officer, and conduct to the prejudice of good order and discipline.

Frémont considered the charge not only astounding but base. He scribbled on a scrap of paper years later, when making notes for his memoirs, that Kearny "should, for himself, and by himself, as a brave man have settled his quarrel with Stockton. Not devolved it upon me, and then charge me with disobedience to a superior officer because I declined to settle it in his favor."

Senator Benton, who acted as Frémont's senior counsel at the resulting court-martial, also regarded Kearny's charges as "absurd," based principally as they were on instances occurring before Frémont had definite knowledge of how the wrangle over authority in California would be settled. Benton wrote to Frémont before the trial, "We shall demolish him with all ease, and overwhelm him with disgrace."

Senator Benton had a fine, vigorous, wide-ranging mind; he also had, now that Andrew Jackson was dead, the hottest temper in the land, and easily outdid Kearny at vindictiveness. Benton and Kearny were old personal friends and St. Louis neighbors; Benton had been instrumental in getting Kearny his promotion to brigadier at the start of the Mexican War; a letter from Benton written early in the war, before he knew of Frémont's operations in California, telling Kearny that he "was to be the civil and military governor of the territory" of California was a factor in persuading Kearny to march on to California even after hearing it was already conquered. All these things only added fuel to the flame.

Benton wrote to Frémont that he had a full view of the case, "Kearny's as well as yours—and am perfectly at ease. You will be justified and exalted: your persecutors will be covered with shame and confusion. The process through which you have gone is bitter; but it will have its Sweet. You will realize what Lord Palmerston said to Mr. Van Buren when he was rejected by the Senate, 'that it was an advantage to a public man to be, in the course of his life, the subject of an outrage.' . . . You may be at ease. The enemy is now in our hands, and may the lord have mercy on them; for I feel as if I could not."

Benton prepared an able defense, but his over-confidence and raging indignation had the net effect of doing Frémont's cause undeniable harm.

Frémont's mother died at her home in Charleston before the trial began. Her death, Frémont believed, was brought on by the shock of the news of his arrest and anguish over the attacks against him circulated by Kearny men in the newspapers.

The court-martial was held in the Washington Arsenal during the winter of 1847-48. It ran for eighty-nine days, attracted capacity crowds, and was a sensation in the press.

Alexis Godey and a number of other Frémont men were on hand as witnesses. A few of these had returned with him at the wheel of Kearny's chariot, some of them had arrived since, and some had come east much earlier, at the height of the struggle for power in California, to carry the Stockton-Frémont side of the argument to Washington.

Stockton arrived to testify for him while the trial was in progress, having traveled back across the plains and been shot in the seat of the pants by an Indian arrow en route. A newspaper report quoted Gassy Bob as relating that he had been wearing at the time, it being a cold night, six blankets, three or four shirts and thick overcoats, two pairs of pantaloons, three pairs of drawers, and three pairs of stockings ("'you were not in a condition to run,' remarked Lieut. Col. Frémont with a smile") and still the arrow had passed through all this and wounded him "under the haunches."

He had two prayers, Gassy Bob stated, "one was, that he might do nothing to injure what little reputation he had, and the other that God would keep him safely and not suffer him to be placed in a condition where the d—d savages would cut his throat."

The press further quoted him as saying, "I will tell all about my conduct; I will tell everything, if I have an opportunity. I want the truth to come out."

To which Senator Benton said, and was quoted, "That's the American people; that's the American people, sir; they will have the truth, sir."

"Animated by no feeling of bravado, claiming no infallibility of judgment, but erect and confident in the correctness of the course I have pursued, I ask for the opportunity of testifying thoroughly and fully," Commodore Stockton told the court, or would have told the court if the court would have listened, but the court limited his testimony rather severely; plainly the Army court took a dim view of Navy Commodore Stockton.

Kearny as a witness willingly distorted facts and recollections and made it painfully clear that he was acting at least as much from a sense of personal malevolence as from a sense of duty. One of the few times Kearny appeared in a sympathetic light was when he complained to the court that "the senior counsel of the accused, Thomas H. Benton, of Missouri, sat in his place, making mouths and grimaces at me, which I considered were intended to offend, to insult, and to overawe me." This brought Senator Benton leaping to his feet and shouting that he had done so because General Kearny had previously "looked insultingly and fiendishly" at Frémont.

Frémont felt certain of victory, but even so he found the trial itself a highly mortifying experience, regardless of how thoroughly he should be vindicated at its outcome. In summing up his defense he remarked, "The trial of an officer before a general court martial (no matter what the event) is the cause of injuries to him, for which there is neither redress nor oblivion. The name of it lives coupled with his name, while history records it, tradition repeats it, or posterity bears it. The daily appearance, as a prisoner, at the bar of the court, is a bitter humiliation. To have one's self sworn against, with-

out the power of reply, is a sickening trial of the human feelings. [Frémont could not under law be sworn in his own
behalf while Kearny the accuser could be sworn and testify.]
The anxieties and distress of friends and family is a serious
aggravation of real evils. Marks of indignity, or degradation,
such as deprivation of the sword, real or virtual imprisonment
in being confined to quarters, or the place of trial, the rear
position in the march; a sort of social excommunication in the
interdiction of official visits, or appearance at public places;
the daily remarks of the thoughtless or the uncharitable; the
exultation of enemies (of whom every man has some), all
these are humiliating concomitants to the state of arrest and
trial. . . ."

All this, needless to say, the court found irrelevant to the
point at issue. The point at issue was whether or not Frémont
had disobeyed the lawful command of his superior officer, General Kearny, the chief instance being Kearny's order countermanding Stockton's routine order at the start of the whole
affair. There was no question but that Frémont had disobeyed
Kearny's order and there was no question but that Kearny
was Frémont's superior officer in rank, but a question existed as
to whether Kearny was Frémont's commanding officer at the
time. This was the main line of the defense, and Commodore
Stockton its principal support, testifying that he, not Kearny,
was then Frémont's commanding officer, and for Frémont to
have obeyed Kearny would have put him in the position of
disobeying Stockton, his rightful commander.

But the court, after several days' deliberation upon completion of the testimony, decided Frémont had had sufficient reason to recognize Kearny's claim of authority to be stronger
than Stockton's, and found him guilty on all charges.

The sentence was dismissal from the service.

3

The verdict was a shattering blow to Frémont. He had endured the ordeal of arrest and trial supremely confident of ultimate victory and vindication. Now he felt he had been publicly and unjustly, grossly, dishonored. The judgment of the court stamped upon his name an official opprobrium for which there was indeed neither redress nor oblivion. The fall from grace was concluded.

For General Kearny, it was a brief triumph. He was sent to Mexico as governor of Vera Cruz and Mexico City (followed all the way by a ruthless cannonading from Benton on the floor of the Senate), fell ill with tropical fever, returned to St. Louis, and died within the year.

For Frémont, the court-martial resulted in the fourth expedition.

Of the thirteen officers who made up the military court, seven recommended clemency. President Polk, after discussing the complex political aspects of the case in two Cabinet meetings, approved the sentence but remitted the penalty, and ordered Frémont to "resume his sword, and report for duty." Frémont angrily refused to resume his sword, writing in a letter of resignation to the Adjutant General: "I do not feel conscious of having done anything to merit the finding of the court. . . . I cannot, by accepting the clemency of the President, admit the justice of the decision against me." The War

Department was laggard in accepting the resignation; Frémont waited a month, and wrote again to the Adjutant General: "I have to request that, at some convenient opportunity, you will take the trouble to obtain the reply, and make it known to me." A reply was fired back the next day, March 15, 1848, that his resignation had been accepted as of that date.

Now the book of the court-martial was formally closed, and Frémont could sit back and look at his life lying in fragments about his feet. His livelihood, the Army, was gone, and with it the sponsor of his career in exploration, the career that had been his engrossing reason for being; now, at the age of thirty-five, that career was suddenly struck down at its zenith and apparently ended. Worst of all, his position, the recognition he had attained, had been soiled and assailed.

As for Benton, he severed relations utterly with the White House and resigned the chairmanship of the Senate Military Affairs Committee, which he had held for twenty years, because he refused to have any further communication with the War Department and Secretary of War Marcy. He denounced Polk's chief advisers as a little group of immoral intriguers, "architects of war and annexation," and opposed Administration desires in the peace treaty with Mexico. He did not go over to the Whigs, as Polk feared for a time he might do, but sulked in his tent as far as party activity in the forthcoming Presidential election was concerned.

There were condolences, although condolences could not change the damning decision of the court and the President. Frémont had gotten a good press during the trial and as a result the public generally agreed with him that he had been wronged. This was gratifying but only served to make Frémont feel the more flagrantly dishonored. The halls of Congress echoed to sturdy expressions in his behalf from friends of Benton, and even from some who were not friends of Benton. ("The courage and conduct of Colonel Frémont have signalized his name," from Senator Crittenden. "I have admired the man from character," from Senator Underwood. ". . . a name which has acquired greater renown in this country than that of any other man of his age who now breathes its air," from Senator Allen. ". . . this gallant and accomplished young officer, with a discretion far beyond his years," from Senator Clarke. ". . . he has established a reputation for himself, by braving dangers and fatigues—a well earned reputation which has extended itself far beyond the limits of the United States," from Senator Rusk. ". . . rare endowments, rare abilities," from Senator Butten. ". . . extraordinary merit and abilities," from Senator Bagby. ". . . I am prepared to bear testimony upon this occasion to the correctness of his whole line of conduct as an officer," from Representative Gorman, Chairman of the House Committee on Military Affairs.) He was offered a place on the faculty of Charleston College, where it had long ago been completely forgotten that he had once been expelled; he was offered the presidency of the railroad from Charleston to Cincinnati, the route of which he had helped survey thirteen years before.

These were all well meant and if they bore unconscious irony it was only in Frémont's own reflection that they could not change a comma of the fact of his disgrace and the ruin of his career. They were all kind tributes that did him honor, but they were not what he needed. For the present he could only be restored by an achievement considerably more spectacular than a professorship or a railroad presidency. The very generosity of such tributes demanded some action of equal grandiloquence to live up to them. For the future he needed a new career, and the West he had traveled (and strewn with settlers in the wake of his reports) offered a more expansive stage for this than the settled and humdrum East. Jessie wrote in later years: "He felt that he was better adapted to carve a future in new lands and conditions, rather than enter into competition with men who were more experienced in the ways of the settled parts of the world."

So the notion evolved that he would move with his family, Jessie and their little daughter, Lilly, and the second child Jessie was now expecting, to California. The pleasant ranch on the coast Frémont had arranged to buy would not be waiting for them; Mr. Larkin had instead bought it for himself and gotten Frémont a vast and worthless mountain tract called the Mariposas—Frémont and Benton for a time considered a lawsuit over this. Nevertheless, perhaps the Mariposas could be developed. Tools and machinery for a mill would be sent around by sea. Jessie and the children would also go by sea. Frémont would gather together some of his men and go across the continent and he would make of the journey one more trip of exploration, his fourth expedition.

The object of the expedition, beyond the immediate object of restoring himself with an incandescent success, would be to complete and connect the surveys of his previous expeditions, and to examine a central route for a transcontinental railroad, for some time a glowing dream in the minds of both Frémont and Senator Benton. To determine that such a route would be practicable both winter and summer, the fourth expedition would plan to cross the central Rockies in midwinter, a plan daring and spectacular enough to suit the most Byronic gesture of wounded pride.

Senator Benton began the delicate maneuver of engineering a Congressional appropriation of $30,000 to finance the expedition.

In the meantime Frémont, living with Jessie at Benton's house, the only home they had yet had, was at work on the belated job of summing up the scientific results of the third expedition. There were the ornithological and geological and botanical collections, sent on from California where Kearny had made Frémont leave them, to be submitted to various

authorities for classification. There was a brief report, called
A Geographical Memoir upon Upper California, concise description and observation, destined to be widely reprinted during the California gold rush. Most important, there was a map
of the far West drawn by his old topographer, Charles Preuss.
This was an excellent map, by far the best of its day, and the
Senate ordered 20,000 copies. (The most prominent error on
this map, incidentally, was in the central Rockies where a
certain river then called the Bunkara was shown far out of
position. This was part of the region the fourth expedition
intended to explore.)

Undoubtedly Frémont and Preuss discussed the proposed
new expedition while they worked on the map; certainly
Preuss would have been one of the first of Frémont's old men
recruited to go along.

Charles Preuss was a stocky little man, German from the
ground up. A master topographer, he had called on Frémont
one evening before the start of the first expedition and asked
for a job. Frémont described him as a "strange figure—a shock
of light curly hair standing up thick about his head, and a
face so red that we attributed it to a wrong cause instead of
the cold and nervousness and anxiety which turned his speech
into stammering." When Frémont found he was not drunk
but only desperate with worry because he and his family were
"actually without means of support," Preuss was hired out of
hand for the first expedition. To keep him until the first expedition was ready to start Frémont got him a job working on
some "astronomical observations remaining unreduced." This
was something Preuss could not do, so Frémont did it for
him, working evenings. "It troubled him greatly that I should
have to do this for him, but it was the only way I could come
in aid; and so it was done. This was Preuss; and this was the
beginning of our long friendly comradeship." Frémont added
that this little kindness was amply repaid "by years of faithful

and valuable service as topographer on my journeys, during
which his even temper and patient endurance of hardship
earned my warm regard."

Preuss did have one handicap; that was Mrs. Preuss. Mrs.
Preuss did not like him to go traipsing about in wild and distant places. This was said to have been the reason Preuss
stayed home from the third expedition. Mrs. Preuss was a
standing joke between Jessie and Frémont, so Jessie once
wrote, immediately springing to mind whenever Jessie began
feeling too sorry for herself or worrying too much while her
young husband was away wresting the bubble reputation from
she knew not what perils of the wilderness.

For the age in which he lived, Preuss had a singular lack
of emotionalism. He did his work and obeyed orders as a
matter of course, in a most prosaic and unpretentious matter-
of-fact way. When (out on the first expedition) he met a
"party of traders and trappers, conducted by Mr. Bridger, a
man well known in the history of the country," he was duly
impressed, but when Mr. Bridger warned that war parties of
Cheyenne and Gros Ventre and Sioux were all over the country ahead, sworn to kill any whites that passed, and advised
Mr. Preuss to turn aside, Mr. Preuss could not consider it,
sound advice though he was sure it must be coming from Mr.
Bridger. Mr. Preuss had arranged to meet Lieutenant Frémont
and the main party ahead, and of course must do so. Mr.
Preuss on this occasion was accompanied by a number of
French engagés and he was astonished at the excitement Mr.
Bridger's news created among them. "In a camp consisting of
men whose lives had been spent in this country, I expected
to find everyone prepared for occurrences of this nature; but,
to my great surprise, I found, on the contrary, that this news
had thrown them all into the greatest consternation; and, on
every side, I heard only one exclamation, '*Il n'y aura pas de
vie pour nous.*' " These engagés were even more disturbed, a

little later on and still deeper into the hostile Indian country, when Mr. Carson gravely made his will; but Mr. Preuss was apparently not of an excitable nature. Anyway, he would have been too busy keeping up the map of the journey each day to have any time left for such frivolous indulgence.

Mr. Preuss deprecated himself, quite genuinely, as any kind of a skilled frontiersman. Being hungry, he shot at a dove in a tree: "But it needs a better marksman than myself to kill a little bird with a rifle." Doggedly following Frémont in climbing Frémont Peak in the superb mountains of equally superb name, the Wind Rivers, Mr. Preuss fell and slid two or three hundred feet down an ice field and "though he turned a couple of somersaults, fortunately he received no injury beyond a few bruises." When the others (yelling Canadian boat songs) shot boiling rapids they gave Mr. Preuss the precious chronometer to carry and keep safe by making his way laboriously on foot over rocks along the bank.

Mr. Preuss sang no rhapsodies of wind and sky, seas of sand and grass and cloud-wrapt mountains. If he glanced up from his stolid industry to be stirred by these things the inarticulate satisfactions remained deep and secret, treasured away where Mrs. Preuss could never find them. Mr. Preuss was not a man of sentiment and romantic fancy. It is not recorded that Mr. Preuss leapt on a quivering steed and chased the buffalo. He was likely to write in his journal instead: "I felt so marode yet, that it was a horrible idea to me to bestride that saddle again; so I lay still." Or of being alone on the plains he wrote: "Uneasy I did not feel, but very hungry. . . . I made a fire, however, lighted my pipe—this true friend of mine in every emergency—lay down, and let my thoughts wander to the far east." This was the extent of Mr. Preuss' dreaming. Where others galloped waving banners Mr. Preuss trudged, square thumb on steel ruler and his mind on his business. If a buffalo skin lodge blew down on him, if he was lost and alone, if he suffered from cold in the snowy Sierra, if in a starving time he could only find food by letting ants crawl on his hands and licking them off (an incident of the second expedition), it was all in the day's work.

And if it was true that Mrs. Preuss kept him home from the third expedition—Jessie wrote that she gave him the ultimatum to "Choose between your home and family over your instinct to wander"—she was not able to hold him back from the fourth.

The court-martial alone, arousing Preuss' bulldog loyalty for his chief, would have been enough to settle the matter. If a fourth expedition, no matter how venturesome, could help to heal the injury of the court-martial, Mr. Preuss was ready to start.

Others of his veterans, his faithful "children of the mountains," as Senator Benton senatorially referred to them, talked to Frémont early in the spring, soon after the trial, of the possibility of a fourth expedition, urged on the idea, and assured him of their fealty. Ned Kern, the artist from Philadelphia, still youthful but now an experienced trail hand and an ex-commander of California forts, would not only jump at the chance to go along again but would bring two brothers, one an artist as good as himself and the other a physician, who would act as surgeon and assistant naturalist. Raphael Proue had been visiting the Kerns in Philadelphia; count him in too, of course, as always before. Several other faithful mountain children were among the Frémont witnesses on hand in Washington for the court-martial; they would like nothing better than to join the colonel in the bold hazard of the new expedition and return with him to California. One of these was written down by the clerk at the court-martial as L. Gorday, although his name was familiar enough in the hard mouths of distant mountain men who could not spell at all: this was Alexis Godey.

Godey was then perhaps thirty years old. He had been in the mountains eleven or twelve years, much of that time as a professional hunter supplying the isolated trading posts with meat, a job Kit Carson and Lucien Maxwell had held before him, or as a trader to the Indians. He had been with the second and third expeditions, and a lieutenant in Frémont's California Battalion; he had been one of a few scouts and sailors sent out into the desert from San Diego to join the approaching General Kearny, and had joined him just in time to take part in the savage little battle of San Pascual, after which Godey led two companions in the tricky business of stealing through the enemy lines to San Diego with a request to Stockton for reinforcements. He could work his way "where there was grass enough to cover a snake," Godey once said, with typical mountain man modesty. The three were captured by the Californios on their return, and Andrés Pico, the Mexican commander, conferred distinction on Godey by refusing to exchange him for a prisoner the Americans had taken. Pico would gladly exchange one of his other prisoners, but not the dangerous Godey.

Frémont made the remark that Kit Carson and Dick Owens and Godey would have been marshals under Napoleon. It was sufficient compliment in itself merely to couple young Godey's name with the illustrious mountain names of Carson and Owens. But Frémont went further still: Godey was "in courage and professional skill a formidable rival to Carson," and higher praise he could not bestow. Throughout his life Frémont never had anything but high praise for Alexis Godey, and they knew each other for nearly fifty years.

Godey was St. Louis French, handsome enough to be a hero in a book, with black eyes, Frémont says, "and silky curling black hair which was his pride. In all situations he had that care of his person which good looks encourage. Once when with us in Washington, he was at a concert; immediately behind him sat the wife of the French Minister, Madame Pageot, who with the lady by her, was admiring his hair, which was really beautiful, 'but,' she said, '*C'est une perruque.*' They were speaking unguardedly in French. Godey had no idea of having his hair disparaged and with the prompt coolness with which he would have repelled any other indignity turned instantly to say, '*Pardon, Madame, c'est bien à moi.*' The ladies were silenced as suddenly as the touch on a tree silences a katydid."

Godey had voyageur blood in his veins. He could never be unhappy long, or solemn or anxious or troubled. He would render unto trouble its due but with not an ounce more gravity than the law expressly required. Life was for living, and living was meant to be an enjoyable business. He could grin the bark off a tree.

Godey was as much the opposite of Mr. Preuss as noon is of midnight; they were as different as a rapier and a mattock; they were millenniums apart, for Mr. Preuss was dull and orderly civilization and Godey elegant savagery.

Frémont wrote, "Quick in deciding and prompt in acting he had also the French élan and their gayety of courage—

'Gai, gai,
avançons nous.' "

Godey was a joyful animal delighted with the good God's splendid world, and especially delighted with the beautiful girls the good God had sprinkled liberally upon it. Vide Poche girls from St. Louis, graceful girls from Santa Fe and Taos, wearing low-necked blouses, rebozos in swirling folds draped from their glossy hair, brown shuck cigarettes between laughing red lips. California girls in scarlet petticoats embroidered with green silk stitching that flashed under satin skirts, Cheyenne girls in sleeveless knee-length dresses of fringed and quill-worked buckskin, worn Dianawise, and best of all, so they said, Arapaho girls, so ardent, kind, and comely. Godey was charmed by them all.

To talk about Godey is to conjure up a creation of Dumas the elder, but Godey lived in a world Dumas never knew, and the lighthearted lover never stopped at becoming a gallantly fierce musketeer but went blithely on to the neolithic happy land of the lighthearted savage. Godey, born too late to hope to reach the stature of a Tom Fitzpatrick or a Kit Carson, must nevertheless be counted among the ranking mountain men, and the mountain men took pride in being more Indian than the Indians.

Godey has to be seen in action to be real, to get desert dirt grimed in his fine black hair and bloody Indian glory in his heart, and twist out of the manicured grasp of M. Dumas, and the action should be the horse rescue, on the second expedition.

The second expedition was coming home from southern California over the Old Spanish Trail in April of 1844. This was a dry, hard, winding route, much of it over desolate desert country where water holes were scarce and grass scarcer, and the cruel and rocky going murdered animals by inducing an ailment called the foot-evil. In the stretch of the Trail running south of what is now called Death Valley to cross the present Nevada line, Frémont and his men came on two survivors of a little party of New Mexican traders. The traders, traveling with their families and a small herd of fine California horses they were taking home to New Mexico, had been attacked by a horde of the Indians who inhabited this section of the Trail. These were a wandering horseless people of Digger type likened by Frémont to beasts of prey. They were equipped with dangerous long bows almost as effective, Frémont wrote, as rifles.

The two survivors were a man named Fuentes and a boy called Pablo. Pablo's mother had been taken away by the Indians and was never seen again. His father had been killed and his body wildly mutilated, the legs and one hand chopped off, possibly in simple anger because he had put up a hard fight. A band of these Indians had eventually captured the horses, which to them represented treasures of food, and driven them away.

Kit Carson and Alexis Godey appointed themselves a counterattacking army of two, and galloped out to win back if they could the stolen horses. Night fell and they rode on, following the trail of the Indians by moonlight, well marked as it was from the passage of the horses. The way led into an upthrust of bald, rocky desert mountains. They stopped at midnight in a cañon, slept beside their horses until the first light of daybreak, and went on. They found the Indian camp just as the sun was rising. The camp was four lodges; this might mean forty people.

They dismounted, crawled as close as possible to the lodges and the horses, and when a spooking horse gave them away they yelled and charged. The Indians boiled out and cut loose with twanging bows; an arrow went through Godey's collar. Carson and Godey fired with their rifles, reloaded and fired again, killed two men, and the rest, men, women, and children, ran away, except one small boy, who didn't get out in time and was caught.

Now Carson and Godey counted coup on the dead and went to work ripping off their scalps. This was not the work of an instant but something of an operation: the scalp was sliced around and then a little man of Carson's size would need to brace his feet on the dead man's shoulders and grasp the hair with both hands and rear back and tear off the scalp, which would give way with a sound like splitting a melon. In this case it developed that one of the fallen was not yet dead, and under the cut of the knife he leapt up screaming and had to be shot and killed again as he ran, while an old woman clambering over the rocks in the distance turned and wailed in lamentation.

Several of the best horses had already been butchered and put to stew in earthen vessels. The small boy captive, as soon as he saw he was not going to be killed, unconcernedly turned to breakfasting off a horse head while Godey tied the two scalps to the barrel of his rifle and Carson gathered the remaining horses.

They set the Indian boy free and rode back to join the Trail and return to Frémont's camp, running the recaptured horses with them. They returned whooping to camp in the afternoon, Godey waving the scalps from his rifle. Besides the prime business of their excursion, the blood-springing few seconds of fighting, they had covered something like a hundred miles in thirty hours.

Frémont added proudly, "To avenge the wrongs of Mexicans whom they did not know."

The recaptured horses were given back to Fuentes and the grief-stricken little Pablo, who continued to travel on with the expedition. But the horses gave out one by one from the foot-evil as they went on, Fuentes gravely cutting off the mane and tail (for saddle girths) of each one as it dropped out, and he didn't get them through to New Mexico after all.

Alexis Godey would be delighted at the thought of a new expedition. He wanted to go back to California anyway.

It would be a hard trip, a winter crossing of the Rockies? Good, he would take along a young nephew, a fourteen-year-old boy named Theodore McNabb, who was hungering to go out West and learn the way of prairie fixin's and mountain doin's. He was big enough to pull his weight and this would give him a fine apprenticeship. (Frémont's first expedition had included a boy of twelve, Jessie's young brother Randolph.)

In marked contrast to both Godey and Mr. Preuss was another Frémont man present at the trial, bearing the unlikely name of Lorenzo D. Vincenthaler. People who met him could not be blamed for thinking his last name two, as they often did, and speaking of him as Haler. Vincenthaler, a native of Ohio, had gone along on the third expedition and in California had been a sergeant in Company C of the California Battalion, but somehow the impression had gotten around since that he was a captain, and he was usually called such. Vincenthaler was not a mountain man; his type was much more common to the land-seeking pioneers and settlers. He had a bourgeois soul, crammed with little moralities to make up for the lack of big ones. He was full of anxious yearning for material gain, on the make and not overly scrupulous about how he made it. To get ahead, to feather his nest, to make his way, he was plentifully willing to be servile and flattering, eager and earnest, and, if need be, cunning. Frémont was very susceptible to this sort of fawning courtier's approach, which encouraged him in excursions into his knightly dream world, and regarded Vincenthaler as a sound man, businesslike and trustworthy.

Vincenthaler would have been prompt in signing on for a return to California. The peril of the proposed expedition would be balanced by the advantage of going to settle in California in the train of Frémont, who in spite of the humiliating chastisement of the court-martial was sure to be a person of influence in the affairs of the new territory.

Among the other faithful children of the mountains in Washington for the trial and consequently on hand during the early planning stages of the fourth expedition were three Missouri frontiersmen, Wise, Ferguson, and Breckenridge, all veterans of the third expedition. Josiah Ferguson and Marion Wise had been present as volunteers at the taking of Sonoma, the curtain raiser of the California conquest, the first action of the Bear Flag revolt. When the California Battalion was organized Wise served in Company A, under Dick Owens, while

Josiah Ferguson served with Lieutenant Godey in the Los Angeles area.

Thomas E. Breckenridge was, like a number of others of the third expedition who later signed on with the fourth, a young man and a Missourian, but one gathers that he had had a previous acquaintance with the mountains and was one of the seasoned mountain hands hired on by the third expedition when it reached the Rockies. As was the case with Kit Carson, Breckenridge appears on the muster rolls of the California Battalion attached to no specific unit and with no specific rank. Breckenridge had come back from California by way of the Santa Fe Trail and there had fallen in with not one but two authors, the youthful American, Lewis Garrard, and the British travel writer, George Frederick Augustus Ruxton. Garrard wrote rapturously of Breckenridge and his companions, ". . . they have stood the shock of more than one Indian skirmish, and have led the van at a sweeping gallop through many a dangerous mountainpass, with rifles cocked and unconfined hair streaming—the mountaineer's pennon."

Ferguson and Breckenridge put their names down for the fourth expedition. A Wise was also a member of the fourth expedition, but in spite of the possibility of confusion in the frequently confused records, this was apparently not Marion Wise. Listed as Henry Wise, of St. Louis County, this man was probably taken on later while the expedition was organizing in St. Louis.

Very likely it was Mr. Preuss who brought in another addition to the scientific corps, which would be the most complete that had ever accompanied any far West expedition. This was Frederick Creutzfeldt, who would serve as botanist and also assist Mr. Preuss with the topography.

Over in Georgetown, District of Columbia, Captain Henry King, late commissary officer of the California Battalion, volunteered and was taken on as "assistant surveyor." King was in

"the spring of life, of cultivated mind, and of the most engag-
ing manners," so said Charles Taplin, who knew him on both
the third and fourth expeditions. King knew the hardships he
was letting himself in for and, as his hometown newspaper
stated, "he considered them over before voluntarily encounter-
ing them again, and his spirit almost faltered; but being possessed of an iron nerve, he concluded to adhere to the determination once made, to accompany his enterprizing officer
once more. . . ." One reason his spirit almost faltered was a
Georgetown girl. King was in love, and the sweet sorrow of
parting had less appeal than formerly.

A strong influence in his decision would have been the flattering fact that Frémont considered him one of his chief lieutenants; another would have been the simple fact that King had
caught the western fever. Like Ned Kern, he was infectious
with it, and before he left Georgetown his brother, James King,
had decided to go west also: he would go around by sea while
Henry went overland with Frémont and they would meet in
California. The entire King family, in fact, went west to California a couple of years later. (Brother James King was destined
for a nod from history—when he arrived in California, where he
took the royal title of James King of William to distinguish
himself from other James Kings, he became a red hot crusading
editor, started the San Francisco *Evening Bulletin* in 1855, and
was shot and killed the next year by a politician he had exposed. It was this murder that led to the organization in San
Francisco of a group that gave a new phrase to the language
and a symbol to the mores of the new West, the Vigilance
Committee.)

Henry King was also probably responsible for the recruit-
ment of another man for the fourth expedition who would be
important to Frémont's plans for the future in knowing how
to make use of the mill irons Frémont was having shipped
around the Horn from New York, for the development of his

California ranch; this was Henry Rohrer, a Georgetown mill-wright who had built a number of flour mills in the vicinity. Rohrer was a settled family man with a half-dozen children. Perhaps he felt some lure of adventure, but it is more likely that young Captain King explained to him the very real lure of opportunity. California needed skilled mechanics more than adventurers and would pay for them with an immediate success far beyond anything the East could offer.

All these, the vastly experienced Godey and his young nephew and Tom Breckenridge, as well as such as Rohrer and Creutzfeldt, valuable technicians although novices to the mountains, weathered and faithful Mr. Preuss and the still more weathered and faithful Raphael Proue, the third expedition veterans Ferguson and Sergeant-Captain Vincenthaler and Captain Henry King, were ready and willing to set out on the new expedition. Nearly all of them were "men of the old exploring party" as Frémont wrote of them; clearly there would be no shortage of tough and able volunteers.

There remained the matter of financial backing before the expedition could emerge to the stage of definite planning.

Senator Benton felt very earnestly that the expedition deserved Congressional support. Its purposes, to complete Frémont's survey of the West and prospect the route of a railroad line across the continent were, he and Frémont both believed, urgently in the country's interest.

In a sense, a new nation had just been born out of the recent acquisition of Texas and Oregon and the empire building of the Mexican War. The little United States had quite suddenly grown up into the giant land of America, stretching from sea to shining sea. This fulfilled the ambitious dream Benton had been hugging to his heart for all of his public life, but it remained to consolidate the winnings of empire with the only bonds empire has ever considered substantial—trade.

California was remote and its hard and fast annexation would remain shaky until it could be welded into a chain of trade that ran to the East Coast. No substantial trade with California itself could be foreseen for a long while, until the region was gradually developed (not even Benton could predict the forced growth of the gold rush then about to begin), but California was admirably situated to serve as a bridge to the then very important China trade; in fact, the underlying purpose of Benton's long agitation for western expansion, a purpose he had inherited from Thomas Jefferson whom he regarded as his geopolitical master, had been to secure a western gateway to this trade of the East Indies and China. He had made so familiar the bit of stage business of pointing west and crying, "There lies the East, there lies the road to India!" that it was carved on the toga-draped statue his Missouri constituents later erected to his memory.

A transcontinental railroad would make magic medicine in effecting the anticipated bigger and better commerce with the Orient, and would immediately establish California as an integral part of that commerce. The railroad would also physically bind the new empire together, literally strap the East and West together with the iron of the rails. And with a railroad, emigrants could stream west in the multiplied numbers that would complete with finality the work of consolidation.

"Nothing," declaimed Senator Benton in a later speech to the Senate on this subject, "is more essential than roads. . . . We know that the Romans . . . never considered a conquered territory added to the republic or the empire until it was perforated by a road. There was no annexation in their idea until there was communication. The idea was well founded, sir. . . ."

With an American road to India, perorated Mr. Benton, "the rich commerce of Asia will flow through our centre," and he instanced Tyre, Sidon, Balbec, Palmyra, Alexandria, Constantinople, Genoa, and Venice—"mere cities" which became "the match of kingdoms and the envy of kings"—Lisbon, Amsterdam, and London, all of whom in their turn "became great in arms, in letters, in wealth, and in power" to attest the ability of "this commerce to enrich, to aggrandize, and to enlighten nations. . . . In no instance has it failed to carry the nation, or the people which possessed it, to the highest pinnacle of wealth and power, and with it the highest attainments of letters, arts, and sciences. . . . An American road to India, through the heart of our country, will revive upon its line all the wonders of which we have read—and eclipse them. The western wilderness, from the Pacific to the Mississippi, will start into life under its touch. A long line of cities will grow up. . . ."

But the route of such a projected road, whether it headed west from the north or south or the central portion of the country, was important. The North and the South were forging into the gun-point rivalry that would result, in a few years, in the Civil War. The solidarity of the Union between North and South was to be considered even before that of the union between East and West. If a transcontinental railroad ran west from the South or the North, the West might tend to grow into a distinct colony of whichever camp possessed the railroad. The possessor of the railroad would provide the mother touch and most of the settlers and could shape the West in its own political image. But such an expansion of either power would upset the precarious equilibrium between the slave States and industry States and imperil the Union. This besides factors of terrain and weather: a northern route would be subjected, presumably, to heavier winters that might make it impassable during much of the year, and a southern route would appear to be an almost constant succession of desert jornadas, over sunburnt sand described by Senator Benton as "sands which creep, like an army of pis-ants, under a gentle breeze, which bury the traveler who lies down to sleep on them—" and

without sufficient wood or water, then considered as much a
necessity for a railroad as for a wagon trail.

For these reasons and, of course, because of his own sec-
tional loyalties as a Missourian, Benton hoped for a railroad
that would follow a central route, running west on a line from
the vicinity of St. Louis. ("Behold the extended and ramified
system of railways from the Mississippi to the Atlantic! What
is it but an expanded fan! the top on the Atlantic coast, the
spokes converging to St. Louis! and the road to San Francisco
the handle to that fan, in the extension of which every western
and every Atlantic road would find its own participation in the
splendid commerce of Western America and Eastern Asia!")
If a central route that was more feasible and more direct than
either a northern or southern route could be put forward, the
great railroad route argument would be over before it began.
The best westward roads generally known were via South
Pass, that lay a little too far north to best suit the desired central route, or the Santa Fe Trail through Raton Pass, connecting in New Mexico with difficult trails that wandered too far
south. There were other passes in the Rockies that Frémont
had traveled, but these too, besides presenting greater engineering difficulties for a railroad, fell north of the central line.

Frémont believed in the superiority of a central route. He
had been over much of it, on both sides of the Rockies. It only
remained to seek out a workable pass in the Rockies nearer
a more central point, a railroad pass that could be used winter
and summer, and on a line that cut as straight through the
mountains as possible, to reduce to the minimum the enormous
difficulties of railroad building in the mountain country.

Furthermore, there were trappers' reports of such a pass, a
good year-around pass that crossed the Continental Divide in
the neighborhood of the head of the Rio Grande, near the desired line of the thirty-eighth parallel. Bill Williams, the old
trapper who lived with the Utes in that country and who had

guided Frémont's third expedition over the Rockies by another pass farther to the north, knew it; it was said Robidoux, the trapper and trader, took wagons over it. It would be the prime objective of the fourth expedition to have a look at this particular mountain region under midwinter conditions, and see if it could get through.

Discussion of a transcontinental railroad was not new. In the early 1830's the suggestion appeared in several newspapers, and at the same time a professor at St. Joseph's College in Kentucky advocated such a notion (following which the college trustees had him declared insane and fired him). In 1842 Asa Whitney began memorializing Congress on the idea of a northern-route road, from Lake Michigan westward, between the forty-second and forty-fifth parallels, and in 1845 the first Memphis Railroad Convention countered by proposing a southern route along the thirty-second parallel. As time went on and the western movement gathered power, more discussions of a transcontinental railroad appeared in journals and were held in Congress and in public meetings. But the fourth expedition was the first step in the project beyond the talking stage.

Senator Benton's request for an appropriation of $30,000 to finance the expedition was undoubtedly handicapped by political overtones. If the appropriation was granted it would appear to be a vindication of Frémont and a rebuke to the Administration that had countenanced his court-martial. Senator Benton being Senator Benton was not the man to ignore this implication; neither were his Congressional enemies whom he thought of as the tools of the "West Point bloc" that had engineered Frémont's ruin. The appropriation resolution received a favorable report from the Senate committee, but was overwhelmingly defeated in the House.

This was a discouraging setback, and another calamity struck during the early summer in Jessie's sudden illness. She was working on the abridged report of the third expedition, the

Geographical Memoir on California, when she collapsed at her desk. Jessie was pregnant at the time; her breakdown was serious and left her health unstable for several years to come. Frémont, deeply worried, saw in her illness still another injury from the court-martial, feeling that it was a direct result of the strain and worry of the trial.

None of these things shook Frémont's determination on the new expedition. It is more probable they would have spurred it on. Money could be raised some place, and as for Jessie, California would be the best of climates for her convalescence, if she was strong enough to make the voyage out. That remained a question for some time, complicated by the thought of the raw world of the West that would face her when she arrived. She was young, accustomed to what was then called refined society; she would have her small daughter and the new baby with her. She was troubled by the fear that she might be more a burden to her husband than a help. The decision was made for her, naturally, by the thought that Frémont's need for her was all that mattered. As she wrote later, "I saw only the proud lonely man making a new start in life. . . ."

4

As any American schoolchild knows, if they still print the picture in the history books, and maybe they do, "Westward Ho!" is not a novel by Charles Kingsley but a painting depicting a wagon train of pioneers in perilous transit. The painting is by Emanuel Leutze, N.A., America's foremost exponent of the school of the grand and glorious that found its highest point in such subjects as the Charge of the Light Brigade or the Battle of Trafalgar or Leutze's own "Washington Crossing the Delaware." The original of "Westward Ho!" bearing the more stately title of "Westward the Course of Empire Takes Its Way," is a fresco on the wall of the west stairway of the House wing of the Capitol, and for it in 1861 the Congress appropriated $20,000, or two thirds of the amount asked and refused for the fourth expedition. In the forefront of the picture a mounted man wearing a slouch hat and a yellow neckerchief, his left hand upraised, is a symbol of the guiding frontiersman. This symbolic frontiersman is a portrait of Ned Kern, a lean man, properly tall in the saddle, cool-eyed and not unhandsome, drawn from his photograph and costumed from his own clothes.

Ned Kern was Edward Meyer Kern of Philadelphia, artist and topographer on Frémont's third expedition, and one of the two artists accompanying the fourth expedition. The other was Richard Kern, Ned's next older brother. The next brother of the family older than Dick was Dr. Benjamin Kern, who went along on the fourth expedition as physician.

If Frémont's leitmotiv for the fourth expedition was relentless determination, that of Ned Kern and his brothers could be called headlong enthusiasm. A later remark attributed (questionably) to Godey has it that the Kerns were "the most strenuous advocates of the organization of the expedition in Washington. . . ."

The Kern family might present a useful microcosm of the world of the eastern seaboard that was losing so many of its younger brothers to the West. The family was long established in Philadelphia. The father was Deputy Collector of the Port of Philadelphia for a number of years. There were nine children, six boys and three girls. The eldest son, John, was for a time a sea captain and then became an artist, and was a teacher of drawing for twenty years at Franklin Institute and at Friends School. The three youngest boys were soundly educated in polite professions, Ned and Dick as artists, Ben at Pennsylvania Medical College, and thus irrelevantly equipped the three of them went West.

There were economic factors in this and spiritual factors, romantic factors both sound and synthetic. In a word, the breath of the time was in their nostrils.

That the family felt itself in some economic ill fortune is revealed by a reflection of Ned's when discussing a personal loss and a hope destroyed—that such was the family luck. Doc Kern at first, as a new young doctor in Philadelphia, set up shop in an office of his own but within a couple of years was practicing from the family home. Ned and Dick joined their eldest brother, the professor of art—he was some fifteen years their senior, and they called him Old Man—in his studio and were taking students in drawing, as he did, and prowling down commissions to make illustrations for medical botanies and microscopic anatomies, and three drawing teachers in one studio might have been a little crowded. While Ned was out West the first time, Dick mentioned in a letter to him that "business is good, and the income certain . . . sufficient for Old Man and self . . ." the implication being plain that it was not always thus. So much for economic impetus, and the Kern boys went West to seek their fortunes.

But here, as the family is representative of its world, tentatively probing new shoots westward, the Kern boys are even more ideally representative of a special and important aspect of that westwardness, the seduction of the sophisticated East by the autochthonous rude virgin of the West. Considered as a symbol of this union rather than as a professional guiding frontiersman, which he was not, Ned was very aptly chosen for the leading role in "Westward Ho!"

For the Kern boys went out to make their fortunes in Frémont's California, and they took paints and pencils and kept notebooks and made scientific collections, and wherever they went, bloody with fresh-killed buffalo on the plains or painting Navajos in the shadow of the Cañon de Chelly, they were to be a temporary little extension of 62 Filbert Street, Philadelphia, but it did not work out that way. At the first blush on the virgin's cheek Filbert Street was utterly forgotten and the West was from that time on their home.

Here is the essential difference between those who merely saw the West, those who merely worked in the West, and those who became the West. To Frémont, whose values and deepest recognitions were fixed at more sophisticated poles, the cowbells at the frontier welcoming the return home would always be sweet music. Charles Preuss, his dogged chief topographer, excellent German craftsman, was too solid, sound, and steady, too much a twentieth-century man, too much a realist, to let himself become possessed by anything. But to many others, and among these the Kerns, home became magically switched around when they stepped into the West, and thus the keenest pleasure of these was never in a return from the Shining Mountains but in the setting out toward them.

This could not have been so much a matter of place as of inward feeling. The Kerns' hope of fortune was lost in the snow with the fourth expedition, but they went on traveling west, in a veritable sense, the rest of their lives, although they did not intend to farm or trade or settle and exploit the new land, or strike it rich in gold—they were next door to the gold rush of '49 and ignored it—and, for all their collections of bird skins and flowers and the real value of their work in ethnology, they did not regard themselves as dedicated scientific explorers. If all life yearns towards its own recognition, then the feeling that held them was simply that here they recognized themselves. The suspicion arises that in the beginning they were not so much going out seeking their fortunes as going adventuring, odd as the word may fall on today's practical ears. And the adventuring itself surely remained as much a part of the home feeling as any place in itself, arched however beautifully among the mountains.

Behind them in the Susquehanna River valley a song was later sung that ran:

"Once on a time there lived a man, his name was Peter Gray,
He lived way down in that there town called Pennsyl-
van-i-a. . . .
Now Peter went away out west to seek his fort-i-an,
But he was caught and scalp-ed by a bloody Ind-i-an. . . .
Blow ye winds of morning, blow ye winds, heigh ho. . . ."

And it is the last line that most fitly applies.

Ned was twenty-one years old when he joined the third expedition in 1845, substituting for Preuss. Frémont's letter to Ned informing him he was chosen began: "I am authorized to appoint you Artist to the Expedition which is about to visit the region west of the Rocky Mts. Your duties will be arduous. . . ."

To get this job Ned won out over a small riot of forty-two zealous artist applicants who were eager to take Preuss's place: a chance to go with Frémont—there was a fitting frame for romantic ambition. Frémont has been likened to a Galahad in the mind of that hour, particularly in the mind of the younger generation of the time, but one Midshipman Edward Fitzgerald Beale, a member of that younger generation ("A real midshipman of the old type," Frémont said, "happy and spilling over with uncontrolled good spirits, as mostly midshipmen are used to be when away from the restraints of the ship"), reached somewhat higher in the hierarchy when he spoke of an assignment in California during the conquest to go ashore and locate Frémont: "I remember the lovely spring-like morning (I think it was autumn, but it ought to have been spring because I was so happy) when I was ordered to command a squadron of boats (what is the Presidency to that at nineteen or twenty?) and go to find Frémont. Sir Galahad going to search for the Holy Grail."

On the third expedition Ned Kern followed the Grail over the prairies to Bent's Fort, the famous trading post of the Santa Fe Trail, on up the Arkansas River to its headwaters on the Continental Divide, across the Rockies, through the mirages of the salt deserts of Utah to the Sierra and California. He stood to his rifle when on the plains a war party of some hundreds of Pawnees and Comanches threatened to attack: Godey rode to meet them and talked them out of it. He looked in the dizzying gorges of the cañons of the Arkansas; he hunted buffalo not only on the plains but high in the Rockies, within a few miles of the highest point in Colorado; he rode his horse through the shallows of the dead and silent Great Salt Lake, the floor of the lake a crusted scab of salt into which the

horses sank to their fetlocks. He rode beside Kit Carson, Joe
Walker, Godey, and Old Bill Williams.

In the big days of the fur trade two Americans had led parties
of trappers across the open-hearth wastes of sand and chapar-
ral and pastel mountains that Frémont called the Great Basin,
between Salt Lake and the snow-capped Sierra that stood like
a two-mile-high signboard announcing California. One of these
was Bible-toting Jed Smith, dead now, killed by the Comanche
lance when Ned Kern was a child of seven, and the other was
Joe Walker, who a dozen years before had passed by here leading a fur brigade and shooting Digger Indians right and left.
In this country, on the Humboldt River in what is now Nevada, Frémont divided his little army of sixty-odd men of the
third expedition, sending the main party of fifty or so to explore the Humboldt to its sink, the marsh where it disappeared
in the desert, and then meet him again at Walker Lake at the
foot of the Sierra, a lake named for Joe Walker; and here the
expedition was immediately split again, as before, to enter
California by two different routes. Ned Kern, as topographer,
was placed technically in command of this main body of the
expedition, with Joseph Reddeford Walker himself as guide,
and what is the command of a squadron of boats to that at
twenty-one or twenty-two?

In California, in the interlude of idling and resting and saber
rattling at the Mexican authorities before the West Coast unit
of the Mexican War went into production, Ned Kern had a
river named after him by Captain Frémont, the Kern River,
which runs from Kern Ridge past Kern Hot Springs through
Kern Cañon and the Kern Lakes in the Inyo-Kern country, past
Kernville in Kern County and Kern Peak in the high Sierra
(11,493 feet). Upper Kern Cañon cuts the western base of
Mt. Whitney, highest in the United States. Just across the
mountain is Owens Lake (Dick Owens) and Owens River in
the Owens Valley and farther south is Owens Peak, near

Walker Pass. Walker Lake is far to the north on the Nevada side of the Sierra, rather near Carson Sink and Carson Pass and Carson River.

In California there were grizzly bear hunts: more than a dozen were once killed in two hours. The voyageurs Archambeau and Basil Lajeunesse tracked down two enormous grizzlies that were estimated to weigh 900 pounds apiece. There was a big bear feast, and rollicking French songs went on all night long. There was a sociable to which were invited some American emigrants camped nearby. Tom Martin, one of the third expedition men, tells about it: "Having received permission from Frémont to have a barbecue we collected a large quantity of bear, elk, and deer meat. Then we took a number of our horses and went down for the emigrants—among those who came were about fifteen ladies. A place had been cleared away and we began dancing which we kept up for two days. On the third day the emigrants returned to their camp."

In California, Ned watched some of his mountaineer companions trade exhibitions of fast and fancy rifle shooting for exhibitions of the finest horsemanship in the world by the Californians—a witness of the time describes a drunk vaquero at a fiesta "mounted on a restive, plunging beast, holding at arm's length a tray of glasses, brimming with aguardiente, which he politely offered to everybody within reach of his curvettings, without ever once spilling a drop." And a little later, in sudden fighting with those Klamath Indians who gained Frémont's great respect, he might have seen Frémont himself ride down a warrior who had an arrow drawn to the head and aimed at Carson, and he might have come on a scalp hung to an arrow planted in the trail, a Klamath scalp: mountain man Lucien Maxwell had left it there. The arrow had been shot at Maxwell as he rode along, but it had missed. And he would have heard the saga of the fight of another member of the expedition, the Delaware, Crane, who battled among the

Klamaths with his clubbed rifle and received five poisoned arrows through the body, each of which he jerked out and cast away as soon as it drove into him, and withal succeeded in loading his rifle and had the cap half on when he fell dead.

The festivities of the California conquest opened, and Ned was named by Frémont a lieutenant in the volunteer California battalion made up of Ned's third expedition companions of the long trail of the past year, including the Delawares (those left alive after the Klamath fighting), American settlers, Walla Walla and California Indians, an irregular company of Dragoons formed of shoregoing Navy personnel under the resounding command of Captain Daingerfield Fauntleroy, USN, a troop or two of native Californians, and anyone else who happened along. The Frémont men in the battalion created something of a sensation among Navy officers who saw them at Monterey and drowned in a lather of J. Fenimore Cooper describing "this wildest wild party" of "true trappers," these "gaunt bony woodsmen of the Far West, dressed in skins," with their "rifles, revolving pistols, and long knives," not to mention the "savage aspect" of "their black beards, with white teeth glittering through."

Ned Kern was left in command of Sutter's Fort, with ringing orders from Frémont to "iron and confine any person who shall disobey your orders—if necessary, shoot any person who shall endanger the safety of the place." Ned organized a garrison, mostly made up from Sutter's Indian cowpunchers, appointed Captain Sutter his second-in-command, recruited emigrants and Indians for service with the California Battalion, set up a regular mail service between the fort and Sonoma, and led his men in sorties against hostile Indians, sometimes imaginary and sometimes real.

He wrote to his brother Dick back in Philadelphia, one July day in 1846 when Commodore Sloat, bound for the States, offered to take mail: "Little did I think when sitting at home in our office . . . that I would ever raise to be a Mil. character, a rale commandante of a Fort. With power to do as I please and shoot people if they do not obey me, and all that sort of thing. . . . Anyhow, strange as you may think it here I am, vested with the aforesaid authority and surrounded by a Garrison of runaway East Indianmen and Indians . . . and the most ungodly horde of the largest and hardest to catch highest jumping and hard biting putting your finger on and not to be found fleas that ever worried man since the days of Adam. They are a staple production of the country. . . ."

Ned added a few words of observation on "this newly acquired Terr. of the U.S. . . . What a field this country will be for those miserable pests the missionaries. Here they can find the untutored child of the forest in a perfect state of nature, women-preachers could do a better business than the men. This is damned unhealthy neighborhood and I'm Dr. I made a mash . . . and liked to have fixed off one of the prisoners, that would have been a bad job as people would have said he had been poisoned. . . ."

And closed his letter with the unmilitary ritual: "But like the old woman who fancied herself an hour glass I must stop being quite run out. Somebody turn me up."

Ned made friends with everyone, with prisoners left in his charge, with George McKinstry, appointed sheriff in those parts, who wrote Ned during the gold rush advising him to "hasten out" and a couple of years later wrote him again, with a sigh, "I presume if you had come and made the almighty pile you would have lost it as the rest of us have . . . ," and even with fiery Captain Johan Augustus Sutter, the little king of the Sacramento Valley who was deposed from the rule of his own fort to make place for young Commandante Kern, a touchy situation indeed; but Sutter wrote to Dick Kern a few years later that when Ned "and myself was together how many hearty laughs we had, and enjoyed ourselves, in our old poor

times. . . . I give not up the hope to have once more the
pleasure of seeing him."

By virtue of his office, during February and March of 1847
Ned helped organize and provision the repeated reliefs sent
to rescue the Reed-Donner party, eighty-nine emigrants badly
advised in their route by "one Hastings author of the Emigrants guide etc as big an ass as runs" as Ned described him,
and now stranded in the Sierra snows, freezing, starving, and
the stronger feeding on the weaker: forty-five were gotten out
alive. He wrote, "It's so seldom we hear of such suffering on
land that it has the appearance of romance and one would
hardly credit it. . . ."

Ned would have reason, two years later, to remember vividly
the horror stories brought out with the Donner party survivors.
But at the time he could read, at the rescue operations base
camp on Bear Creek, George McKinstry's double-entendre
jokes about the man-eating women up there—McKinstry was
"full of fun and wit," as Captain Sutter said.

For all his youth and blithesomeness, Ned proved himself a
surprisingly capable officer in California. He kept careful,
accurate records of the business of his district. He demanded
responsible authority for orders and decisions, and had little
sympathy with the freebooting temper of the times. He wrote
of the Bear Flag revolt: "Had the revolutionists been left to
themselves a few weeks would have settled the business by
their defeating themselves. A few honest and well disposed
persons among them who really intended the movement for
the best, but the majority moved by nothing but the chance of
plunder without the slightest principles of honor to guide them,
they would have defeated the cause. . . ."

After Frémont's downfall in California, Ned Kern returned
home by sea. At the court-martial Frémont and Benton tried to
show that General Kearny had willfully hindered both Kern
and Henry King from accompanying Frémont back to the

States, presumably to handicap Frémont's defense against Kearny's then unrevealed design of the court-martial. The two men and the records they had kept were important, Frémont asserted, to the over-all background of the case, which included all Frémont's operations in California under Navy authority. Kern's testimony was also wanted to support the contention of the defense as to the pattern of malice prepense in Kearny's behavior, for example, in taking approximately a thousand horses and mules from "Frémont and Lt. Kern and other places without receipts," thus leaving Frémont and his lieutenants empty-handed but still responsible for the animals to the ranchers from whom they had been requisitioned. It was definitely established at the trial that Frémont had asked permission of Kearny to summon Kern and King before setting out for the States, and that Kearny refused the permission. However, both men were near at hand at the time and, as it happened, started out four days behind Kearny and Frémont, hoping to catch up to them, but couldn't, and had to turn back.

Probably the trial was drawing to a close when Kern and King arrived in the East by ship, and it may be that there they learned for the first time of the charges brought against their recent commander. Neither is listed as a witness in the proceedings of the court-martial, although their possible whereabouts are discussed in the testimony.

So Ned was home again, temporarily, after more than two years in the West, and he appeared transformed into that new thing on the horizon of the family home at 1 Olive Street and Old Man's studio on Filbert Street, a westerner.

There was no doubt that he had seen the elephant, that he had found what he had gone to seek. He had heard the songs of the voyageurs and the hee-ya-hay! of the savage skulp yell and the heart-stopping thunder of stampeding buffalo and the suspended silence of the Sierra snows. He had learned Spanish, and would have become familiar with the lingua franca of the plains and the mountains, the Indian sign language, one of the more marvelous developments of their neolithic culture, vestiges of which are still in use today, particularly among Pueblo commercial travelers to the Navajos trading raw turquoise for silver work—nobody can learn Navajo, the Pueblos say. His ear would have been bent, too, to the language of the mountain men, the mixture of Walter Scott English, Spanish, voyageurs' profane French, words from Indian dialects, and the lustiest cant the slang-loving American people have ever produced, the workaday terminology of the trappers, who drove up to Green River in a mess of boudins and shouted that's beaver! for fat cow when they meant buffler and to discuss tactics of a skirmish might remark, "We'll cache here and see how them pelados' stick floats and if they want hair we'll talk Hawken. Wagh!"

He had learned something of the science of exploration, entailing an observation of rocks and soil formation, flowers and grasses, shrubs and trees, birds and animals and weather, and above all the science of the course, the run of the land and its waterways, the determination of position and altitude, arduous work to be faithfully pursued in spite of all the interfering multifold duties necessary to stay alive, and if a poor camp had to be maintained in an uncomfortable site for two or three nights until the skies cleared sufficiently for a fix, so be it, for that was the ultimate purpose of the camp and the entire expedition in the first place. The earnest, indefatigable pursuit of this science was the one thing at which John Charles Frémont excelled, within the emotional limitations of his time bound round as it was by the romantic baldric, and at which he would have been an inspiring preceptor.

Already a superlative draughtsman, Ned would have learned the added special art of mapmaking, but beyond this his artist's eye would be dazzled by the magnificence it had seen, the massive mountains cloaked in pure deep green of spruce, topped

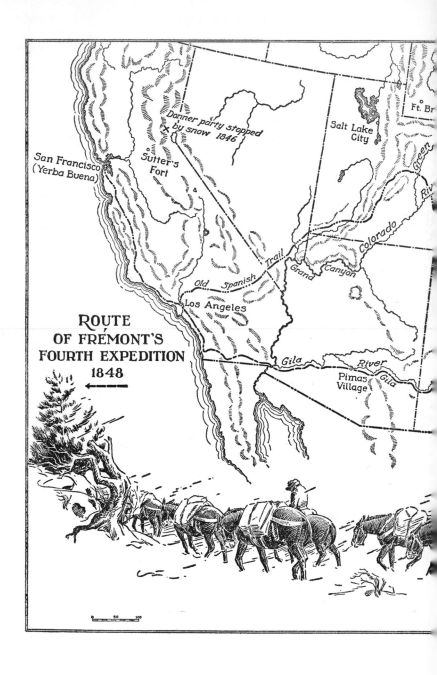

ROUTE
OF FRÉMONT'S
FOURTH EXPEDITION
1848

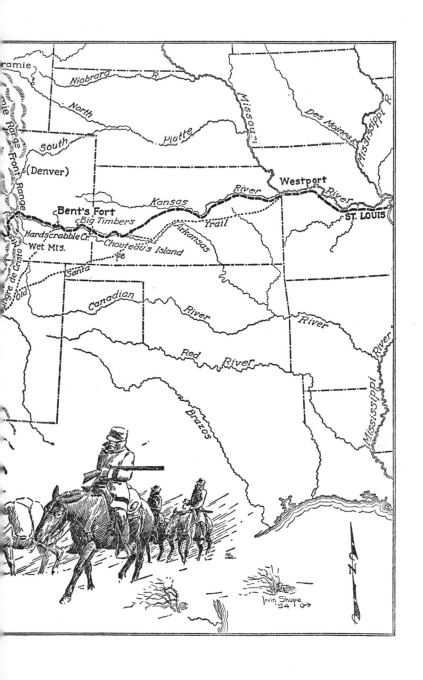

Niobrara R.

North

Platte

South

Missouri

Des Moines R.

Mississippi R.

(Denver)

Front Range

Laramie

Range

Kansas River

Westport

River

ST. LOUIS

Bent's Fort

Big Timbers

Trail

Hardscrabble Cr.

Chouteau's Island

Arkansas

Wet Mts.

Santa Fe

Sangre de Cristo

Old

Canadian

River

River

Red River

Mississippi River

Brazos

Irvin Shope
'54

N

with great stars of snow splashed on their naked peaks, the still and breathless beauty of high mountain parks, quiet rippling meadows stretching for miles among the crags and forests, or the sky on fire in a desert sunset, glory bought at the price of blinding dust that hung among them step by step, caking on faces and eyes until friends were unrecognizable, and the ivory smoke of campfires hanging in curling plumes against the soft palette of the afterglow. And the trembling chill of dawn, when gun-colored fantastic cliffs reared out of the dissolving darkness and were swept with a sudden vermilion veil at the first light of the rising sun, when the feeling would be strongest that surely no other voice had ever before spoken in this awesome place, this silent immensity glittering with a newness that had waited here undisturbed for so many millenniums; and a whiskered compañero, ready to mount, held his rifle between his knees and lit his clay pipe, and the day was started.

Ned's stories, and the presence in the flesh of some of the heroic characters who had figured in them, when various third expedition men visited the Kerns in Philadelphia after the trial, must have been enough in themselves to strike fires of enthusiasm in brothers Dick and Dr. Ben, but it was undoubtedly the dream of California that settled their hash: California, the acknowledged major prize of the Mexican War, round brown hills blanketed in poppies and shaded by holly-leaved oaks, washed by the blue South Sea, warm and tranquil in eternal sunshine, "the land where," as Sutter put it, "1000 chances are for one in comparison with an old country." Americans who had settled there under the Mexican regime had already prospered remarkably enough, and now that it was American territory there would be opportunity unlimited, especially for anyone who went out there with Frémont, because out there, why, Frémont was the biggest man in the country. Furthermore, if the fourth expedition succeeded—and

Frémont's expeditions always succeeded—the Kern boys, as members of the scientific staff, would share in the rewards and glory; and if its success should actually bring a railroad in its wake, then certainly California would become the land of the future.

For the fourth expedition, then, Ned was a veteran, and Dick, twenty-seven years old, was a wide-eyed greenhorn possessed of the midshipman soul that had been Ned's three years before. Doc, at thirty, was a little too old, a little too much settled in dignity, to share that spirit. Dick was malleable and ready to embrace the coming experiences that would work a chemistry of change in him, but Doc remained Doc, more sober and reflective, as observant in his way as his artist brothers, but alone of the three Kern boys observant to the last as the man he had been at the beginning, sober-sided Doc of Philadelphia.

And when Congress refused to finance the new expedition, the zeal of the Kern boys was such that they offered to go along without pay.

This doubtless opened an interesting avenue of thought to Frémont, and it appears that he may have made the same arrangement with some others of the personnel—to serve without pay, in the hope that Congress would reverse its decision and pay the bill in the face of a brilliant success. One of the fourth expedition men wrote later, "He promised us no wages, but said that when the work was finished Govt would pay us." If this was so it reveals a considerable stretch of loyalty indeed, dollars being inexorably dollars even among faithful children of the mountains. The usual scale of pay ranged from a very few (fifteen to twenty) dollars a month for mule packers to as much as three dollars a day for technical experts—Ned's salary on the previous expedition—or the $100 a month Frémont had paid Kit Carson as a guide.

To raise money for equipment and supplies Benton wrapped

his cloak about him (the Senator had a long cloak and a silk hat and the nose of a brooding osprey, enough to fill out anyone's picture of an imperial figure) and went home to St. Louis, where he drummed up financing from railroad enthusiasts, interested friends, and doubtless his own pocket. Frémont himself was broke. Army pay does not make for riches, and he had realized no income from his best-selling reports (proclaimed Benton: "His work is public; his journals are public property; his maps are public property. He took no copyright for anything which he did while in the service of the United States. . . .") although he was to be paid by the Senate for the *Geographical Memoir* and map worked up after his resignation. Apparently the bulk of his savings had been the $3000 used by Larkin in California for the unwanted purchase of the wild Mariposas. Counsel fees for the court-martial were estimated before the trial by Benton at $2000, which would be "such as you could not pay," as he wrote to Frémont. The mill irons and agricultural equipment shipped from New York for California were paid for by loans from Benton and friends in the East; Frémont still had a way with wealthy and influential friends, and even though he would start on the new expedition with no money of his own it is probable he was armed with sizable commissions from such friends for investment in California.

As Benton knew, St. Louis was railroad hungry. In the railroad fever of the 1830's eighteen companies had been chartered at a railroad convention in St. Louis, with capital stock totaling eight million dollars, to put in local railroads. The panic of 1837 had stopped all that for the time and it was to be 1851 before the first rails would be laid in the state of Missouri, but railroad was still a magic word there, and Benton and Frémont were magic names. Three St. Louis businessmen, Thornton Grimsley, O. D. Filley, and Robert Campbell, underwrote most of the fourth expedition's outfitting and expense.

Grimsley was a saddler, with an "unequalled establishment, giving constant employment to from sixty to seventy hands," the maker of the bridles, saddles, and Grimsley X-tree pack-saddles used on the expedition. Filley was a manufacturer of camping equipment. Robert Campbell, called Colonel Campbell, the usual title in those parts for any man over forty with a clean collar, was one of the West's great merchant adventurers, veteran of the fur trade, builder of the first Fort Laramie on the Oregon Trail fifteen years before when he had been in the mountain trade in partnership with Captain Bill Sublette (Cut-Face to the Indians, and a peer of the realm in the Rockies), and knew the West as a mountain man. His participation as a backer speaks of his confidence in Frémont as well as of his interest as a trader in the dream of a far west railroad.

In the summer of 1848 Kit Carson came to Washington, carrying dispatches from California, and stayed at the Benton home as a guest of the Bentons and Frémonts. In late July Jessie's baby was born, a boy, their first son, named, naturally, Benton Frémont. The baby, perhaps as a reflection of Jessie's recent illness, was frail and unwell. Kit Carson was on hand as sponsor when little Benton was baptized, August 15, at the Episcopal Church of the Epiphany, in Washington.

The expedition was in process of preparation while Carson was staying with the Frémonts, and certainly Frémont must have talked it over with him at length. It is scarcely credible that Kit objected flatly to the notion of driving over the Rockies in midwinter along the line of the thirty-eighth parallel. Even in Frémont's present state of mind, snapping at dreams of bold venture as a wolf snaps at a wound, Kit Carson's opinion would have swung too much weight to ignore. Carson had stood too high in Frémont's councils on too many trails for too long a time; Frémont valued his advice beyond any other. It is much more probable that Kit said maybe, depending on the weather, depending on the condition of the animals when they reached the mountains, depending on the look of things ahead, depending on many things. The decision could only be made on the spot, when the time and the mountains were at hand.

It is more than likely this is the way the matter was left, as far as Carson's opinion was concerned: that Frémont would try to take the expedition through the mountains near the head of the Del Norte, the Rio Grande, if it seemed feasible when he got there, and if not that he would swing down south into New Mexico and pick up the familiar Old Spanish Trail.

Carson, however, was not going along. As in the case of Godey, Frémont and Carson remained lifelong friends, and in later years Kit stated: "I was with Frémont from 1842 to 1847. I find it impossible to describe the hardships through which we passed, nor am I capable of doing justice to the credit which he deserves. . . . I can never forget this treatment of me while I was in his employ, and how cheerfully he suffered with his men when undergoing the severest of hardships. His perseverance and his willingness to participate in all that was undertaken, no matter whether the duty was rough or easy, are the main causes of his success. . . ." Nevertheless, the embittered Frémont who came out of the court-martial was a different man from the Frémont Carson had known on the earlier expeditions, and perhaps some such psychological factor had something to do with Kit's absence from the fourth expedition. Perhaps.

What seems much more reasonable is that Carson merely wanted to spend the winter at home for a change. He had sold out a New Mexico rancho, at a sacrifice, to answer Frémont's call and join the third expedition. During the war President Polk had given him a lieutenancy in Frémont's regiment of Mounted Rifles, this had kept him on duty in California and away from home still longer, and Carson had just now learned that the Senate had refused to confirm his commission, probably a piece of political sniping in the spite campaign between

Benton and the Administration that had grown out of the court-martial. The reason given for denying the commission was that Kit could read and write only haltingly if at all, and was deficient in book learning and similar cultural advantages, although a fortified degree of literacy was scarcely a prominent requirement in the Army of the forties, nor even in the United States Senate. Due to the technicalities of the situation, incidentally, Carson had no pay coming for his past year's tour of duty.

In any case, he was out of the Army and a free man again, and except for three brief visits when he had passed back and forth through Taos on official missions, Kit had not been home since August of 1845 and this was August of 1848. He would be thirty-nine years old his next birthday. He owned considerable property in New Mexico, brought to him by his wife, Josefa Jaramillo, who was well dowered as well as beautiful. ("Her style of beauty was of the haughty, heartbreaking kind—such as would lead a man with the glance of the eye to risk his life for one smile. I could not but desire her acquaintance," wrote eighteen-year-old Lewis Garrard.) Carson might well have desired her acquaintance also and might justifiably have cherished thoughts of settling down for a time, after so many years of constant wandering. This appears to have been the assumption circulated among the mountains as to why he was not with the new expedition.

Senator Benton, during the couple of weeks following the baptism of his namesake Benton Frémont, was in Washington plotting a very typical Benton maneuver, typical because it was brilliantly adroit, drastically hot-tempered, and would kill a whole flock of birds with one stone. It would give still a new purpose to the expedition, lend added importance to Frémont's return to California, embarrass President Polk's now-hated Administration, attack Kearny and his successor as military governor of California, Colonel Mason, and it would force the issue on the establishment of territorial government in California, the concealed chief purpose behind the whole thing.

Due to many petty political reasons, but principally the touchy question of slavery in new territories, California had been left by Congress without any provision for legal and authorized government. Benton had been ferocious in demanding territorial government there, sensing a danger in leaving this prize maverick unbranded. The temporary military government set up under wartime authority had legally ceased to exist upon the signing of the Treaty of Guadalupe Hidalgo ending the war, and that had been months ago, in February. Garrisons remained in California to hold the country but had no legal authority there, and there was no civil government. President Polk, more cat-footed than ever, said only that he was powerless and that Congress had to act. He was in no mood for cracking the Administration whip; a Presidential campaign was in progress, and at such a parlous time every little party congressman has a meaning all his own. Benton felt that in such a critical matter Congress should be forced to act by every means in the Administration's power, and if the Administration wouldn't crack the whip, he would.

So on August 27 Senator Benton wrote a letter to the people of California, advising them to form an independent government of their own until such time as Congress should act. He outlined the form of government they should adopt and wrote that "the edicts promulgated by your temporary governors (Kearney and Mason, each an ignoramus), so far as these edicts went to change the law of the land, are null and void . . . for the laws of a conquered country remain in force until altered by the proper legislative authority." The letter was dated as "written at Washington City . . . and sent by Colonel Frémont." Frémont was to bear it westward on his expedition, and the hint was inherent that the Californians would do well to choose Colonel Frémont as their governor.

This mine exploded in President Polk's face when the letter was published in the New York *Herald* a month later. Polk wrote in his diary of this "extraordinary letter" assuming to "speak as from one in authority," and "calculated to do much mischief." He noted that "It is sent by Col. Frémont . . . and the inference is plain enough that he means they shall make Col. Frémont the Governor of the Independant Government they shall form. Indeed I think it pretty clear that this was the main object." (Frémont's popularity in California at the time is ironically attested in a letter written some months later by a young easterner in Los Angeles: "It is generally supposed at the north that Frémont is very popular here, but that does not seem to be the case. *They say* he gave rowdy balls and so became popular with the lower classes, but the best families *could* not attend them and consequently were not influenced by them. . . .") President Polk, reacting beautifully, wrote that the "arrogance and whole tone" of Benton's letter were "offensive and must do harm, unless the people of California have assurances from the Govt that they will be taken care of by the Govt." Thus Polk took the bait with a rush, and three Cabinet meetings at the end of September and early in October were devoted to the Benton letter and to drafting an official letter to California from the Secretary of State, designed "to persuade the people of California not to abrogate" the present de facto military government until the President could "earnestly recommend" the establishment of a territorial government at the next session of Congress.

Now autumn and the hour of the expedition were at hand. By September plans had been completed in Washington and Frémont was making arrangements to start west for St. Louis. Jessie, with five-year-old Lilly and the new baby and Aunt Kitty, their colored nurse, would go to the frontier with him to see him off, and then return East to sail on her own voyage to California. Two cases of amputatory instruments were purchased in Philadelphia, doubtless by Doc Kern, although ordered in Frémont's name. Frémont would have assembled his chronometers and sextants, refracting telescope and compasses and barometers and thermometers. Another man may have signed on in the East before Frémont left, Julius Ducatel, the son of a Baltimore doctor. The historian Hubert Howe Bancroft lists Ducatel as also a member of the third expedition but this seems doubtful. Ducatel was young, probably another youthful easterner who wanted to go West, perhaps a "gentleman." A sprinkling of gentlemen, traveling for sport or health or business, accompanied most of Frémont's expeditions; and very commendable, these gentlemen, Frémont once remarked, but sometimes a nuisance.

Over in Georgetown, Henry King married his girl two weeks before he left for St. Louis.

In September the Frémonts traveled west by steamboat from Buffalo, Frémont a lithe little man in civilian clothes, looking somewhat more worn and old than his thirty-five years, with hunting-dog eyes and a short black beard and long hair, frontier style, the temples brushed with gray. He had written Jessie during hard times on a previous trip that his hair was turning gray before its time; now there had been the graveling court-martial and even casual spectators on the boat could see, or thought they could see, the bitterness it had left. Jessie, persistently gay and surprisingly youthful, devoted herself to trying to chase his somber mood away.

5

With St. Louis began the metamorphosis of the expedition from idea into reality, the assembling of equipment and supplies, and the gathering of still more old Frémont boys, and still more new men, attracted by the remembered glamor of his name, who wanted to go along. In St. Louis was the first breath of the frontier, and long-haired rheumatic old men with bloody mountain memories might be met at Jake Hawken's gun shop, where were made the famous rifles that had given a superlative ("that's Hawken!") to the trappers' vocabulary. St. Louis was the old capital of the mountain fur trade and still the gusty capital city of the westward spirit. In St. Louis was the Benton home, and the town or the country roundabout was the home or adopted home or mailing address between mountain sojourns of more than half the men of the fourth expedition.

Thomas Salathiel Martin was typical of one group of Frémont veterans, veterans by virtue of being graduates of the third expedition, that signed on at St. Louis for the new expedition. The second son of a large Tennessee family, Tom Martin went to St. Louis in his early twenties and lived in the vicinity for five years. He was a backwoods boy, he wasn't long on reading and writing, but he knew something of hunting. He also had a traditional backwoods tendency toward some exaggeration, especially of the feats of Tom Martin, judging by his memoirs dictated years later. When the third expedition was making up in St. Louis, Thomas Salathiel got letters of introduction to friends of Frémont in the city, who "in turn furnished me with similar letters to him," doubtless recommending Tom as a good rifleman and packer. A good rifleman he may well have been (he says he won first prize in a shooting match on the expedition) but a packer he was not; as far as the mountains were concerned he was, as were most of the third expedition recruits, "comparatively green."

He described his equipment for the third expedition, which may be taken as typical for an expedition of the time, as consisting of "1 whole stocked Hawkins rifle, two pistols, a butcher knife, saddle, bridle, pistol holsters and 2 pr blankets. For his individual use each man was given a horse or mule for riding and from one to two pack animals to care for," a job that was considerable of a chore for Tom for several weeks until he began to get the hang of it.

When General Kearny was preparing to take Frémont back East from California, Thomas Salathiel, by then ex-Trooper Martin of Company A, California Battalion, expected to go along but, he relates, Kearny "told us that if we wished to go back we would have to go back with him, which we refused to do. He then told us that we could go back with Frémont, but that Frémont would be under his orders." Upon which, with a few others "of the company," he returned across the plains with Kearny and the vanquished Frémont. He went on home to Manor County, Tennessee, for a couple of months of walking tall, and then back to St. Louis.

He was there when the St. Louis *Reveille* announced, on September 5, 1848, that "Col. Frémont, on his arrival in St. Louis, will employ men to form an escort to California. He is to continue his explorations of the country, on his own hook."

Upon which "I again joined Frémont. . . . The company was composed almost entirely of our old men and Frémont told me that he was going to survey for a RR through to Cal."

By then Tom Martin was thirty years old and a man of the world, mountain style.

Such as Thomas Salathiel were a number of others from the last expedition and its California doings, greenhorns no longer after two years' apprenticeship.

There were Billy Bacon from St. Louis County, and probably Benjamin Beadle (the newspapers have it Bedell) of St. Louis was also a third expedition man. Such were also, it appears, young Carver from Illinois and young George Hubbard from Iowa, spelled Hibbard by most of the journalists except Frémont.

There was Joseph L. Stepperfeldt, who may also have gone west with the third expedition three years before but more likely was in California beforehand and joined up with it there. It would seem Stepperfeldt was "Stepp, who was a gunsmith, and knew as well how to make a rifle as to use one," who was with Frémont and the small picked group of third expedition men that fought off the night attack by Klamath Indians in which the brilliant French scout Lajeunesse and the great Delaware warrior Crane were killed. It was Stepp who later, in a seagoing operation in San Francisco Bay, spiked the ancient Spanish cannon at the Castillo of San Joachim. He is listed on the roster of Company A, California Battalion, as Chief Armorer. This was the "Step" the youthful author Lewis Garrard met in company with Breckenridge, riding east on the Santa Fe Trail when coming back from California; Garrard went hunting with Stepp, on a buffalo crawl.

There was John Scott, English-born westerner, another California Battalion man. He had been a lieutenant in Company A, which numbered so many of the third expedition explorators in its ranks, but there is some evidence that he had come to California as an earlier emigrant, and was a "hunter in Copay County" before the expedition arrived.

Charles Van Linneus Taplin was ready to go again—Captain Taplin, of both the second and third expeditions, the California Battalion, and the U.S. Army. Like Kit Carson, Taplin had been given a Regular Army commission, brevetted captain soon after, and soon after that resigned, a week after Lieutenant Colonel Frémont resigned his commission at the close of the court-martial. Taplin, not yet thirty, was by now old with skill and experience.

There were three other friends from California, three California Indian vaqueros, Manuel, Joaquin, and Gregorio, who had come East in Frémont's service and would go back with him. The British travel writer Ruxton described the one of them he met the year before on the Santa Fe Trail: ". . . a young centaur, who handled his lasso with a dexterity which threw all the Mexican exploits I had previously seen into the shade." Joaquin—Frémont calls him Juan—and Gregorio were Tulare Indians. Manuel was a Cosumne, which is to say his people were from the Cosumne River. He had been to Washington with Frémont.

One of the new men Frémont accepted was Saunders Jackson, a free Negro, a servant in the Benton household, to go along as Frémont's personal chef and orderly—in the Army terminology of the past, his striker. Frémont had taken another of the Bentons' colored servants, Jacob Dodson, along on his second expedition. Saunders was a steady hand and a good cook and he too had worries of his own, and hopes and aspirations for the vague bright future in California. He was free but his family was still in slavery. Their owner would sell them for $1700 and maybe California would somehow provide him a chance of accumulating the money—so many other people of the expedition blithely expected to carve out fortunes there.

Another new man was Micajah McGehee, son of Judge Edward McGehee of Woodville, Wilkinson County, Mississippi, going West bright-eyed for adventure, and to hear the winds of morning.

Two others were a father and son from St. Louis named Andrews. The son was Elijah T. Andrews, a midshipman with seven years in the Navy, who had been detached in the summer of 1848 and given permission to go to California. He was tubercular. It was beginning to be understood that something about life in the open air was sometimes good for tuberculosis. Senator Benton himself was of a tubercular family and had arrested the disease by living a vigorous outdoor life as a young man. The Andrews were "well known citizens" of St. Louis, and quite possibly friends of the Benton family.

And three old voyageurs were hired, bearded coureurs du bois, of the type of Raphael Proue, standard trail hands for western travel for two generations—the employee contracts for Frémont's first expedition were written in French. These three Canadians, as Frémont calls them, were a man named Longe, and Vincent Tabeau, called Sorel or Sorrel and so apparently red-haired, and Antoine Morin, who had been with the third expedition and served in Companies A and B of the California Battalion. In accounts of the fourth expedition he is variously referred to as Moreau, I. Morel, Joseph Moran, and Mosel. He was an old man, full of experience and know-how, and much respected by all the others.

One of the culls of the third expedition, sent home from the Pueblo, was a young Missourian with the whole-souled Missouri name of Ike Cooper. What he lacked as a potential packer he made up as a lively witness when a few years later he published, under the highly un-Ike Cooperish name of "François des Montaignes," a description of as much of the trip of the third expedition as he had seen.

Of such as old Morin, François des Montaignes wrote: ". . . let me edge in a word or two about the Canadian engagé or hired hand; that last remnant of the old voyageur, the last button on his ancient capote. Like a man of metal, he stands out in bold relief, the personification of much of that stoical philosophy, for which the western voyageur was famous—the snows and tempests of time scarcely silvering his raven locks, running the gauntlet of danger and toil, and going down beneath the grass of the wilderness, as though he went to his long rest to the sweet music of the chapel bell of his native village. No; we cannot do justice to the Canadian engagé; too much cannot be said in his favor. . . . With his possible sack, containing all he possesses, perhaps, his blanket, his steel, his pipe and his tobacco, he is fully equipped for any trip or voyage, it is immaterial to him in what direction; for he subscribes as freely for a five years' sojourn on the upper Missouri as for a three months' cruise among the Caws. He looks upon life as a lease at will, and as such not necessary to be retained forever. He, consequently, is careless of danger, reckless of limb, and, for a few dollars per month, will rove from the borders to the mouth of the Gila, or the head of Behring's Straits. The prairies and the Rocky mountains, with their buffalo, their beaver, their snows, and even their Indians, exert a strange power of fascination over this class of adventurers. . . . And here, ensconced in some elk-skin lodge, or maybe camping beneath the shelter of some mountain crag, he strikes his steel, and puffs away whatever care he may have, in the curling smoke of his mackinaw. . . . The engagé, however, like his predecessor, the vieux voyageur, has almost performed his trip; one disappeared with the cordelle and the bateau, and when the buffalo ceases to roam over the great plains, and the Indians' fire no longer smokes amid the mountains, the engagé's term of service will have expired; knocking the ashes from his short pipe, he will wrap him in his blanket, and enter that unfathomable futurity, from which romance and remembrance only can invoke him."

One other new man was taken on in St. Louis, a young

British sportsman named Andrew Cathcart, Captain Cathcart
of the 11th (Prince Albert's Own) Hussars.

Cathcart was a friend of George Frederick Ruxton, the Byronic British author who published in 1847 his *Adventures in
Mexico and the Rocky Mountains,* and in 1848 his *Life in the
Far West.* Ruxton was in England, and ill, in the spring of
1848. He thought the Rockies would cure him and planned
a hunting trip in the American West with Cathcart, who had
recently sold his commission and was at leisure. They arrived
at the Planters House in St. Louis in August and Ruxton fell
sick with dysentery, a variety of which was epidemic in the
town that summer, and died within two weeks. Ruxton had
been a boy-wonder soldier of fortune (wearing the Cross of
San Fernando with title of knight when he was seventeen, in
the civil wars in Spain; a lieutenant in the British Army in
Ireland at nineteen), and had traveled in Morocco and South
Africa and Canada and coursed energetically back and forth
over western America and Mexico. He had gone after adventure with all the eagerness of a hungry colt eating a carrot,
and died at the age of twenty-seven.

Cathcart saw to the unhappy business of his friend's burial
and had a monument erected over his grave, thought gloomily
of going back home, but decided to go on and have a look
at the West after all, and fell in with the organizing fourth
expedition. This winter journey under its rather desperately
daring leader would have been attractive to him, offering precisely the sort of sporting chance he wanted at the country.
Frémont was glad to have him, and Cathcart went along.

From the beginning he was a special friend of the Kerns.
Dick Kern made a sketch of him—all nose and outswept mus-
tache and blazing eye. It is not fashionable to hint that stand-
ardized motion picture notions might contain any validity,
but it must be confessed the sketch looks remarkably like a
younger version of the late C. Aubrey Smith. More subtly

typical of the British Army still, Cathcart was not English but
an Ayrshire Scot. He was of the Cathcarts of Carleton, an old
family that still preserved, and still does preserve for that
matter, the early fourteenth-century grant of the estate, written
by the order of Robert the Bruce. His eldest brother was the
fifth baronet. His childhood home had been historic Killochan
Castle, a few miles up the Girvan valley from the rocky coast
of Ayr. He was thirty-one years old at the time of the fourth
expedition.

Cathcart had been a soldier for eleven years, and had put
in seven years of that time in horse regiments; he had seen
service in India; very possibly, in spite of his single-minded
interest in hunting, he was a useful addition to the expedition.
His wealth and position, exotic and ergo impeccably romantic,
would not have been lost on Frémont either. When, years later,
Frémont scribbled notes for the story of the expedition that he
never wrote, he began the roster by writing: "Capt. Cathcart
and personnel of the party—"

At the end of September Colonel Frémont was ready, according to the St. Louis *Reveille*, to leave for "Upper California, to complete his explorations of that region. The present
survey is taken at his own private expense, with the view, of
course, of future remuneration from Congress. . . ."

And on October 4 the *Reveille* stated that the "gallant Col.
Frémont with his party, left the city yesterday, on his way to
the Pacific. The lady of Col. F., distinguished alike for her de-
votion and her fine accomplishments, accompanies her husband to the borders of the wilderness. . . ."

They took passage by steamboat for Kansas Landing and
Westport, the present-day Kansas City, where the expedition
would put itself together. On board the boat, two days up the
Missouri, the Frémonts' infant son suddenly died. The baby,
still less than three months old, had never seemed entirely well
and strong. Both Frémont and Jessie felt that the loss of the

child, like Jessie's previous illness, stemmed from the ordeal of the court-martial. This was the final blow, if one was needed, to make the start of this expedition a desperately heavyhearted time for both Frémont and his youthful lady, no matter how much they tried to conceal it from each other. Jessie wrote later that it was so different from the other times, the other separations that began the other expeditions. She said, "When one has had to meet death and treachery, the sense of security never returns." But this new anguish, to be sure, would only leave Frémont more determined than before to bring that sense of security soaring back on the wings of a brilliant success for the expedition.

The day before the expedition landed at Kansas, President Polk's Cabinet met again in Washington. Secretary of State Buchanan's letter to the people of California had been whipped into shape with all possible speed, and its final draft was studied and approved. The military department of California had been hastily reorganized, and Secretary of War Marcy had prepared fresh instructions for the officers in command there. Two days later all these papers were ready for dispatch to California and President Polk could take a deep breath and write that Mr. Buchanan and Mr. Marcy—Senator Benton's particular foe of the War Department crowd—"took a family Dinner with me today."

Kansas Landing was a rock levee on the river, a row of loading pens for cattle, and a warehouse for furs maintained by the Chouteaus, the St. Louis tycoons of the fur business. In the spring it was a busy place, piled high with goods destined west, when the emigrants and traders made their start. At this time of year, in the autumn, few trains were heading out, although one had departed a few weeks before bound for Bent's Fort and Santa Fe, led by the trader Ceran St. Vrain and accompanied by the mountain man Tom Fitzpatrick: the fourth expedition would overtake it on the way.

Westport, a village four miles inland from the river, centered about at what is now Fortieth and Main Streets in Kansas City, was the frontier, a collection of stores (one was run by a nephew of Daniel Boone), wagonwrights, horse and mule and cattle dealers, gunsmiths, and saloons all devoted to the business of the wild plains and the wilder mountains on beyond.

Ned Kern, three years before, had found Westport "a dirty place filled with Indians, Spaniards, Jews, and all sorts and sizes of folks." Francis Parkman, the historian, described the Indians' "little shaggy ponies . . . tied by dozens along the houses and fences. Sacs and Foxes, with shaved heads and painted faces; Shawnee and Delawares fluttering in calico frocks and turbans. . . . Whiskey circulates more freely in Westport than is altogether safe in a place where every man carries a loaded pistol in his pocket." And here Ned Kern had found sprouting the Indian curio business, moccasins with bead doings for five bits, befringed skin pants for five dollars; and an Indian from the Shawnee Indian Manual Labor School, missionary-operated three miles out of town, announced he was Methodist, God damn you.

When he arrived with the fourth expedition Ned, too old a hand now to have time for sightseeing, went up to Westport from Kansas Landing with the aristocrats Godey, Taplin, and Cathcart, bought horses, and selected the campsite at Frémont's old jumping-off place, Boone Creek, some three miles out of town. The rest of the men would be busy making order out of the chaos of equipment and supplies and animals, and greenhorns such as Ned's brothers or the gentlemanly young Micajah McGehee could look on and hear new swear words by the bale. Conceivably some of them followed the example of François des Montaignes and his buddies on the previous expedition, who all got "in a most pitiable condition of gloriousness in the tavern at Westport" and rode happily out to camp singing "Old Dan Tucker" and "Lucy Neal."

The Frémonts stayed at the nearby Indian agency, guests of the agent, Major Richard M. Cummins, and his wife. Frémont had made the acquaintance of Major Cummins at the start of his second expedition, and ever since then a few hunters from the Delaware Nation had been "chosen" at Major Cummins' agency to go along, sometimes part of the way and sometimes for the whole trip, with his expeditions.

Frémont and Jessie spent their nights in a log house at the agency, and their days at the site of the camp, where Jessie watched the work of preparation from a tent pitched for her under a cottonwood tree. She was young, pretty, bereaved, and the colonel's lady, and the men of the expedition were attentive. It is recorded that the hunter John Scott turned his polished talents to shooting quail for her.

Eleven days were spent readying the animals and equipment. Besides the instruments and the professional tool kits of the artists and surveyors and the special necessaries of botanist Creutzfeldt and the surgical hardware of Doc Kern, there were flour and sugar and coffee, molasses and macaroni, bacon and vermicelli, cordage and picket stakes, blacksmith tools and mule-shoe iron, tin pans and cups, coffeepots and frying pans, blankets and guns and powder and shot, saddles and pack-saddles, panniers and bridles, spare bits and stirrup irons, blankets and tents and clothes and books, needles and thread and candles, shovels and picks, axes and knives, boxes and barrels and trunks. Everything had to go on the mules; there would be no wagons this trip, not even on the first leg across the plains.

Such an expedition depended absolutely on the animals, the horses or mules, or if there were wagons, the oxen. The usual practice was to set out across the plains in the spring, when the good was in the grass and grazing would keep the animals up in sound condition all the way to the mountains. If an animal found poor grass or was overdriven he became, as Fré-

mont said, what "is called in the language of the country
resté," and if the animal was a horse he could not recover from
this without time for convalescence, and had to be left along
the trail. But "with a mule it is very different. He may be resté
at night, but give him plenty of good grass and water and he
is ready for service in the morning." This was one of the
reasons mules were so much used by the mountain men, and
by all sorts of mountain travelers from early Spanish times on.
Horses may look better in the movies, and they looked better
too to the romantic easterner of that day, but mules were dearly
beloved by the men who habitually staked their lives on their
backs. They were tougher than horses, surer footed than
horses, and more intelligent than horses (when they were contrary they usually had good reason), and if you came on starving times mule meat tasted better than horse meat. Mules were
less high strung than horses, and less likely to give away, by
whinnying or jingling bits or spooking or stamping, the position of a trapper or two hiding from an Indian war party. Some
mountain men claimed their mules could smell Indians, hos-
tiles, that is. Horses had the advantage of speed, and so were
preferred on the plains—when it wasn't too far between grass.

For the fourth expedition, facing both mountains and winter,
there was no consideration of anything other than mules. A few
horses were bought at Westport and came in handy doubtless running buffalo on the prairies of the Kansas, but most
of the animals at the start were mules, and after reaching the
foot of the mountains no horses at all are mentioned in the
journals, indicating that by then the horses had been swapped
for more mules.

But mules were a caution to handle. François des Montaignes
said his mule was a very devil, and had to be knocked down
with a rock to be packed. The usual method was not so easy.
The mule was caught up, blindfolded if he plunged and kicked
too much, short-hobbled if necessary, the girth cinched up

until it looked like he was being cut in two, and packing commenced—but if the blindfold slipped before the packing was
done the mule unwound and strung pack and packers over the
landscape for rods around. This battle royal of packing would
continue each morning after they got under way until the
mules, most of them (there'd be a few free souls that would
never quit resisting) eventually resigned themselves to the
routine. The packing up, though, was only the part that came
after the catching up. Remarked François: "These same mules
are tremendously stout in the neck; a common little Spanish
mule can make off with a strong rope tied about his neck and
a greenhorn holding on to the end, at the rate of about 8
miles per hour," and he gravely asserted he had frequently
seen roped mules flying across the hills and hollows assisting
the transit of half a dozen men in a manner "at once rapid and
salubrious," or a mule trailing a "long cable with a number of
stout explorers for cars attached. . . ." Tom Fitzpatrick said
there were two kinds of mules, "beat out and balky." Another
affecting memory of François' was that they were always informed of the first break of day by "the musical throat of every
mule on the ground. . . ."

To the men laboring day after day in the bawling confusion
of preparation this embarkation was different too, as it was
different for Frémont and Jessie, from other departures in the
past.

Most of the people of this expedition expected, like Frémont,
to stay and settle in California, that fat and sunny promised
land, when they reached the West Coast. (There were even
items in the papers claiming that now gold had been discovered out there on Sutter's ranch, and that fabulously rich
samples had been brought east by none other than Ned Beale
—passed-Midshipman Edward Fitzgerald Beale, the ex-commander of boats. But this kind of newspaper talk wasn't taken
too seriously. Someone always thought he was finding gold in

those rust-streaked metallic cañons and glittering stream beds. Frémont recalled later that on the third expedition Brecken-ridge had brought him a handful "of some large grains that I carelessly told him were sulphurets of iron. These too were probably gold. . . .") This sense of finality, of going away this time to be gone for good, was different from the previous ex-peditions, which had set out with an air of holiday feeling, gusto and exhilaration, school days over and adventure ahead and a sparkling big world beckoning, all this made subtly more lightsome and carefree for many by the distant anticipa-tion of galloping uproariously home again. But this expedition would be more than an interlude. To all those who were plan-ning to go West this time to stay it was a decisive severing away of the past, and so the leave-taking of the lives they had known took on a fitting size and threw a sober mood over the expedition's beginning.

Further, this trip had a specific, pinpointed purpose: ex-ploration for a railroad pass through the Rockies as near as possible to a line laid down on a map in Old Bullion Benton's study, and that was different, that was very different; other expeditions had merely meant to get from here to there by any route at all, and if the way ahead looked too rough, Indians or guides were earnestly questioned for an alternate.

Finally, and this was the most sobering point of all to those who knew the mountains best, the expedition was starting in the fall to explore the anticipated pass in the dead of winter and thus prove its practicability in any season. Traffic stopped in the mountains in winter; the trappers and traders holed up, for the most part, and the mountain Indians went into winter camp in sheltered valleys.

These things, a winter expedition, a mule expedition, giving plain notice the way was expected to be hard, a one-way expe-dition, all would have combined to make even the lighthearted French engagés feel a certain solemnity, a touch of grimness, feel perhaps a little heroic, perhaps a little fearful. One account written later says that a man named McDowell (no one else has his name on the expedition's roster) turned back the first week out, prophesying "much hardship . . . and that not half the men would ever reach California." As in all accounts written after the event this has the suspect value of hindsight. On most of Frémont's expeditions he occasionally discharged men at their own request, sometimes requested because of cold feet and probably sometimes accompanied by dire predictions muttered to someone. Such predictions are seldom remembered except when something dire does happen—if they're not actually invented or retailored at that time to please the human yearning for an orderly plot sequence. This McDowell was possibly James McDowell, a cousin of Jessie's who acted as an agent for Frémont during the formation of his expeditions and occasionally went along part of the way across the plains, in which case he would have been intending to go only a short distance when he started. But rumor has room to move around in a mounted party as large as three dozen men, camping in various separate messes, with various duties, and castes, and the inevitable semblance of a chain of command. A man detaching at the head of the column and turning back may mean anything they please to make of it to those at the rear of the column, particularly when significantly remembered in time to come.

Nevertheless the mention of McDowell proves at least that in the later imagination of the imaginative youngster who mentioned it (Micajah McGehee), a grave sense of moment accompanied the setting out of the expedition.

Frémont's own frame of mind, depressed, defiant, and on edge, would have been a keynote during the time of preparation in the camp on Boone Creek. Once started, once out in the open where he could get a deep breath and where galling thoughts would be worked on by the tonic of a long sky, his unhappiness might be soothed and diminished, but packing and readying in a turmoil of flying dust and fighting mules would have been a bad time for his brooding spirit.

On October 20 the expedition saddled up and got under way; to tickle the sensitive ganglia of the superstitious, it was Friday. It was also a clear and pleasant day. They moved only five miles and camped on Mission Creek, nearby the house of a Delaware.

Frémont's parting from Jessie was unsatisfying; they were both anxious and uneasy about the future and about each other; they had dwelt too much on the sorrows and resentments of recent months, which made good soil for foreboding. After the expedition was gone Jessie got Major Cummins, kindly old Major Cummins as the Frémonts invariably spoke of him, to take her over to the deserted campsite at Boone Creek. The cottonwood where her tent had been was bare of leaves, she said, and she spoke of a desolate wind whispering in its bare branches. This could be a touch of poetic license, as less fanciful observers on the expedition saw leaves on other cottonwoods until many days later. However.

That night Frémont made a ten-mile round trip back to Major Cummins' agency to see Jessie once more, for a second farewell to blot out the lackluster shadow of the first. A typical impulse, carried out with the moonlit grace and dash of the period. Jessie was flattered and delighted, the despondency of the day's parting vanished, and the future took on a fondness that left it not so frightening after all.

There may be something to be said for the romantic gesture, for husbands and wives at least.

Part Two

THE APPROACH

6

There were thirty-five men and more than a hundred mules. The mules were brawny and big, the best that could be found, of the developing type that later came to be called the Missouri mule, bred from the fine jacks that came east from New Mexico and California as a profitable part of the Santa Fe trade.

There were the third expedition men, such as Tom Martin and Josiah Ferguson and Sergeant-Captain Vincenthaler and the well-trained bright young men, Ned Kern and Henry King. These made up about a third of the company.

There were the veterans of more than one previous expedition, such as Mr. Preuss and Raphael Proue and Captain Charles Taplin, and the more seasoned westerners such as Breckenridge and John Scott. There were the three California Indians, and the three men of metal, the old St. Louis French engagés. And there was Alexis Godey. These, the elite in experience, made up about a third of the company.

There were the new men, Dick and Dr. Ben Kern, Creutzfeldt the botanist, Saunders Jackson the ex-slave and Captain Cathcart of Prince Albert's Own Hussars, and the three or four young gentlemen from Baltimore and Mississippi and St. Louis. These made up about a third of the company.

The expedition moved out, leaving the sorrowing Mrs. Frémont under her mourning cottonwood tree, and trailed westward along the Kansas River, through pleasant country farmed by the Delawares, timbered along the creeks, the coming prairie hinted at in rolling reaches of grassland. After the clear and frosty night of Frémont's second farewell to Jessie, and another round of mule fighting in the morning—it was ten o'clock in the morning before they got moving on Saturday, the second day out—they pushed on for twelve or fourteen miles and that evening Doc Kern, enjoying a swim in Mill Creek on which they were camped, was called out to dress Morin's lip, cut in two by a kick from a mule. This was a gloomy omen, this injury at the beginning to a skilled old man who should know how to keep from injury, so the wise heads said.

The next day the sky was low and leaden, and it began to rain. They made more than twenty miles, through steady rain, and now the train was shaping up and starting to move along as it should. That night, camped in the rain (one of the more miserable experiences for new men was the first rainy camp, and not too enjoyable for old hands, who had to wrestle rain-soaked packs and that quickly, before the resentful mules could roll them in the mud), they were joined by a party of Delawares who were to be their guides to the Smoky Hills, a few days distant. Some of these Indians were old acquaintances to Ned Kern and the other third expedition men, and they were under the leadership of Jim Sagundai, whose name had been made familiar to eastern readers through Frémont's reports.

In the morning the rain stopped, and in place of it the prairie was on fire around them. Doc Kern was given the job of helping Tom Martin drive a mule loaded with a keg of powder; they picked their way across the burned ground and dodged the blazing areas, and got in burning high grass and escaped the fire by four feet.

These things, eating in the rain and bedding down in mud, mules that stubbornly persisted in running the wrong direction even if it meant dancing mulishly up to a fire with a powder keg, putrid drinking water at Rock Creek, where the water was full of dead leaves, strayed stock discovered gone at breakfast time, and an hour spent to bring them in again, and prairie fires—these things were entirely routine. Prairie fires, for all their fearsomeness, the wave of smoke billowing across the world and spouting up like spray against the sky, the racing, crackling sweep of flame, did not too much alarm men without wagons. The flames could be outridden or avoided, or if necessary could sometimes be ridden through—at the right spot. Frémont impressed the men of one of his other expeditions by riding up to them through a prairie fire in this same country. Regarding the common occurrence of prairie fires at the season of the year when the grass had cured dry on the stem, the word Kansa, tribal name of the Kansa Indians, connoting burning or smoking prairie, gives some testimony.

Colonel Alfred S. Waugh, the peripatetic portrait painter who tried so hard and so unsuccessfully to join the third expedition, pursued it out onto the prairie and caught it after it had been four days on the trail, to have at Frémont with still another futile letter of recommendation. He wrote of that expedition in motion: "Already had the duties of the Expedition wrought a change in the personal appearance of the men, they looked dirty, greasy, and toil worn, and were with much difficulty recognized by those of our party. This, I must confess, did not impress me very favourably. It was plain to me that those engaged, found it rather a different sort of thing from that of a mere hunting excursion, a party of pleasure, or a pic-nic. In a word, the poetry and romance with which I had, in my warm fancy, clothed it, fled like the baseless fabric of a dream with the light that now broke on my newly awakened sences. Not that I ever entertained the idea of its ease and comfort, but, although I knew that it was attended with many discomforts not to say dangers, yet I did not realize its true character until that moment. And if this was so perceptable at the commencement, what was to be expected as it progressed?"

These wearing and greasy duties became routine and so did the strange, unpeopled look of the land, the grasslands rolled out endlessly under a windy sky, patterned with sailing light and shadow. (Confessed Colonel Waugh, when he came upon the prairie: "Never before did I feel so absolutely lonely as at that moment, and for the first time I began to feel myself growing old.") The prairies and the knouts of miniature mountains flung out from the Smoky Hills were more red than brown, and in the distance they were purple, and Doc Kern rode behind the train to enjoy their beauty alone—this was very near the present Abilene, Kansas, a Hell's half acre cowtown a generation later when it was the goal of the great cattle drives over the Chisholm Trail and ruled by the pistol artistry of Marshal Wild Bill Hickok, and a quiet wheat-farming town a generation after that, when Dwight Eisenhower lived his childhood there.

This was the beginning of what the principal published authorities before Frémont had called the Great American Desert. Washington Irving compared this country to "the wastes of the ocean or the deserts of Arabia." Zebulon Pike thought there was game enough on the banks of the Arkansas to "feed all the savages in the United States territory one century," but he thought the country could never support white men because there was not enough timber. Naturally Lieutenant Pike could scarcely foresee a Kansas City that would be for a time one of the great lumber centers of the country while loggers ripped into the distant forests drained by its railroads. Major Long in 1820 reported there were "no agricultural possibilities" here, and various other army officers who crossed the great plains outdid each other in declaring them worthless. Army officers habitually find remote places worthless, otherwise they might be given duty there. Frémont, however, observed that here was soil of superior quality, a land with an agricultural future. He thought the fourth expedition's route over the plains, following the Kansas River ("to avoid the danger of snow storms upon the more exposed Arkansas route") and bearing south on its left-hand fork, the Smoky Hill, to reach the Arkansas and the orthodox Santa Fe Trail near the western edge of the present state of Kansas, offered "by far the most eligible" approach to the mountains, and he believed it would afford continuous and good settlements for 400 miles; and with his reports, as has been pointed out so often, the myth of the Great American Desert was demolished.

And the Kerns made notes of the colors, the fringes of timber tinted by autumn, green clay in the creek banks, the masses of willow and plum, and the water plants nestled in the pools of the creeks—and this too became all routine.

One of the secrets of success in moving a train through the early West lay in how quickly all activities fell into fast, accurate routine, routine that minimized confusion and delay in making and breaking camp and kept the train moving as rapidly as possible. In a party made up principally of experienced men this routine of the trail was a habit of years. The animals were rounded in to the camp, unpacked and hobbled or picketed—the wilder ones always picketed, and a really contrary animal was sometimes capable of fighting the picket rope until he impaled himself on the picket pin. Hunters came in with their meat and fires bloomed in the dusk. Guard was set and the camp slept, and Saunders kept coffee hot while the colonel worked with his notes or recorded measurements by the moving stars. The men rolled out of their blankets and robes an hour before daylight and made ready to be on the march before sunrise. Picketed animals were turned out for some breakfast grazing under the watch of the horse guard, fires were stirred up for breakfast, armloads of buffalo chips were brought for fuel, and if no one set a new prairie fire (as Carver did one day while cooking—a not infrequent occurrence among overland parties in the dry season) and if none of the animals had strayed, packing up was under way before all hands had finished breakfast, plunging mules kicking dust into stirrup cups of coffee. There was the yell, "Catch up, catch up!" (probably from Godey or Taplin) and men scrambled for their mules with coiled ropes, warmed bits in their hands and teased them between the mules' averted teeth, heaved up saddles, lashed packs with cold fingers. The day's first wave of exasperation reached its crest while the cuss words, sparkling blue creations in three languages, could almost be seen shimmering in the pale bitter air of dawn, and then they were on their way, an occasional shod animal striking sparks from the frozen November ground.

And the trick was, once started, to keep going, jogging wearily in the saddle at a steady quick pace for twenty miles, twenty-five miles, thirty miles, thirty-five miles, before rounding up to unpack and drop beside the fire at the next camp. Few such trips were ever leisurely. Things happened, in the way of weather and Indian trouble and coffee giving out and grass drying up, if time was wasted along the way. Hurry was in the air, hurry became routine. If a river was to be forded it was done swiftly, with no time-consuming discussion and planning and doubting and considering and looking before the leap, done in a lashing bedlam of yells and straining animals, and if it had to be rafted rafts or bullboats were made with expert haste, and if a whole day or God forbid two whole days were spent crossing a river the leader wrote words of despair in his journal.

The chief cause of the many troubles of emigrant trains was delay. The emigrants often took too long a time to settle into a routine even remotely resembling the hurry-up spirit of a traveling fur brigade or Santa Fe trading caravan or any experienced group. Military units, too, could dawdle, in the time-honored way of officialdom. The march of Kearny's Army of the West to Santa Fe at the start of the Mexican War has been justly honored as a rapid maneuver—the leading elements of the great column of more than 1500 wagons and nearly 20,-000 animals made it across the plains to Bent's Fort in thirty-three days, only a week longer than it took the Frémont fourth expedition. But when Kit Carson was commandeered as guide of Kearny and his dragoons on the way from New Mexico to California, he told them that at the rate they were going they wouldn't get there for four months, and so he took them through in two.

The routine of incessant haste was of course wearing on a greenhorn. If they rode through fogs and he got fever and chills, he was dosed with cholagogue or quinine and kept on riding. If he made his pack improperly and had to stop to make it over, he was left behind, and had to catch up on his own. Like a ship in a wartime sea, the party was loath to circle back and pick up a man washed overboard.

And after the first long day or two in the saddle when the greenhorn's knees locked because he hadn't yet learned to sit down and take his weight out of the stirrups, when he made his bed in the dark and was roused up in the dripping dark to wolf a greasy breakfast and catch up his mule and ride on again, he may well have begun to suspect that this unreasonable haste was insane. What was the point of it? What was the difference, if they took a few extra days to get to Bent's Fort? There was not even a shortening season to race, for the fourth expedition—they deliberately intended to meet winter in the mountains.

But it was really not the time that counted so literally as the routine itself, the hurry-up push-along routine that once formed and welded into iron habit became a machine, an automatically driving group superself that was more than the sum of the various selves of the party. And of course it would not do to adulterate the fuel of the machine, its routined will, with even a drop here and there of watery human dilatoriness, however excusable, because the routine was basically a delicate thing, interleaved and interbalanced of many conditioned wills and spirits, and only a little defection could cause it serious damage.

Game was plentiful, turkey and ducks, and Captain Cathcart did a great deal of hunting along the way. Also, on the second day out, he caught a catfish, which gives rise to a question: Why was fishing so little practiced among the trappers and other travelers of the West in early times? Fish would seemingly have been forced to the consciousness of men working streams killing beaver, and yet the literature of the period only infrequently mentions fishing, except in the neighborhood of the various fishing-Indian communities, chiefly in the Northwest. Men starved on the banks of streams that were full of trout. (Lieutenant George Douglas Brewerton, writing of an overland journey with Kit Carson, speaks of trout so thick in a Rocky Mountain stream they were killed with clubs.) Curious.

Eight days out, as they wound into the Smoky Hills, they came upon the supreme excitement of buffalo. The first bands they saw were all bulls. Several were killed; Doc Kern preferred turkey. However, the next day, when brother Ned killed a young bull with some fat to his chine, Doc admitted it was pretty good. The day after that, a Tuesday, when Godey finally brought in a cow, Doc confessed they had a feast.

(On this same day, back in St. Louis, General Kearny died. Jessie wrote that on his deathbed he asked for her to visit him and forgive him; she couldn't bring herself to do either one.)

Buffalo bulls were notoriously bad eating—too tough. In buffalo country it was hard times if you had to eat poor bull; what was wanted was fat cow. Fat cow seems to have been one of the healthiest diets ever known; mountain men and buffalo Indians customarily lived on fat cow and fat cow alone, gorging themselves at their two meals a day, if not all through the night, for days or weeks at a time—as long as they could get it, and they thrived and accomplished mighty feats thereon. Poor bull, on the other hand, was not only tough and tasteless but also was accused at times of being downright toxic. On a previous expedition several of Frémont's men fell sick, including Carson and Maxwell, who could seemingly stand anything, and Frémont attributed the illness to the meat of a buffalo bull.

The frontiersman, incidentally, ate game hot oftener than not, that is, immediately after it was killed. The liver was frequently cut out on the spot and eaten raw, seasoned with gall, an old Plains Indian custom. Commonly the buffalo was butchered up by bracing the carcass upright on spraddled forelegs, ripping off the hide, from the backbone downwards, taking then the meat of the hump, considered extra delicious, and the strip of fat along the backbone, sometimes as much as fifteen pounds of this. These and the tongue and the entrails were the chief delicacies. Sometimes the blood was caught in a kettle and drunk. The marrow was good too, especially for mixing with jerked meat to make pemmican, or tasajo, which made a favorite Cheyenne dish when pounded together with wild cherries (stones and all).

The fresh meat was hung about the hunter's horse—either horses were generally more blasé about the smell of blood in those days, or the hunter didn't consider his frightened spooking worth mentioning, and the latter was probably more often the case; for although a good buffalo horse was highly prized, a hunter would jump on anything that could run if need be, and there must have been many green horses that objected considerably to packing quarters dripping blood, but such troubles are rarely recorded—and the meat was packed jubilantly flopping and bouncing back to camp, and immediately stuck on sticks and roasted and eaten, in marvelous amounts, after which the boys wiped their hands on their shirts and lit their pipes and stretched out with their feet to the fire and belched and smoked and lied to each other until they fell asleep.

Nowadays most hunters like to let their game hang awhile at least before having a go at a steak, and many cowhands living off the range in remote camps believe that if they don't wait overnight after butchering a beef before eating any of the meat, it will certainly make them sick.

Ned had no hesitation about declaring his delight at coming upon buffalo again. He stated happily that he had a glorious mess of guts. He rode with Godey, running buffalo. Doubtless Ned, the veteran, the westerner, was big in his older brothers' eyes, and doubtless too, since Ned was human from hocks to cowlick, he showed off a little for them. But a few days later staid Doc himself was running buff. He found it rather scary.

Hunting buffalo from horseback was acclaimed by most of those who tried it as the highest excitement going, the uttermost top of the shelf in big game hunting. It defined the word thrill. One had been told the buffalo was big, but he was always larger than expected. He was gigantic. He was enormous and hairy and humpbacked, and furious little red eyes gleamed out of his shaggy head, and in the dusty sky above him buffalo still more gigantic bobbed and ran in grotesque mirages, and the earth shook to his lunging hooves. The buffalo band was a sea of tossing humps and a strong wild smell and swaying great heads tossing foam. One had been told the buffalo ran fast but he always ran faster than expected. The horse was in a hard lope and then a dead run, heedless of rocks and holes, and the world was filled with the kettle drumming of the racing herd. The horse was among them and they were on all sides, running shoulder to shoulder, almost within arm's reach, incredible in size and speed. The first shot always missed. The mountain men had advised a big bored fusil rather than a good rifle, because it could be reloaded without a ramrod. One hand shook in powder. If the horse began to lag behind he was frantically kicked and lashed. A ball was spit into the gun. The piece was given a shake, to set the ball and charge and knock powder through the blowhole to the pan, and this time the hunter leaned from the saddle and stabbed the gun almost against a mud-caked coat and fired and this time, perhaps, the beast stumbled and collapsed in a storm of dust and tumultuous collisions, and a kill had been made.

Invariably the first-time hunter was left shaken by his own insane recklessness. It seemed the thrill brought on a kind of drunkenness in which nothing was important except to make the horse fly fast enough to catch up and keep up.

Now and then hunters came to themselves to realize they had traveled so far they were lost. This happened to Frémont when he first chased buffalo, on the upper Missouri, when he was an assistant on Nicollet's expedition of 1839. As Frémont worded it, ". . . the interest of the chase became so engrossingly intent that we were sensible to nothing else." When he woke up he was lost and he stayed lost on the prairie overnight. Now and then a hunter awoke from his enchantment to find himself far from camp and an Indian war party materializing in the middle distance, and then he became the game. Now and then the horse did cross his legs or step in a badger hole and go down. The first time Frémont saw Kit Carson run buffalo—and Kit was a professional; he had held the contract, in earlier years, to supply Bent's Fort with meat—Kit killed one cow and went after another, when his horse took a beautiful spill. It could happen to anyone.

On the Sunday that they first saw buffalo, Captain Cathcart leapt joyfully to the chase with the experienced hunters Tom Martin and John Scott. The buffalo ran to the river (the Smoky Hill Fork), jumped down a twenty-foot bluff to the water, surged over to the other bank, and ran away across the plain. Caught up in that glorious madness of the buffalo run, Cathcart jumped his horse down the twenty-foot cliff after them, half drowned the horse, lost his revolver and one shoe and powder flask, broke his ramrod, and rolled himself out handsomely in blue clay. He came into camp in his stocking feet, a most melancholy Don Quixote, Ned Kern said, but Dick Kern added that he took it all philosophically. He was out again the next day with Ned and Godey.

The sadness of Ruxton's untimely death was in the past and Cathcart was living as he had dreamed of living, and it is obvious his enjoyment was generous and infectious.

The Kerns hunted with Cathcart and Godey, with Martin and Scott and the botanist Creutzfeldt, and Ned sketched dying buffalo bulls, each a symbol of indomitable power to the last, when finally the trembling legs would buckle at the knees, the blood gush from the nostrils, and the great body rock and fall. One of the bulls sketched had been hamstrung by a pack of wolves before Cathcart arrived to kill it as an act of mercy.

One of the Tulare Indians, Joaquin, brought in a duck. The other, Gregorio, turned a herd of buffalo stampeding on the camp; they passed within 150 feet and Thomas Salathiel Martin, firing from beside his cookfire, dropped one. Cathcart killed four coons for an evening's supper. In the buffalo country, eleven days out, at the Smoky Hills, their Delaware harbor pilots dropped out and turned back for home.

The Kerns noted buffalo grass, much eaten, and the endless network of buffalo trails, and cactus, and the soil growing sandy, and huge croaking ravens, silken black and sinister, and empty brush huts, called by the Spaniards ramadas, left by Pawnees on their summer buffalo hunt, and Doc and Ned and the recent bridegroom, young Captain Henry King, fell behind to gather fossil shells.

The nights grew colder. There came a morning when the wind blew a gale and a plains snowstorm swept down on them, and the march was stopped at noon and camp made and the mules warmed by the fires. This same storm cost heavy losses in frozen animals to other trains then on the Santa Fe

Trail. Doc Kern and King and the Indian Joaquin hunted in the driving snow, in which the running buffalo were ghostly and picturesque. In the snow, Doc shot at a distant wolf and missed, and in the snow Carver saw two Indians, unidentified. Many of the mules had just been shod, in preparation for the sandy, gravel-ribbed country they were entering, where there was little soft footing of sod, and the snow balled in their new shoes and they had hard going, and Dick Kern was thrown. The next morning it was clear and cold, twelve above zero at daybreak.

Now they were swinging down across almost treeless plains country to join the Arkansas. They began to see bands of antelope as well as buffalo.

And each day they made twenty-five miles, or twenty-eight miles, and one day forty miles, and one day fifty-two. They angled across the Pawnee Fork of the Arkansas and it was a chilly evening, but Ned and King had themselves a bath.

They reached the Arkansas River in the area of the present town of Garden City, Kansas. The country of deep rich loam and rolling prairies and creeks cool with the shade of overhanging elms was far behind them and below them; they had been steadily climbing since they had started, although the slant of the flatlands was too gradual to be noticed; they had climbed almost 3000 feet. They were on the tableland of the high plains, where creeks (when they existed) were little gullies and incipient cañons, and cactus writhed in the curling fuzz of the buffalo grass, and the soil was wind-blown sand and glacial drift and the bare floor left by the immense beds of fossil lakes. This was the front yard of the still invisible mountains.

This is sugar beet country today, along the river, a country of irrigated farms inhabited by people who crawl on their hands and knees along endless rows with beet hooks, weeding beets. It is wheat country here and there, and grazing country here and there, and here and there it is trying to be oil coun-

try. This is the western fringe of the land of the suitcase
farmer, the gambler who leases large tracts, invests in seed and
hired mechanical equipment, and bets on one big crop, and
to hell with the topsoil if it dries up and blows away after
his plowing. This is the land of the land speculator in many
different disguises since the days when the "good road to Bent's
Fort, much traveled" was civilization's umbilical cord to the
unknown Southwest, and consequently this is the land of dust-
bowl memories.

They turned up the Arkansas River—occasional fringes of
ice scalloped its margins—and crossed to the south side of the
river, which had more the appearance of desert than the north
bank, but cottonwoods grew in the sandy draws and afforded
firewood. The river here was wide and shallow with frequent
flat, weedy islands that sometimes grew a few trees among the
dead cottonwood trunks of better years gone by. On one such
island Auguste Chouteau, of the great fur trading family, had
fought off an attack by 300 Pawnees, one of their earliest intro-
ductions to American rifles, and had established there for a
time a fur-trading post. The island still went by the name of
Chouteau's Island and was a usual camping place along the
Bent's Fort route of the Santa Fe Trail. It is today just beyond
the present Hartland, Kansas, a day's march past Garden City
and a day's march short of what is now the Colorado state line.

At Chouteau's Island they came upon a sizable community
of Indians on the move, Comanches and Kiowas. These were
real Indians, wild Indians, the wildest of wild Indians, in fact.
And now, unquestionably, the expedition had arrived in the
West.

Ned Kern, the disdainful young old-timer, said, ". . . children of nature, bah!" But his elder brothers were still too close
to the beautifully romantic primitivism of Rousseau to cloak
their excitement with sensible disparagement, although they
tried. Dick Kern thought they were wild-looking rascals, carry-

ing bows and arrows, wrapped in ragged black buffalo robes so that men and boys looked like so many master and apprentice chimney sweeps.

The expedition had driven hard getting to Chouteau's Island and that day a few mules fell to trembling and refused to go on with their packs; the weak among the animals would be disclosed by now and could be culled out. The Indians came to the Frémont camp and traded until dark and probably these resté mules were traded to them. The Indians moved along with the expedition to the next camp, and were a nuisance to their routine. One stole a saddle blanket, and that night (the Indians camped with them again) an old chief named Little Wound stood on a river bank bluff and made an impassioned speech to his people about honesty.

These Indians, 100 lodges, which is to say 100 households of them, were on their way to Big Timbers, another day or so upriver, to the winter metropolis of the high plains, where thousands of Indians of various tribes customarily made a winter base. This year they would find a solemn occasion awaiting them at Big Timbers, a great feast and a great talk with the official representative of the American government, the recently appointed Indian agent, Tom Fitzpatrick, the mountain man.

Fitzpatrick had been named the first Indian agent for the wild tribes of the plains two years before. These people, particularly the Kiowa, Comanche, and Apache, had been greatly feared in the Southwest for many years. Before the Spaniards had come to New Mexico the highly civilized Pueblo Indians had dwelt in fortified villages and danced ancient prayers for protection against these fierce and foot-loose barbarians of the plains. Among the Spanish colonists the Comanche became a symbol of dread and ruthlessness. They swept down like sudden storms, burned and killed, took children to lives of slavery, women for wives, and other captives to furnish entertainment with hideous tortures, and in the dusty towns New Mexicans wept and wailed in their churches. But at the next fiesta there might appear for trade in the markets the trinkets these raiders had torn from their victims; and in New Mexican families, the families of the ricos who could afford them, Comanche and Apache slaves were plentiful—and were not unheard of in American families after the American occupation of the country; and the traders who fenced their stolen goods did business with them steadily for generations, as long as they saw a profit, in the long-established tradition of the border businessman.

With the Mexican War and the arrival of American dominion in the Southwest, promises had been made in New Mexico by General Kearny that the Americans would put an end to the constant Indio bravo menace. Traders using the Santa Fe Trail, too, were demanding some action about the increasing losses from Indian harassments. Wagon trains went in constant fear of the terrifying cry of "Comanche!" or the perhaps even more terrifying cry of "Kiaway!" The Kiowas were credited with having killed more whites in proportion to their numbers, which fortunately for the whites were never very large, than any other tribe. Comanche, Apache, and Kiowa were all famed for excessive cruelties, and there would seem to be more just evidence for the indictments than was usually the case with anti-Indian propaganda disseminated by the invading white man.

Only a few months before, while Frémont was planning his expedition in Washington and Captain Cathcart was taking ship in England with his friend Ruxton, a large war party of Comanches and Apaches had attacked a detachment of U.S. soldiers at Coon Creek, on the Santa Fe Trail.

It was Tom Fitzpatrick's job to make the hearts of these people good, instead of bad, and establish a peace with them. Fitzpatrick was a man of honor and known as such among the Indians, and famed among the mountain men as an Indian diplomat. His talks here and there to such groups as the winter camp at Big Timbers were only preliminaries to a sweeping peace conference he hoped to set up, and did, within a few years, a Great Council such as was seldom seen on the plains.

The Comanches and Kiowas journeying to Big Timbers were in high finery and holiday mood. A good time was expected by all, games, feasts, dancing, visits with friends not seen since the preceding winter, wonderful free gifts from Fitzpatrick and fascinating dickering and window shopping with the peddling traders, and speeches upon speeches that would provide the deep delights of storytelling, for most of them would include recitals of the stirring acts of valor of the speaker and the speaker's clan.

Those of wealth were loaded with jewelry hammered out of silver money—Doc Kern counted nineteen dollars on one child —mirrors, beads, and sea shells. These ornaments hung from their necks, their hair, their blankets, their ears. Dick Kern saw several Spanish children who had been stolen from Monterey three years before. Ned and Dick made sketches. At sundown Little Wound made his long oration exhorting honesty; the language sounded to Ned like the cries of wild ducks. Old Bill Williams, who could speak with fluency a hatful of various Indian tongues, once said of the Kiowas that "no man on earth can talk their language," and said it was "all like dropping stones in the water; punk! punk! punk!" Frustrated linguists have similarly abused, and still do today, various other related Apache dialects of Athapascan stock.

Encamped with the Indians at night, Dick Kern (already lost forever to Philadelphia) was awed by the wildness of the scene. There were ruffled curtains of cirrus across the sky and a white, brilliant moon, and around the fires the Kiowa soldiers sang and shouted, eyes bright with excitement, silver foxtails dangling behind. Dogs and horses and mules joined in, and the expedition men picked up the exuberance and yelled and sang, and one of them—it might have been Ned, a little withdrawn and superior to all this—"was playing most dolefully on the flute, 'Home.' "

Now the expedition had crossed the present state of Kansas from east to west and was over what is now the Colorado state line. Little Wound, having done his righteous duty by the honesty totem the white men affected to reverence so sternly, gave them the honor of his personal company when moving on the next day, and all the Indians trooped along about them as they followed up the river. Along the sandy road the expedition passed and repassed wagons bound for Santa Fe, the train led by St. Vrain, who was camped ahead with Fitzpatrick.

They entered the long stretch of cottonwoods that was the Big Timbers. This parklike district, floored here with sand and there with grass, shaded by grove after grove of majestic cottonwoods, some as much as eighteen feet around, extended for thirty miles along the Arkansas. Its center was near where the prosperous farmers' town of Lamar, Colorado, now stands. Here was the site of a ford where the trail the expedition followed, which had crossed and recrossed the river, crossed to the south bank once more. At one such crossing Wise got left behind and couldn't catch up to the expedition again until the next day, when Vincenthaler went back to him with a fresh horse. The way was miry, and this time it was Doc Kern who was thrown by his struggling mule.

Big Timbers was home grounds for the Cheyenne and Arapaho, and Comanches and Apaches often wintered there.

In the middle of the many Indian encampments—some 600 lodges, all told, or about 6000 people—was Tom Fitzpatrick. Fitzpatrick was a very famous man out here; out here, much more famous than Frémont himself. He had a crippled hand, from a gun that had blown up; his hair was bleach white—it had turned white suddenly, it was said, during a nerve-racking escape from Gros Ventres sixteen years before: he had hidden among rocks for two days and a night while warriors prowled and snuffled within stone's throw, and he had concluded his escape with a 200-mile marathon on foot, armed only with his knife, living on roots, and had appeared at rendezvous (so the story went) a skeleton with flowing hair of pure white. He was thirty-three years old at that time. As a result of these marks put upon him by his past, the Indian nations knew him by the name of the White Head or the Broken Hand.

Broken Hand was another of Frémont's most respected guides of past years, and at Big Timbers Frémont had an opportunity to get his opinion on the intended passage of the mountains. The expedition made two short marches here, lingering, while Frémont counciled with Fitzpatrick and the best informed of the Indians present.

Frémont says nothing in his letters of what Fitzpatrick may have recommended. He merely takes occasion, in a letter to Senator Benton, to recommend most highly to the Senator's good offices and influence, "our friend Major Fitzpatrick," found in the exercise of his official functions as government representative among the Indians of this district, and demonstrating himself a most admirable agent. "I hope you will be able to give him some support."

Undoubtedly Major Fitzpatrick said, "Depending," as Kit Carson had probably said. Fitzpatrick laid no claim to an intimate knowledge of that section of the Rockies about the head of the Rio Grande. That was the Robidoux country, the Leroux country, the Old Bill Williams country. In a letter written to Mrs. Frémont some weeks after he had talked to Frémont, Fitzpatrick said, in describing Frémont's plans as he understood them: "Col. Frémont will fall immediately on the Rio del Norte, and a considerable distance north of the New Mexican settlements; from which place I believe it is his intention to steer directly for California, leaving the two hitherto traveled routes, one north and the other south of him, and passing midway between the two; and which, if he is able to find a practicable route, will be much more direct and shorter than any hitherto traveled."

There was a little snow among the trees at Big Timbers, just enough to be charming and cool, like the sheepskin pants of Tom Bolynn. There were some Arapaho present, receiving gifts and preparing to black their faces and ride forth to fight the Pawnees and capture horses, and Doc Kern treated one of their old men "for trade"—he found syphilitic ophthalmia "very prevalent." The Indians hugged him and brought him three fine mules in payment.

The expedition had done with idling through Big Timbers and went on up the river. Doc had equitation trouble with his new Indian saddle mule and this time the mule ran away and Alex Godey obligingly charged out after it and caught it up again.

On Wednesday, November 15, they arrived at the famous trading post of the Southwest, Bent's Fort, a day or two up the river from Big Timbers, and 560 miles from Westport, although they had added some miles to this (they were inclined to zigzag for a while after their Delaware guides left them). The distance is 563 miles by railroad and 565.6 by highway today, to the dirt road that turns off U.S. 50 in Colorado to the site of the old fort. Various logs kept on the journey indicated total estimates to Bent's of from 568 to 624 miles. The expedition had been out twenty-six days, and that was very respectable time, considering the pause at Big Timbers. The machine of the push-on routine was winching along in excellent condition.

Snow fell throughout the first night they camped near the fort and most of the next day. It was twelve above zero the morning after that, and Doc took a skillet of coals into his tent for a warming pan.

And from Bent's Fort they had a good view of the mountains ahead, crumpled and blue under a creamy topline of snow.

Frémont wrote, "They look imposing and somewhat stern. . . ."

7

Fitzpatrick rode up from Big Timbers to Bent's with the expedition, and King and Godey sat in on conferences with him at the fort. Kettles of food had to be sent over to them from camp, as the fort was nearly deserted and almost out of provisions. There were only four Frenchmen, employees of the trading company, on hand; for the moment, all the trading in the area was going on down at the Big Timbers. But the expedition did buy from the engagés there a taste of butter—strong, but still a delicacy; and everyone washed with warm water and soap. "Quite an epoch," Dick Kern said.

Talks at the fort continued for a couple of days, perhaps around the large telescope mounted in the tower above the fort's four-foot-thick walls. Letters were written; this was the last call for homegoing mail until California. And at Bent's the elder Andrews, the father of Midshipman Andrews, dropped out, to go back home when a passing trading caravan offered the opportunity.

Many of the men usually stretched linen tents at night for shelters; these thin flies were all right for one to sleep under, wrapped in blankets, but Frémont "found it almost impossible to work in a tent. After the fatigue of a day's ride, with the anxieties which winter exploration in an unknown country bring upon me, and with the demand upon one's strength which the mere resistance to cold always makes, it requires an exertion of courage to take astronomical observations, and then calculate them at night, in a linen tent, tired and cold, and make up the notes of the day." And besides his own work, "the Kerns have their drawings and paintings to make—Preuss his field sketches to finish." So at Big Timbers Frémont had traded with the Indians for a conical skin lodge with a smoke-hole at the top, "admitting of a fire in the centre." This was put up for the first time at the expedition's camp across the river from Bent's Fort, "greatly to the delight of our *compagnon de voyage,* Capt. Cathcart, who is eloquent in its praise for the comfort it secures."

On the last day before leaving Bent's, the luxurious new lodge was given over to letter-writing, Frémont writing to Jessie and her father, Ned Kern perhaps adorning a letter with a sketch, King doubtless writing to his new bride and Mr. Preuss dutifully to Mrs. Preuss, and "Cathcart also" was present, Frémont said with negligent ostentation, his scratching pen making contact, presumably, with distant grand and aristocratic addresses.

Their emotions would have been filled with home and their thoughts with the expedition's prospects in the light of information and advice so far received. There was one disquieting piece of information: the weather forecast. An unusually hard winter was being predicted.

Frémont wrote to Benton, "Both Indians and whites here report the snow to be deeper in the mountains than has for a long time been known so early in the season, and they predict a severe winter. . . ." He added that some men just come into Bent's Fort from farther up the river "say they have never known the snow so deep in the mountains so early, and that there is every prospect of a severe winter. But this does not deter us. I have my party well prepared, and the men are all made as comfortable as possible, and expect to overcome all obstacles."

He was "nowise discouraged," Frémont wrote from beside the fire in his new lodge, "and believe that we shall succeed in forcing our way across. We will, after crossing the chain before us" (between the Arkansas and the Rio Grande), "ascend the Rio del Norte to its head, descend to the Colorado, and across the Wah-satch mountain, and the Great Basin country, somewhere near the 37th parallel. . . ."

The later explorer Frederick Dellenbaugh says of this region, "A large portion of this country was unexplored even by trappers. . . . A portion was not explored till 1872 when a party I was with went into it from the southwest, for the purpose. From the head of the Rio Grande, about longitude 107°, to the west line of the High Plateaus of Utah, about 112° 30′, between the thirty-seventh and thirty-eighth parallels, we know now there lies some of the most difficult country to traverse within the limits of the United States. Even today it is formidable."

That it was unknown country was of course what made it the best of objectives.

The party was in good health and spirits, Frémont reported to Benton, and the animals in good condition, after the breathing spells of leisure at Big Timbers and Bent's Fort. There was a "small store of provisions for hard times." The instruments were in good order, "barometer inclusive."

It was true the men were in good spirits, at least most of them, according to the tone of the day-by-day journals. They were hardened to the routine of the machine, the inexorable piston the expedition had become. The green hands had by now been shaken down into place as conditioned and habituated units that performed as steadily if not yet as skillfully as the experienced men. They believed in Frémont and they believed in themselves, and so they believed they could succeed in going on across the snows of the Shining Mountains.

Frémont believed they would go through, and intended that

they would go through, in spite of the warnings and the reports of heavy snows. Any explorer grew accustomed to warnings that what he intended could not be done. Hadn't the Indians told him he couldn't cross the California Sierra in the winter? (Rock upon rock; snow upon snow.)

He wrote, "A vigorous effort, we trust, will carry us over."

But morose shadows could still be glimpsed through his electric determination. "I think that I shall never cross the continent again, except at Panama. I do not feel the pleasure that I used to have in these labors, as they remain inseparably connected with painful circumstances, due mostly to them. . . ."

And he concluded his letter to Old Bullion at headquarters by appending a timetable: "Should we have reasonable success, we shall be in California early in January, say about the 8th. . . ."

The letter was written under date of November 17. Frémont had written Jessie on his third expedition that he could now ride from the Fontaine qui Bouit River (two days farther on) to Captain Sutter's in California in thirty-five days. Thus he was allowing exactly two weeks extra in his calculations for the difficulties the winter snows and the new mountain pass might present.

The expedition moved on, pushing at a fast trot to make up for lost time. King and Alex Godey and Ned Kern camped together, probably to talk over the plans and strategy and intelligence bulletins discussed at Big Timbers and Bent's. Now the front yard of the mountains had been crossed and they were on the doorstep. The character of the country had become shaly, and the gulches deep and crooked. This is fine farm land today along the river; Rocky Ford, twenty miles beyond the site of Bent's Fort, has given its name to the brand of melon developed and grown there. The country still looks barren to the eye but irrigation makes it bloom, not only in truck farms and still more acres of sugar beets but literally in blooms, for there are flower farms along here, wide fields of zinnias and marigolds in a brightly colored patchwork quilt upon the land.

Now they could look up from scraping snow out of the tents to see clearly the Spanish Peaks, Wah-to-yah, the Breasts of the World, off on the left hand, entirely white, and Pike's Peak bearing on the right hand. In the mornings they saw ice in the river, sheets that tried to form overnight and broke away and spun like stars in the pools. The morning they pushed on from Bent's Fort it was ten above zero.

They made the seventy-odd miles from Bent's to the little mountain-man settlement called the Pueblo in three days, and anyone could tell they were trending uphill now. They were at almost 5000-feet altitude, and some of the mules were already weakening from the steady going, and the first range of the mountains, called the Wets, swelled up close ahead. There was game to be had: Scott killed a deer, and Breckenridge supplied antelope. Doc was tossed one more time; his mule started before he got settled and sat him on the ground.

The Pueblo was sometimes called by a full name, Pueblo de San Carlos on the Fontaine qui Bouit. Boiling Springs Creek, the Fontaine qui Bouit (some mapmakers made it "qui Bouille" with the mistaken notion that was more correct; correct would be "qui Bout"), flows down from the north to join the Arkansas River at this point. In 1842 a handful of mountain men and their Indian or Mexican families began a more or less permanent settlement here, looking for something better to do than the faded business of beaver trapping. They put up an adobe fort of sorts, kept cattle, traded, farmed, and hunted. The population had an unsteady floating air: trappers and Mexicans who drifted in to winter or try for a while the unappetizing occupation of scratching around at farming or have a fling at the business of bootlegging aguardiente to the Indians.

The expedition reached the Pueblo at noon of Tuesday, November 21, one month and one day out from Westport. Camp was made near a string of log cabins, then still called Mormontown in memory of some westering Saints who had wintered there two years before, on the south bank of the Arkansas. The clumsy fort of the Pueblo proper across the river was a tatterdemalion place, livestock, poultry, and dogs living together with the families of the residents in the littered courtyard. A few other adobe houses had been built around the fort by retired trappers. There were quite a few families all told: perhaps sixty men, nearly all having wives and a few possessed of two. There were children attending milk cows, a pleasant sight.

There was a light dust of snow on the ground.

Among the old mountain men settled in Pueblo for the winter was the almost legendary Old Bill Williams, one of the few acknowledged experts on the region of the Rockies the fourth expedition intended to assault. In the afternoon Old Bill came across to their camp, and conversations with him and with the other trappers and traders wintering there continued on into the night.

One of these was John Hatcher, known for years as Bent's best trader among the Indians, a stumpy little man called by the Cheyennes "Freckled Hand," and called by young Lewis Garrard the "beau ideal of the Rocky Mountain man." Hatcher knew Frémont from times past, as did Old Bill Williams; Hatch had been with a detachment of the third expedition for a time as a hunter. He told Frémont that it would be impossible for him to get through the mountains at the place he wanted to cross at that season of the year, and Hatcher said later that all the others who were living near him who knew the country said the same thing.

And the oldest and most experienced of them all, Hatcher said, Old Bill Williams, also had his doubts.

Another of these men, Lancaster Lupton, West Point graduate, fur trader, and builder of the trading post of Fort Lupton, writing a few days later to Senator Benton, said, "The snow is unusually deep in the mountains, and many old mountainmen here have expressed a doubt whether he can get over with so large a cavalcade—about one hundred horses and mules and thirty-odd men; but I think he will do it. He has experience himself, with energy, patience, and perseverance, and many of his old comrades. Carson and Maxwell preceded him a month, to see their families in Taos; but Godey, full of experience, resolution, and resources, is with him, and others, all experienced and determined. . . ."

In spite of these warnings, Frémont not only remained determined on the attempt but talked Old Bill Williams himself into coming along as guide. The next day the expedition broke camp and crossed the river to the Pueblo and hung fire there for part of the morning, and Old Bill came out with his packs and swung aboard his mule and when they rode on he went with them.

Another little settlement, called Hardscrabble, twenty-five miles upriver, was reached early the next day. Here some of the men from the Pueblo Home for Old Mountaineers did their summer farming, and the name of the place indicated what they thought of their labors. There were a few adobe houses, corrals, and the summer's crop of corn stored in cribs. Frémont had made arrangements at the Pueblo to buy as much of this corn as the mules could carry, to take along as feed for the animals over the snow of the mountains, and the expedition camped at Hardscrabble for a couple of days while the corn was packed up and the mules given a chance again to rest and strengthen.

The Wet Mountains were now within arm's reach, or so they seemed in the brilliant air of the beautiful springlike weather that held for the stay at Hardscrabble, and beyond the Wets were the much higher Sangre de Cristos, sending up a wall of eight peaks that were over 14,000 feet, and beyond the Sangres the valley of the upper Rio Grande del Norte, and on the other side of that valley the beginning of the virtual unknown with the towering, jagged San Juans, which wore the crown of the Continental Divide.

Hardscrabble was the final jumping-off place, and at this point Longe, one of the three old Frenchmen, turned back.

Something that was fairly common in that day seems to have become rather rare in more modern times: a sense of historical importance. It was often evident, not only among members of exploring expeditions, but also among early settlers from Iowa to Texas, among traders and teamsters and soldiers. In diaries, letters, journals of the time the implication may be found again and again that the writer felt he was doing something of historical importance and that his adventures would have significance for others who would later come his way in greater numbers. For the feeling seems to have sprung from a lively certainty not only of continuing expansion but a certainty, an assured inborn belief, in the simple fact of continuity itself, a faith now not quite so certain in the bewildered spirit of today. That awareness of the significance of the moment was to some degree indicated in the mere act of keeping a journal or diary, no easy job in the midst of weariness and tension.

Frémont was especially adept at mesmerizing his men into feeling their historical oats. (At least six and probably several more of the less than three dozen men of the fourth expedition were keeping journals.) The true romantic regularly stood off and saw himself panoplied in the significance of the passing moment, and fairly quivered at the greatness of it all. Frémont performed this rite with utter sincerity and even humility, and was a marvelously inspirational example. He dreamed with the pedal down, and the men of the fourth expedition were swept up heart and soul in the fiery hope and glory of the music. This cannot be doubted; otherwise more of them would have turned back with Longe.

They had listened to Tom Fitzpatrick, John Hatcher, Old Bill Williams, men of vast experience and no lid to their courage. They had listened to the Indians, the Comanche, who had fought their relatives, the Ute, in these mountains throughout a racial history; the Arapaho, who ranged with their great allies, the Cheyenne, from the mountain slopes to the prairies, and who were also ancient enemies of the Ute on the battle-grounds of the Rockies; the Mountain Apache, called the Jica-rilla, who lived their lives on these mountain trails.

Many of these people had shaken their heads at the pro-jected route for this time of year, and all of them, so Frémont himself had written, had given warning that all signs pointed to an exceptionally bad winter. The trappers and voyageurs of the expedition knew by witness of past mountain winters what that could mean, and their entrails must have contracted in some dread from what they nevertheless rode on to meet. Those of the expedition who were new to the mountains would have heard awesome stories of the furies they were about to face, and certainly had looked furtively within to question secretly their nerve and hardihood.

Against this were balanced Frémont's glittering reputation and the determination, forged in the fires of his trial and pub-lic downfall, that whipped him on; and, now, the presence of Old Bill Williams, a most powerful factor for confidence among the others, reluctant and querulous and pessimistic though he may have been.

And there was the magnificent picture of themselves march-ing like heroes in the eye of history.

History is a recognition of relatedness, the leap of a spark that closes the circuit on what Kierkegaard called "presenti-ment of participation in the eternal"—past and future. The figure in Giovanni Bellini's "Madonna of the Trees" casts a shadow and that is important to the history of art, but only the withered academic husk of thought will find the painting stirring for that reason alone. But, casting a shadow, the Madonna emerges to a reality, to a human grandeur of reality and dignity and self-determinism and thus to an expression of the leaping spark of the Renaissance, and the beholder, vainly scratching matches from picture to picture along the wall, finds one that strikes, and sees in its light a simultaneousness, a relatedness, that cuts through time. The yearning then of the artist and the yearning now of the beholder touch hands and recognize one another.

The men of the fourth expedition cast bold shadows. The Indians warned them with ominous full-arm gestures, as though they played blaring trombones and clashing cymbals, but the Stone Age faces would have looked at them with an undeniable respect. And the mountain men were shrewd and whiskered faces, with the eyes in Stone Age masks, and they looked on with an impatient contempt for foolishness and yet with an undeniable respect too for foolhardiness and, it might be, a drop of envy. They wouldn't want to be along; they'll be gone horse and beaver sure . . . but won't it be some doings if they make it? These marks of recognition fostered a certain stubborn pride that had its perils, a pride that made it always harder to turn back than to go ahead. And history was watching, and the presentiment beating in their blood.

8

It has been suggested that a high point of freedom in the career of humankind was attained with the mountain man.

One of the freest of these, in certain literal respects at least, was William Sherley Williams, called Parson Bill, Preacher Bill, Old Solitaire, and Old Bill, and named among various Indian peoples at various times as Red Haired Hunter and, later in life, Lone Elk.

The Williams family came from North Carolina to St. Louis when William Sherley was a boy of five or six, and while St. Louis still belonged to Spain. The boy was raised on a farm near St. Louis. He was seventeen years old before Thomas Jefferson bought that country for the United States as part of the Louisiana Purchase. He grew up in close association with the Indians, Osage particularly, who were numerous around the home farm. He learned to hunt with a bow as well as a rifle.

His mother was a devout Baptist, and at the age of seventeen or so the boy felt called to the ministry. He became a wandering Baptist preacher, working the backwoods of that early-day Missouri. He was tall, rawboned, freckled, red-haired, and the description calls up an ungainly youth, probably self-conscious, earnest, uneasily searching, it may be assumed, for the fulfillment of some emotional need. The emotional religion of that day was full of such youngsters, but the religion of any time is an emotional experience—faith must be an intellectual absurdity or there is no reason for faith—and religion of any time has always had a special appeal during that teetering, insecure interval while youth is a creature of two worlds. The youth who responds with burning eyes to the appeal gives more of revelation than he receives.

But young Parson Williams' eyes did not cool sufficiently for grace to get a good hold. He was in his early twenties when he drifted away from preaching. He gave more of his time to hunting and trapping, and perhaps he took a turn at school-mastering; he had some learning. Then the everlasting peace that passeth understanding fluttered before him one final time and he moved over to the Osages, lock, stock, and barrel, and became a missionary among them. But the hovering dove fell before Indian existentialism, and the Osages converted young Parson Williams, rather than the other way around. He became a member of the tribe, married an Osage girl, fought, hunted, danced, trapped, and traded with his foster people, and came to a place of some importance acting as a government interpreter in Indian negotiations. He fathered two children, daughters. He lived with the Osage until he was thirty-eight years old.

At this time the Osage were shuffled out of their far-spreading country by a typical government "treaty." It was assumed Bill Williams' two daughters would be provided for by lands granted them individually under the terms of the treaty. His wife had died. This was 1825, the Santa Fe trade was beginning to open up, and Senator Benton had pushed through a bill calling for a survey of the Santa Fe Trail, to promote this sprouting western trade that was of importance in Benton's vision of the future. The principal commissioner appointed to conduct this survey, Major George Sibley, offered Bill Williams a job as guide and interpreter. Bill took it.

The most important work of the survey was getting easements from the Indians for free passage along the Trail. This was Bill Williams' special job. He arranged a big council with the Osage at the spot known forever afterward as Council Grove, and another with the Kansa Indians. Eight hundred dollars' worth of presents were passed over to each nation, and the Trail had bought itself a right of way. This was a bargain price; the survey commission had as much as $20,000 to spend for the purpose. Pawnee, Comanche, Kiowa, Apache, were not consulted, for valid reasons: the Pawnee made summer hunts in the region of the Trail on sufferance of their stronger Indian neighbors, and the others ranged principally in what was then the bailiwick of Mexican authority.

The survey party broke up at Taos, and Bill Williams stayed in the Rocky Mountain country. Except for a rare visit or so years later, he never returned to the Missouri and civilization again.

Before 1822 the Indian trade (which meant the fur trade) had been chiefly a government monopoly, carried on through government factors. George Washington had set this policy, the idea being to assure the Indians fair trading and thus wean them from the commanding influence of the British trading companies, the Northwest Company and Hudson's Bay. This socialistic interference with private enterprise was fought for years by private trading interests, led by John Jacob Astor, the American shogun of the fur business. Senator Benton was Astor's mouthpiece in Congress. In 1822 the Benton bloc succeeded in getting Congress to cut off appropriations for the Indian factories (they ran at a loss) and the riches of the fur trade were wide open to private competition. This threw the Indians to the lions but it stimulated enormously American activity and ergo influence in the beaver country of the West, which was what Benton and his expansionists wanted.

The first Ashley fur-hunting expedition went out that same year, 1822, and with it the immortals Jim Bridger, Tom Fitzpatrick, and Jed Smith stepped on the stage of the mountains, along with nearly a hundred other Ashley men. Other companies, large and small, boiled into the field with trappers and traders, and many hundreds of men crossed the wide Missouri to hunt the distant mountain streams. The first grand rendezvous in the mountains was officially opened on July 1, 1825, on Henry's Fork of Green River, and that year Ashley brought out a fortune in furs, $75,000 worth.

Beaver fever was in the mountain air. Bill Williams knew trapping, hunting, and trading; he had operated trading posts of his own in the Osage country, judging and buying peltries. He had spent more than a dozen years living as a blood brother with a tribe of Indians who were proud of a reputation as champion hunters. He had learned enough to have forgotten more about wilderness craft than the average man who called himself a scout ever knew—and he was just beginning the career that made his name familiar around mountain campfires for many years to come. At thirty-eight he had already lived to a riper old age than many mountain boys managed to reach before they went under. He was considerably older than any of the other Americans who became celebrities at rendezvous. (A few months after Bill Williams came to Taos, a runaway boy from Missouri, Kit Carson, age sixteen, showed up there.)

So Bill Williams, Pah-hah-soo-gee-ah of the Big Hill band of the Great Osage, went out from Taos as an independent trapper.

The mountain men were a variegated, highly individualistic breed, much more so than any vocational group in the confines of civilization. Their lonely, self-sufficient lives developed separatist tendencies, and they were apt at any moment to be subjected to unique experiences for which the group had provided no adjustment, thus inducing bizarre modifications in individuals—which is to say each man lived in his own hide, hair side out and plenty of it.

There were men from what are called good homes among them and scrapings from the muddy waterfronts of the big rivers from New Orleans to the Yellowstone, intelligent men and mental defectives from backwoods slums, men straight-forward and sly, cautious and reckless, frolicsome and dour, men with black souls and men with white, in short, heroes and victims and villains and clowns and all the shades be-tween, and the shades in sunburst colors, heightened and brightened to the wearer's pleasure.

They had in common only a constant insecurity and a bound-less freedom, both of such dimensions as to be appalling to those sheltered by a civilized world. They assuredly did not possess freedom from want or freedom from fear but they came very near, many of them, those who had the size, to realizing a naive notion of individual freedom that had existed as a dream for centuries before Jean Jacques Rousseau reduced it to concise statement thirty-three years prior to the time Bill Williams was born. Rousseau's sentimental celebration of primitive man, besides giving birth to the romanticism that has ruled literary salons ever since, must also be found guilty of error in its choice of example. The noble savage, the natural man dancing in the forest primeval, was, of course, not free and unoppressed. Totemized aboriginal life is restricted by a maze of law, ceremony, caste and ritual, bound round with repressive fears that may lend to any bush or breeze a spectral terror. Rousseau's elegant fancy flourished mightily—Chateau-briand was enthusiastically pumping out novels of the impas-sioned and untrammeled North American Peau Rouge the year Bill Williams went to Taos—but in reality Neolithic man, being Neolithic man, could not bear it out. The mountain man, however, did literally approach the status of exalted free-dom which the fantasy portrayed.

Freedom apparently entails challenge and is achieved, not bestowed. The achievement of the mountain men was to go

where others had not been, in the face of a constant challenge
from an awesome and unbroken wilderness. They were repaid
in freedom, a freedom they could accept, not being fettered
by the rigid taboos and fixed, complex, clan-ridden life patterns of the Indians. They were the freedom fantasy made
flesh, even to an uncanny identity with the incidental details
of Rousseau's picture: preoccupation with savagery, violence,
sensation, and megalomania. Beaver was only a reason for a
beginning; unconscious contempt for the tangible rewards of
their achievement was demonstrated by many of them over
and over again at rendezvous, when a year's catch went for
a few days of Old Sledge, aguardiente, and bells and beads
for the woman in the lodge, and it was back to the mountains
empty-handed. The mountain men were rewarded by their
way of life.

Francis Parkman wrote: "To him who has once tasted the
reckless independence, the haughty self-reliance, the sense of
irresponsible freedom, which the forest life engenders, civilization thenceforth becomes flat and stale. Its pleasures are
insipid, its pursuits wearisome, its conventionalities, duties,
and mutual dependence alike tedious and disgusting. . . . The
wilderness, rough, harsh, and inexorable, has charms more
potent in their seductive influence than all the lures of luxury
and sloth; and often he upon whom it has cast its magic finds
no heart to dissolve the spell, and remains a wanderer and an
Ishmaelite to the hour of his death."

The civilization of which Parkman spoke was in a period
of transition in which romanticism was dominant, the worn-
out life beat of Renaissance humanism was dying in rococo
convulsions, and the age of science was emerging. Science in
the nineteenth century drove the God of its fathers deep in
the woods of transcendentalism and then made textbook paper
of the trees, and it was confidently expected science would go
on to order all nature. Transition talked in forthright political

language in the year of the fourth expedition, 1848, which was the Year of Revolt in Europe. A line can be drawn from humanism to the American idea—the idea of revolutionary America, supporting human dignity by placing authority on the side of individual liberty and the pursuit of happiness— and the line can be continued to the mountain men, a final, remote flowering of revolutionary America. It is eminently suitable that they were instrumental (all unknowing, while they hunted beaver) in accomplishing a continental America before they vanished. But they were the end of an offshoot vine, a high point reached in, if not what men today think of as freedom, what was dreamed of as freedom in a simpler time.

To some, the lack of restraint and the challenge resulted in the realization of lives of monumental stature, lives which inevitably stamped their mark on the changing world, and afforded to an extraordinary degree that inner recognition of a reason for living, the feeling that here and for this one had been born, the sense of recognition and fulfillment, the intimation of immortality, for which all life strives.

Such were Jedediah Strong Smith, the triumvirate of Bridger, Carson, and Fitzpatrick, and a number of others.

These names are the shining reliques of their era, but in the hour of the mountaineers' leathery blue-blazing reality there were many for whom the lack of restraint only led to lives that were orgies of unrestraint, and the room they had to strive in was never recognized. They were accustomed to coming upon dismembered bodies of their companions—the head put up on a stake (with the hat on) and shot full of arrows—so they might go among wounded Indians after a battle and butcher them in grotesque fashion also. Or they might indulge the vacuum of restraint by simply yelling. They yelled when they fought Comanches and they yelled when they fought grizzlies and they yelled when they dashed to meet strangers ("yelling in wild excitement," Frémont wrote); they sang and shouted around a nightly feast, just to fill up the infinite starry space with noise. They yelled when they stampeded and stole horses and when they chased and stole women. They killed anything that moved on the slightest provocation, including each other, and sometimes for no reason at all, as when Jim Higgins of Ewing Young's company felt an urge while in his cups to shoot and kill Big Jim Lawrence, and did so. Likewise, the unrestraint compelled them to gamble their own lives for little or nothing, perhaps no more than a moment of slapstick.

On Joe Walker's famous California expedition of 1833 one of the men, Bill Craig, went swimming in the Humboldt River (then Ogden's River; Frémont later changed its name to honor the geographical baron). Craig stopped to investigate the stream before he jumped in and found it only a skim of water over a pudding of mud. He catwalked his way to a deeper pool in the current of the river, and then down to the bank came tough Joe Walker, the captain, begrimed and hot after the dusty day, and called out to ask how the water was. Craig said, "Joe it is just splendid." He couldn't help himself. The temptation was too great and inhibition had been gone too long. Captain Walker came on the run and dove in headfirst, his glossy black whiskers streaming, and half buried himself in the mud. Craig got out of the river and went into the brush like a jack rabbit. Joe Walker wallowed his way free and got his rifle and went looking for Craig and spent some time looking for him to kill him, before the rest of the men talked him out of it, and then Craig could come in to supper and put his clothes on. At least that was the story told (they loved to tell stories about Joe Walker), and the place was named Walker's Plunge.

Ruxton's much quoted passage on the western trappers, written in 1847 ("Not a hole or corner in the vast wilderness of the 'Far West' but has been ransacked by these hardy men

. . . the beaver hunter has set his traps in every creek and stream."), is preceded by a passage that has not been so much quoted, which runs, "Constantly exposed to perils of all kinds, they become callous to any feeling of danger, and destroy human as well as animal life with as little scruple and as freely as they expose their own. Of laws, human or divine, they neither know nor care to know. . . . They may have good qualities, but they are those of the animal; and people fond of giving hard names call them revengeful, bloodthirsty, drunkards (when the wherewithal is to be had), gamblers, regardless of the laws of *meum* and *tuum*. . . . However, there are exceptions, and I *have* met honest mountain men."

Tom Martin, steamboating into St. Louis with some of the other California company boys of Frémont's third expedition, found that "we were obliged to lie on board a steamer ten days as the hotels would not admit us. They said the mountaineers cut up such shines and were so rough that they would drive away all the boarders."

Bill Williams was a boy evangelist no longer; Parson Williams had died a missionary to the Great Osage, and he owned to the most unrestrained reputation in the mountains and was proud of it.

Captain William Drummond Stewart, a British sportsman adventuring in the mountains, wrote that since Bill had preached and taught all the religion he knew in the States, he "naturally appeared without any in the mountains of the West."

(Captain Stewart also objected to Bill Williams' indiscriminate spitting—thereby effecting solidarity with Frances Milton Trollope and most other British gentlefolk of the time who had opportunity to remark on the domestic manners of Americans—and Bill told him that in America there were two sexes, those that spit and those that didn't, and as for him he would go on spitting until hell froze over and then spit a couple of days on the ice—or words to that effect.)

David Brown, who met Bill Williams at the Green River rendezvous of 1837, wrote: "Next to Bridger, sat Bill Williams, the Nestor of the trappers. A more heterogeneous compound than this man, it has never been my fortune to meet withal. He was confessedly the best trapper in the mountains; could catch more beaver, and kill more horses, by hard riding, in so doing, than any that had ever set a trap in these waters. He could likewise drink more liquor, venture farther alone in the eager pursuit of game into the neighborhood of dangerous and hostile Indians, spend more money, and spend it quicker than any other man. He could likewise swear harder and longer, and coin more queer and awful oaths than any pirate that ever blasphemed under a black flag. . . . He could shoot (so he said) higher and deeper, wider and closer, straighter and crookeder, and more rounding, and more every way than 'ever a son of ——— of them all.' "

Bill Williams lived much among Indians; tradition has him a naturalized citizen of most of the Indian tribes of the Southwest, at some time or other. It seems clearly established that he did live among the Ute, and had a wife there, or maybe more than one, and possibly a family. He probably knew best the Tabeguache tribe, which ranged west of the headwaters of the Rio Grande, and the Moache, which held as its hunting grounds the country up the Rio Grande just north of the New Mexican territories. The mountains of these two domains were the mountains the fourth expedition intended to cross.

Bill Williams seems to have had a facility with languages, and was fluent in a number of tongues and dialects. This entails, particularly with primitive speech, an ability to enter to some degree the mental attitudes, manners, customs, superstitions, the culture of which the language is a spinning mirror. Bill Williams picked up a whole parcel of Indian ideas that he carried with him to amuse his solitude. He had decided that a transmigration of souls was a very probable theory, and that his would migrate into an elk, and the elk would be marked just so, and his range would be in such and such a park, and he asked his friends not to shoot him after he was dead and they saw him as an elk. He had concluded that he would die shortly after being touched by a bear, so he was not bold with bears. Jessie Frémont wrote, "He was full of fanciful superstitions and odd performances. . . . One of his peculiarities was an antipathy of having accidents or misfortunes spoken of—'No! No!' he would remark, moving away from such propinquity, 'don't tell about things, they'll happen to you sure, if you do.'"

Throughout the years after his arrival in Taos, Bill turned up in various trappers' brigades, sometimes as leader, sometimes as guide, from New Mexico to California to the Columbia River, Salt Lake, the Wind River Mountains, rendezvous at Brown's Hole, far and wide over all the West, ranging an area that would embrace a half-dozen Englands with a couple of Frances thrown in. But he was most often seen in the Rockies of what is now Colorado, so much so that that region, generally south of the principal trapping activities of the larger companies, can justifiably be called the Bill Williams country.

As time went on Bill Williams got a reputation for liking to travel alone. Parties of trappers would customarily break up to work the streams in small groups, but they liked to move and camp together. This meant added protection against Indians, help in case of injury or disaster, more hunters to bring in meat, and the human satisfaction of companionship. Bill Williams went much alone, without even taking along a girl in his lodge; if he had a woman in a Ute village he left her there. Companies of other trappers occasionally came across him in deserts or mountains, far from a base, and wholly alone.

He was secretive about his trapping grounds. If Bill Williams was the envy of the shaggy, independent mountain men because among them he was the most independent, the shaggiest, the dirtiest, and could go on the biggest sprees, he was also envied for the rich loads of furs he brought to rendezvous or Bent's Fort. But only he knew where he had trapped them, and so an air of mystery was added. Stories were told of his trail wisdom, his witchery at trapping—beaver were not easy to trap—his supernatural skill in hunting, at which he outrivaled the predatory beasts of the forests; his hair-trigger instinct for danger—but Old Bill himself magnanimously gave credit for this to his mules—his bravery and ferocity in a fight, and the scalps he had taken, and the wounds he had received; his pranks and his monumental Taos sprees; and his solitudes, and it was this last that impressed the mountain men more solemnly than all the rest.

Micajah McGehee of the fourth expedition, putting down what he heard of Bill Williams, said he was the "most successful trapper in the mountains . . . full of oddities in appearance, manner, conversation, actions . . . he was generally alone in the mountains . . . a dead shot with a rifle . . . an expert horseman . . . he loved the excitement and dangers of his life." McGehee reported that he signed his name, "Bill Williams, Master Trapper."

He was a tall, gaunt, stalking man, over six feet. His face was weatherworn and pock-marked. He had picked up the Indian manner of declamation, as did many of the trappers, which was one of few words and gesticulation to the point of pantomime. (Some Utes, once asked for food, said nothing, but opened their robes and showed the racks of their ribs in their starving bodies.) If the stories are true, he had unbelievable strength and endurance, even for a mountain man. If the stories are true, he was a rabid killer and a lawless marauder and he was kindly, warmhearted and generous and true, for all these things were said of him by various contemporaries.

Ruxton described him, hunched in the saddle under an old slouch hat, stirrups so short his bony knees were akimbo, his heavy rifle carried across the saddle horn grasped in one gnarled hand, dressed in shrunken buckskins shiny with grease and adorned with barbaric bead-worked accouterments, powder horn and bullet pouch slung on a shoulder strap, an awl and a worm for cleaning his rifle at the back of his belt, together with a bullet mold and a little antelope-horn bottle of medicine—his private preparation of castoreum, or oil from the musk glands of the beaver, used for baiting traps (it is used in perfume manufacture today).

Ruxton wrote that his "face was sharp and thin, a long nose and chin hob-nobbing each other; and his head was always bent forward giving him the appearance of being humpbacked. He *appeared* to look neither to the right nor left, but, in fact, his little twinkling eye was everywhere. He looked at no one he was addressing, always seeming to be thinking of something else than the subject of his discourse, speaking in a whining, thin, cracked voice. . . ."

Ruxton garbed Bill Williams in buckskin—some references say he was partial to elk hide—at about the same period that Bill was a guide with Frémont's third expedition. But Frémont said the mountain men of his time didn't wear buckskin—with the exception, of course, of the necessary leggings, the forerunners of the cowboy's chaps: "Many years before . . . they wore buckskin clothes, made from the skin which they dressed themselves or traded from the Indians. But that was long ago. In later years, when trading posts were established within easier reach, cloth, which was warmer for the winter, and lighter stuffs for the summer, were always worn by hunters and trappers. 'Bill Williams' even, whom I had with me as guide for a time and who had spent the greater part of his life and until he had become an old man trapping alone in the mountains, never wore buckskin; and he was the most careless and slovenly of all the mountain men. Of course, as these men are exposed to all weathers, their clothes are frequently wet, and buckskin shrinks and dries very hard. A buckskin dress in these days, so far as my knowledge goes, is worn only by amateurs to produce some scenic effect; a pair of leggings, perhaps, but nothing more in the country where the real work is done or the real hunter lives."

Frémont certainly knew Bill Williams, and Frémont would surely not have taken him out of romantic buckskins and put him in cloth and lighter stuffs unless that was how it was. It may be that Frémont saw him at a time when he was flush— with the pay he would get as Frémont's guide—and decked out in newly bought red flannel overshirt and comfortable hard-wool breeches thonged at the knee; and that in hard times when his finery was threadbare he went back to the old dressed hides that never wore out. However, Ruxton makes it clear that he only describes Old Bill from hearsay—lively and life-like though the description may be. "Do 'ee hyar now," Ruxton has him say, as a constant expression. "Do 'ee hyar now, boys, thar's sign about? this hos feels like caching." And "Do 'ee hyar now, boys, thar's *Injuns* knocking round, and Blackfoot at that; but thar's plenty of beaver, too, and this child means trapping any how." And the trappers, scattered at work on the streams, are attacked, and one of the boys staggers into camp, dripping blood, with a Blackfoot arrow in his back. Old Bill, graining a skin, looks up from his work to say, "Do 'ee feel bad now, boy? Whar away you see them darned Blackfoot?" The wounded trapper not unreasonably tells him to first pull the arrow out of his back and then he'll feel like talking, and Old Bill, going on with his work, says, "Do 'ee hyar now!" And Old Bill, all alone in the mountains, makes himself known to a startled trapping party by rising out of the brush six feet away and saying,

"Do 'ee hyar now? I was nigh upon gut shootin some of e'e—
I was now; thought e'e was darned Rapahos, I did. . . ."

All the stories about him were agreed on one point. As Jessie
Frémont, putting down what her husband told her, says it,
". . . the best guide in the country . . . a man whose name
was a synonym for mountain knowledge and trapper's lore—
Bill Williams." Ruxton wrote that he was "acquainted with
every inch of the Far West, and with all the Indian tribes who
inhabited it. . . ." On occasions when he did join a band of
trappers, Ruxton said, he "naturally assumed the leadership."
And "all felt perfectly secure under his charge . . . he managed, with admirable dexterity, to take advantage of the best
line of country to follow—avoiding the gullies and cañons and
broken ground, which would otherwise have impeded his advance. This tact appeared instinctive, for he looked neither
right nor left, whilst continuing a course as straight as possible at the foot of the mountains. In selecting a camping site,
he displayed equal skill: wood, water, and grass began to fill
his thoughts toward sundown, and when these three requisites
for a camping ground presented themselves, old Bill sprang
from his saddle, unpacked his animals in a twinkling, and hobbled them, struck fire and ignited a few chips (leaving the
rest to pack in the wood), lit his pipe, and enjoyed himself."
Tributes to Old Bill's knowledge of the country are documented over the signatures of many men who knew the mountains and the mountain men well. Long before this, he had
been promoted from Bill Williams to Old Bill Williams, the
patriarch of the wilderness. He was one who might almost
have truthfully said, in an expression of the country, that a
ten-prong buck wasn't done sucking when he last sot on a
cheer. He was the wise old man whose trailing skill and pathfinding cunning and intimate acquaintance with the mountains
verged on the marvelous; the "Old" to his name was a title
of honor.

It appears that everyone in the mountains who could spell wrote something of Old Bill Williams. As early as 1834 a young easterner, Albert Pike, published a little book of western travels in which Bill Williams figured as a literate man gone feral and possessed of "no glory except in the woods." But as "a specimen of the genuine trapper, Bill Williams certainly stands foremost." And Ruxton made Old Bill a character typed so strikingly that he has lived ever since in western fiction—the old man of the mountains, the past master frontiersman who has seen more things with his faded eyes than can be dreamed of in tenderfoot philosophies, the eccentric old-timer, full of hard liquor and ancient reputation, who saves the wagon train in between comical jets of tobacco juice.

But Old Bill Williams was more enigmatic than comic, and, toiling, godless, worn Ishmaelite, he was essentially more pathetic than either. One old trapper, remembering him in later years, said, "Poor old fellow . . . I hope he is happy."

Schopenhauer parabled the social structure in his story of the porcupines, who huddled together for warmth, in spite of being pricked and tormented by each other's sharp quills: it was better to suffer the annoyances of the crowd than to be cold and alone. They fell into a pattern, these porcupines, a tight little knot of the coldest and most dependent in the center, surrounded by somewhat more independent porcupines not quite so close together, and on the outermost fringes those few individuals, proud and strong, who could stand the cold best of all. These might represent the mountain men. And the one farthest apart from all the rest was Old Bill Williams.

During the Mexican War, when volunteer Missourians were marching to New Mexico and fighting scurvy, Old Bill distinguished himself, if the story be true—it was one heard by McGehee—by playing Indian and throwing a patrol commanded by Captain Philip St. George Cooke into a turmoil. Old Bill, he would have lacked a few months of being sixty years old at the time, was in high glee, but when the scared patrol finally caught him Captain Cooke, who was a humorless man who talked through his nose, was not amused and took him in custody for a spell. It could have happened, during the march of the Army of the West to Bent's Fort (at Bent's Captain Cooke was sent ahead with the fifth columnist James Wiley Magoffin), but it's cause for suspicion that Captain Cooke is made the goat, Philip St. George Cooke being anathema to Frémont men—Cooke was one of Kearny's chief red-hots in the California feud.

Aside from having fun with the green soldiers, Old Bill apparently sat out much of the conquest time, 1846-47, with his people, the Utes. After the spring fur hunt in 1848 he went down to Taos with packs of skins the Utes had commissioned him to trade for them, sold them, and spent all the money on a beautiful drunk. He then went to work guiding detachments of the 2nd Regiment of Missouri Mounted Volunteers, the garrison force in New Mexico, in punitive expeditions against the Jicarilla Apache, who had been raiding the rancherias above Taos. He took part in one skirmish in June and in a sizable little battle in July, at Cumbres Pass, fighting on the side of 150 soldiers against a large party of Apaches who had been joined by a number of Bill's own people, the Utes. Thirty-six of the Indians were reported killed; two of the Americans were killed, and three badly wounded, and Old Bill was one of these: his arm was shattered by a bullet "most horribly," but he kept on fighting. The major commanding stated in his report that Old Bill "behaved himself gallantly" in spite of being seriously wounded.

It was August when he was brought back to Taos with his shattered arm, and he had hit the alcoholic's rock bottom in first blowing in the money belonging to his long-time friends, the Utes, and then leading the soldiers against them, and he knew it.

It was less than four months later, up at the Pueblo on the Arkansas, that "not without some hesitation he consented to go" with the fourth expedition. He was a month or so short of his sixty-second birthday. It was his twenty-fourth year in the Rockies, and it was nearly forty years since he had withdrawn himself from civilization. Any weakness remaining from his most horribly shattered arm of a few months before is not mentioned.

Oral tradition in the country states that Frémont played on Old Bill's vanity in urging him to come along as guide. Frémont pictured the importance of the expedition, the railroad dream, the eye of history. Frémont was a man of world-wide fame and it was flattering that he thought so highly of Old Bill; Old Bill was the only one who might have a chance of successfully taking them through, everyone said so. And all this has an authentic ring. Frémont would have said it, and it would have been highly persuasive to the disheartened old mountain man.

And there was the chance that they might get through. Old Bill would not have been confident of this, no mountain man was ever confident of getting where he was going, the life was all uncertainty, but he would have been confident there was a chance. He knew the passes, all of them. He knew the weather, and what could be risked against it. In a mild winter, you could go through without trouble; in an average winter, it might be rough; in this winter—well, they'd see when they got there.

Further, he knew a number of the men of the expedition. He knew Godey, of course, and he knew him for one of the best in his profession. He would have known Proue, and probably the old coureurs du bois, Morin, and Tabeau called Sorrel. He might have known Taplin, Scott, Breckenridge, all these from times past. Perhaps he would remember Ned Kern, Tom Martin, Henry King, and some of the others from the third expedition. The majority of these men were young, hardened, capable, and a sufficient number of them were experts. That meant a great deal.

Also, the expedition was extremely well equipped. The wealth of equipment must have appeared splendid to Old Bill, remembering the more primitive gear and not much of it of the trappers' brigades. In the first place, there was a great advantage over a trapping company in that there was no excess weight of traps and peltries, a considerable item. And there were the fine animals of the mulada, not cow-hocked mountain stock but the very best that could be found on the Missouri. Packs upon packs of emergency provision, bacon and macaroni and flour, plenty of coffee and sugar, the mountain man's special delights, bales of goods and tents and trunks and Filley's finest Dutch ovens and pots and pans and axes, spades, and shovels, rifles, shotguns, pistols and handsome pistol holsters, powder and lead and blankets galore . . .

Good men, well equipped, and with plenty of spirit: they might be able to make it.

And beyond all these things, Old Bill sure needed the money.

Part Three
THE ATTACK

9

From now on it was all mules. Mule and horse trading had gone on at Big Timbers, Bent's, the Pueblo, and probably at Hardscrabble. Some later accounts and hearsay reports continue to speak of "the horses and mules," but if there were any horses left after Hardscrabble, even an old bell mare to lead the mule train, there is no specific mention of them in the day-by-day journals kept on the spot by men of the expedition. These talk only of the mules.

The mules were packed, all of them, even the colonel's own riding mule, with the expedition's baggage and with 130 bushels of shelled corn loaded aboard them at Hardscrabble. This was to carry them over the deep snows of the high mountains to the creek bottoms west of the Continental Divide, where they might hope to find sufficient grass again.

The logistics of feed for the animals was a crucial matter at this point, a matter for careful planning and nice decisions, and Frémont evidently gave it much thought. By packing along all this feed the mules could be sustained longer in snow-covered country, but the men would have to be walking for a time and thus the going would be harder and slower. If Frémont had been disposed to gamble on finding mild snow conditions and open country for graze, he would have taken less feed and kept the men mounted and depended on a quick crossing, allowing only a narrow margin of time for getting over the mountains. Instead he took all the corn he could carry, giving them a wider leeway of time than it would seem they could possibly need, even against the worst of winters.

Some grass had to be counted on, of course, along with the corn. Mules customarily want a lot of roughage, more so than horses. Habitually grass-fed mules will break down on a diet of grain alone; some mountain mules were so unfamiliar with grain they refused to eat it when it was offered them, unless on the stem in a field. And some grass was sure to be found, along the slopes and bottoms of sheltered draws, especially in the lower reaches of the mountain country. Allowing for the scantiest of grass, assuming the corn would have to be fed every day, it would still last a number of days that would certainly be more than enough for crossing the mountains. It was possible to calculate this number of days with some exactness.

A full ration of grain for traveling mules, fed in conjunction with grass and browse, will run approximately three quarts per animal per day. On this basis the 130 bushels of corn would carry the mules up in good condition for something like twelve days. But this ration could be cut in half and still the mules would survive, granting always the necessary minimum of grass and browse along the way. The factors were variable, because the mules would be working hard, so hard they might break down regardless of the amount of feed they received, and as their strength failed their resistance to the cold weather would be lowered and they would be more likely to freeze. But if the mules were handled and husbanded with care, the corn would provision them, humoring in all the variables to get a mean figure, for an outside limit of twenty-five days. After twenty-five days, if they had not reached grasslands beyond the worst of the mountains, the mules would be dead.

(And Frémont had written that he could ride all the way from the Pueblo to California in only thirty-five days—in the summertime.)

To get across the several mountain ranges and the Continental should take, even against snow and storm and winter delays, no more than two weeks. The actual distance from the last good grass east of the mountains to a prospect of good grass in the valleys of the western slope would be something less than 200 miles, perhaps as little as 150, and much of that would be across valleys between the mountain ranges: the Wet Mountain Valley between the Wets and the Sangre de Cristos, and the fifty-mile-wide San Luis Valley, or valley of the Del Norte, between the Sangres and the mountains of the Continental Divide. In the summer the three mountain ranges could easily be crossed in a week or even less, and even a slow wagon train, idling along and taking time for side trips, could make it in considerably less than twenty-five days. Trappers told of sometimes traveling these passes in winter and finding only a foot or so of snow, nothing worth talking about (but it was true that trappers also told, and some of the men of the fourth expedition would previously have had the experience, of spending as much as ten days laboring through a single pass during a heavy winter). But feed for twenty-five days almost doubled the generous estimate of two weeks, surely a wide enough margin of safety.

It is clear that Frémont thought it inconceivable they could be as long as twenty-five days getting to the grassy bottomlands of the streams beyond the Divide, whatever the obstacles, but Tom Fitzpatrick, hearing down at Bent's Fort of his preparations, wrote that "he procured a sufficient supply of forage to support his animals in crossing the mountain which lies between the Arkansas river and the Rio del Norte." Or in other words, only halfway to the other side of the Divide. Probably Broken Hand heard a garbled report of the preparations, but it could be he understood them well enough and merely took another view of the winter ahead.

The men of the expedition stayed in comfort at Hardscrabble

for two nights and in the afternoon of Saturday, November 25, they marched out up Hardscrabble Creek, driving the corn-laden mules.

Item, from this day's issue of the Santa Fe *Republican:* "We have just learned that Colonel Frémont is not to pass through this city, as he has taken the other route." Indicating that some-one, if not Kit Carson, had previously given the word in New Mexico that the new Frémont expedition might come that way by an optional route. And indicating that Frémont had ob-viously given such an idea of a safer optional route scant house room in his thoughts, to decide against it in the face of the unanimously adverse reports of the winter he had received at Big Timbers, Bent's, and the Pueblo. Naturally. He very much wanted to cross the mountains on the line he and Benton had chosen, he very much wanted to find his railroad pass, he wanted a clear-cut, resounding success this time as he had never wanted success before, and none of these things were to be won by tamely swinging down through New Mexico along well-known trails.

From now on the men were all on foot, until the mules should gradually eat enough of the corn to make room on their backs for riding. But everyone was rested. They had slept in the vacant adobe houses at Hardscrabble, houses furnished with the comforts of tables and benches, and to complete the picture of fat farm living they had feasted on chicken and baked pumpkin.

Ever since the Pueblo the weather had been fine, like April, some of them said, and like October, some of them said, cotton clouds in a sapphire sky, the mountains ahead in gorgeous blues and coppers, spangled with snow. Screaming, bright-colored birds darted among the sunlit pines and junipers; Doc Kern gathered specimens for his bird-skin collection, including a magpie, big and fearless and vivid white and black, the typical bird of the country. Now and then it had rained at night, be-

cause after all these were the Wet Mountains, the Sierra
Mojada, approaching, and the rain froze to sleet; when it became a skiff of snow instead it was welcome.

The first day out of Hardscrabble they moved only a few
miles, three or four, and made a camp in the foothills along the
creek, and now at last they had left the Arkansas River that
had been their highway for so many days across the plains.

The Wet Mountains belong in New England. They are rolling, blue with timber, and compared to the ranges beyond
them are not high. Their slopes are spread with pretty flowered
meadows and cut by steep-banked wooded creeks that are
scarcely cañons until they are followed to their upper reaches,
where they can become narrow and precipitate and twisting,
and very rough indeed.

The weather continued pleasant, springlike, autumnlike,
and the men slept in their blankets on the crisp snow at night
without bothering to put up tents. In open places the snow was
melted away and good grass could be found, but they waded
through more and more snow as they wound higher into the
mountains, in places as much as two or three feet deep.

They spent two days getting up "Wet Mountain" (in the
language of the time a range of mountains was a mountain
singular to the men who traveled them, and thus the San Juan
Mountains were the St. John Mountain, the White Mountains
were the White Mountain, and to Jed Smith the California
High Sierra was the St. Joseph Mountain). While they were
working up into the mountains a couple of trappers from the
Pueblo caught up with them and wanted to join the expedition, but "Col. Frémont being in no want of their services
they returned," as Fitzpatrick heard it at the time. (The departure of these men was remembered later by some of the
others as another incident full of dire omen, complete with
calamitous prophecy.) These unsuccessful volunteers got back
to the Pueblo two days later and Lancaster Lupton hastened

to add their information to the bulletin he was sending Senator Benton:

"The latest accounts leave Frémont within five miles of the summit of the first range of mountains, forcing his way through the deep snow, and up the steep mountain, and with every prospect of getting over."

Fitzpatrick talked to these same two trappers down at Bent's a month or so later and wrote in his letter to Jessie: "From these men I learned that they came up with the party ascending the mountain through very deep snow, Col. Frémont being in advance, with a few of his ablest men, breaking a road for the horses and mules to follow. They were then within six miles of the summit of the mountain. . . ." Fitzpatrick himself seems to have been confused as to which mountain the expedition was here ascending. When these letters were published in due time in the East they gave the impression that this preliminary assault on the humble Wets was the main event itself, and that the expedition was within five or six miles of the summit that meant decisive victory or defeat, and victory therefore appeared a foregone conclusion. This was the last news civilization had of the expedition for many weeks.

On the second day in the Wets, beating a way up and over the top at 9000 feet or so, the going was not easy. The creek, probably the north fork of Hardscrabble, became a deep and rocky cañon, choked with snow and thick stands of the columnar white boles of aspen. The mules floundered and ripped off their packs among the trees, or fell and their packs had to be removed before they could get up again. They went higher and the creek disappeared and they camped without water, except what could be made by melting snow, a lack that would have been keenly felt by the tired mules. This had been a hard day, costly in time and strength and the precious corn, but at the end of it they were over the top of the Wet Mountain pass, with the descent to the Wet Mountain Valley before them, and across that the first real mountain challenge, the sky-sweeping Sangre de Cristos.

Old Bill led them into the Wet Mountain Valley and down the valley to the south, skirting the eastern base of the Sangres. They found a little game along here and had a taste of deer meat again. Since leaving Hardscrabble they had been living pretty much on their store of flour, which they knew should be saved for the harder times ahead, but there was no help for it if there was no meat to be made. Beyond the Sangres, they thought, hunting might be better. Zebulon Pike and his half-starved party had had the same trouble, no game, on the same trail at about the same time of year, in January of 1807.

The floor of the valley was hilly, there was enough snow to turn soggy in the warm sunshine, wet and slick underfoot so that each step forward slid a half step back and walking was a tiring business. In the middle of the day it was warm enough to sweat but freezing cold at the first shadow, and at night the thermometer fell close to zero. They camped again without water, except for snow melted and skimmed of dirt in the camp kettles, and some of the thirsty mules got away during the night and went looking for a drink, which made for a morning delay while Vincenthaler and John Scott and Tom Martin and the Indian Joaquin scoured back to find them. The baggage the mules should have carried—kitchen gear—had to be left to be packed on them when they were caught and brought up.

They found occasional patches of grass, where snow thinned away and revealed it, and it was good grass. The valley is fine alfalfa and potato country today, dotted with barns. And there were still no storms; for that the men of the expedition were grateful and encouraged. They were not moving as fast as Frémont had hoped, perhaps, for it took two days' marches to travel thirty miles down to the southern end of the valley, but they were all still on foot (with their buckskin leggings wrapped flopping and cumbrous around their boots and moccasins to keep their feet dry), and presently, when they were mounted again, they would make up time. They were not too far behind schedule; their one bad day crossing Wet Mountain had been their only serious loss so far.

There is a pass across the Sangres at the southern end of the Wet Mountain Valley, called Music Pass, crossing the mountains only a few miles below the great upthrust spires known as the Crestone Needles. If this pass was known to the trappers and traders it was seldom used by them, and for good reason, as it is a tortuous road, winding and hairpinning and doubling back on itself so the traveler covers as many miles coursing and toiling back and forth in the mountains as he does getting across them. The traders went still farther south along the Sangres, down the full length of the Wet Mountain Valley and across the sweeping hills, now called Promontory Divide, that separate the Wet Mountain Valley from the valley of the Huerfano River south of it, and here at last, in the Huerfano Valley, trails began branching off to the right and leading up to the three principal passes over the Sangres.

The first of the passes was generally known in that time as Williams Pass, after Old Bill, who had traveled it for many years. In earlier days it had sometimes been called Pike's Gap, for here Zebulon Pike and his men had almost frozen to death crossing the Sangres. Today it is called Medano Pass and contains an old wagon road dating from the days when the country over the mountain was flushed with mining fever and freighters made fortunes hauling supplies.

Ten miles or so below Williams Pass was Robidoux Pass, where the old trader Antoine Robidoux had kept a wagon road, more or less, to travel on his way to trading posts he maintained west of the mountains. This pass is now known as Mosca Pass (Fly Pass), its original Spanish name. Another ten or fifteen miles farther south was the pass of Sangre de Cristo Creek, now La Veta Pass, and the highway route through the Sangres today.

The expedition was heading for Robidoux Pass for several reasons: Old Bill knew it to be less steep, especially on the eastern grade, than the one bearing his name, so it should be a good prospect to examine for a railroad pass over this range; and the country around the opening of Robidoux Pass offered a good place to camp and stoke up for the push over the Sangres. The Huerfano Valley here became a real valley, a little round park called by the Indians the "place of green grass," where the mules would find water and feed and where there was usually good hunting.

From the crest, fringed with pine, of Promotory Divide they could see the valley and Robidoux Pass, but there was again a delay while Vincenthaler and one of the Frenchmen, Sorrel, went back after more runaway mules, and it was another day's weary walking through snow a foot or two deep before they got into the little round park near the entrance to the pass.

In later years various men of the expedition reminisced about the trip, and it is a revelation of the anatomy of memory to compare their recollections with, say, the journals kept by Doc Kern and Dick Kern day by day while they traveled. Tom Breckenridge, for example, related the story of the expedition for publication in a magazine in his old, old age, more than forty-five years later, and Tom was dreaming in the sun of the giants the mountain men were in their youth, and of the giants that were the mountains with which they wrestled, and a mist curled up out of the years that was still terrible with furies of wind and snow and still shining with the golden bravery that made men feel twice as much alive. Tom's memory said there were continuous driving snowstorms when there were not snowstorms, but his memory was striving to make articulate a time of striving and suffering that could not be made articulate to the editors in their offices and to the readers in their lamplit homes. And so in frustration his memory repeated, There were storms, there were storms you could not walk against.

But no such incantation, no matter how many times recited, can slide back the years and reveal a glimpse of the living men in the living picture as clearly as three words scribbled by Doc Kern, crouched over a cottonwood fire, his pencil cramped in cold grimy fingers, his thumb on the fluttering pages of his notebook to keep them from tearing in the wind: "All very tired." This in the little round valley, close against the roots of the tall Sangres, the weather winter-cold but still pleasant during the day, although that morning it had snowed a little while they waited for Vincenthaler and old Tabeau called Sorrel to find the strayed mules; this before any of the high mountains had been entered, and after a short day's march of only ten miles (on slippery footing that knotted leg muscles at each step). The simplest of observations, but enough, if Doc had lived, to have started again the salt of fatigue in his muscles at any rereading in years to come.

Unfortunately the little round park was bare of game. And again the next morning the camp waited while Vincenthaler and Sorrel went back to chase down mules, waited until almost noon and then moved only three miles, plodding up the snow-streaked slope of the little round valley, the expert Proue this time hanging far behind to drive the last of the straggling line of mules, to pitch camp again at the beginning of the pass, because it was now too late in the day to start into it. A few of the men were riding again by now, an ominous sign, revealing that the corn was already dwindling—not much, but little by little to fill out the uneven grass, plus one full day of corn feeding, a price of something more than half a dozen bushels at least, that had been paid to get over the deep snows of Wet Mountain.

This was the first of December. They camped overnight to await the climb the next morning into Robidoux Pass of the Sangres, and here for the first time they met the wind. The wind blew from the west, from the high unknown mountains they were marching to meet, the distant and still invisible mountains ranked on the other side of the broad valley that lay beyond the Sangres. It brought up against the lofty barrier of the Sangres raging and impatient to find a way through. It rushed into the passes and funneled through them in a constant screaming and triumphant gale. At Sangre de Cristo Pass, the next pass to the south, the valley at the eastern gate of the pass was called by the mountaineers Wind-trap Valley; the wind, hurling itself through the pass, was caught in the valley and spun round and round and never got out, so the mountain men said, and thus it blew wildly from all directions at once, and instantly blew out and scattered a fire if you were foolish enough to stop there and try to make one. A few miles north, above Music Pass and near the Crestone Needles, the wind has found a secret and mysterious mouth in the Marble Mountain Caves. One of the caves, La Caverna del Oro, is thought to run in a continuous passage through the subcellars and foundations of the Sangres to come out some place on the western side (according to legend it also leads to an old Spanish mine). Unquestionably it pierces far enough through the mountains to be found by the seeking fingers of the wind on the other side, for a tempestuous cold wind gushes up out of La Caverna del Oro. It will blow out a lantern, and it is said that if you wrap a rock in a blanket and throw it down into the cave, the wind, deep in its den, will presently untangle the blanket from its weight and fling it back up out of the shaft.

At the entrance of Robidoux Pass the expedition camped off on a side slope among pines for shelter, but there was no escape from the booming, freezing wind. They could not sleep. In the morning they lashed on the mule packs while the wind numbed faces and hands, ballooned blankets and tarpaulins, and plucked up hats and sent them sailing. The dawn was ragged and gray and now it began to spit snow, gusts and blasts of stinging snow flying on the wind.

They climbed into the high hills that launched the pass, probably following pretty much the present old road that hangs on the left-hand wall of the cañon of what is now called May Creek, but the snow was deep in the higher regions, where it had fallen and lain undisturbed for many weeks, too deep in places to follow Robidoux's old wagon trace, and they detoured in scattered groups, seeking passage along steep open pitches where the wind kept the worst of the snow scoured away. Old Bill gave them the cheerful news that two trappers had frozen to death here the previous winter. The mules shook from the cold and when they could run they ran, heedless of their packs, and the men ran with them. Early in the afternoon Frémont called a halt. Willows were chopped and heaped in the crackling fires, and the tired mules crowded among the tired men, stretching their quivering noses to the warmth and skinning their teeth and bleating, one may be sure, that pleasure in physical comfort which a mule, perhaps as compensation for the loss of sex drive, seems capable of feeling more keenly than other animals.

Snow fell during most of the night, and the traveling the next morning was across the steepest roof tops of the mountains. And here at last from the summit of the pass they saw the valley of the Rio Grande del Norte, set in the midst of a sea of mountains.

They stood on the top of its eastern wall, the Sangres (the sun had shone on these mountains with a resplendent ruby and frost effect that had looked like the blood of Christ to a pious Spaniard, so the story goes), but better known to the mountain men as the White Mountains, the Sierra Blanca, because of the striking whiteness of their rock formations. The Sangres

sweep up from the valley floor without any preambling foothills, very sheer and awe-inspiring; farther south, down in New
Mexico, they become more orthodox and suckle foothills, but
they remain all the way a rugged, handsome range, because, as
mountains measure age, they are in all the freshness of their
youth.

On the other side of the valley, fifty miles or so away across
the valley floor, they could see the next range of mountains to
be crossed, a galaxy of snowy peaks that was the principal
rampart of the main body of the Rockies. There was the Continental Divide. There, someplace, was to be located the railroad pass that was the expedition's chief objective.

Almost due west across the valley the Rio Grande ran from
deep in those mountains, its cañon knifing a gap into them for
more than sixty miles. The river drifts from the mountains out
into the center of the valley, splitting into ribbons that join
and split again, and turning south in a wide bend flows down
into New Mexico. The valley is shaped like the head of a
royal eagle, with its beak the gap of the Rio Grande where it
plunges into the western mountains. It so appears on present-
day maps, and it so appeared to Dick Kern, who drew the map
reproduced in the end papers of this book.

The mountains that followed up the Rio Grande and curled
around its headwaters were the San Juans, famous then and
now for some of the roughest mountains in America, with more
than a dozen peaks reaching above 14,000 feet. (It was on one
of the fearsome rockslides in the San Juans that in later years
Kit Carson was caught under a falling horse and received the
injury that is presumed eventually to have caused his death.)

The west wall of the valley above the gap of the Rio Grande
is made up of what are called today La Garita Mountains and
north of these, at the upper corner of the valley, lie the Cochetopa Hills, and here could be seen the low saddle of Cochetopa Pass. The trappers generally called those western moun-

tains above the intersection of the river the Chow-atch or Saguache or Sawatch, considering them the tail of the great Sawatch Range that splits central Colorado north of the valley.

All these mountains, the Sangres on the east of the valley, the Sawatch, the Garitas, the San Juans on its north and west sides, are various ribs and thigh bones of the Rockies.

The valley is called the San Luis Valley today, and was so known to the New Mexicans then, named for a creek that rises at its northern rim and runs a little way down into the plain and sinks in a series of shallow lakes before it can reach the bend of the Rio Grande. In the days before irrigation canals the sinks and ponds of the San Luis River made much of the upper valley floor marshy and difficult to travel, especially in summer. The mountain men called the valley the valley of the Del Norte, common abbreviation for the Rio Grande del Norte, the river's full and proper name.

There was very little snow in the valley, and that was heartening. The men of the expedition were making their way through more than four feet of snow when they looked out over it. Maybe, as they had hoped, they would find game in this valley of the Del Norte, and grass for the mules, although the valley looked more like an arid desert of sagebrush than grassland. Just below them, at the foot of the Sangres, they could see the famous sand dunes, tremendous piles of sand in hills more than a thousand feet high, a little corner of the valley turned into a miniature Sahara, or a playground for preschool children of Eblis. These were covered with snow.

The wind was not as cold as it had been the day before, but it snowed off and on during the day and they ran into very tough going in the narrowest stretch of the pass, which was clogged with fallen timber thrown across the road by some previous storm. Such blowdowns, fallen across each other, can form an interlaced log jam that is, in the old saying, impassable and not even jackassable. If it extends any distance there is no crossing on top; the blowdowns are too limby. Especially when they are slick with snow and ice the attempt is dangerous; a slip may mean a fall of ten or twenty feet down through the maze of interlocked and splintered snags. With animals, of course, it is necessary either to find a way around or chop a way through. The blowdowns and the snow hampered them and took time and effort and they would not have made much more than five miles during the day, but they got through the pass, and the descent, down the cañon of Mosca Creek, was steep but easy. Frémont called for an early camp again, to give men and mules a rest. In spite of the wind and snow and below-zero cold and the blowdowns they had made the pass in two days (they had "taken the mountain," in the language of the mountain men) without losing an animal, and that was an achievement.

They made camp at two in the afternoon on a little creek, doubtless the present Medano Creek, running between the mountains and the sand dunes. They were in timber: juniper and cottonwood, so the mules could have tasty cottonwood bark along with their corn, a considerable help in restoring their strength. The night turned extremely cold, with snow and furious winds. The blanket of snow on the sand hills was spun into the air in clouds and by morning the dunes were swept clean and the sand itself laid down in a new day's pattern of ripples and waves. The mules suffered from the arctic cold of the night, turned their rumps to the wind and hopped in their hobbles before it, blindly seeking deeper shelter and the dream of a blade of grass.

In the morning the camp dug out from under the snow and spent half the day tracking down the mules and driving them in to pack, and the day's march, plunging through waist-deep snow in the hollow between the mountains and the high sand hills, into the wind that was veering northerly and turning steadily colder, was less than five miles. Again they camped in

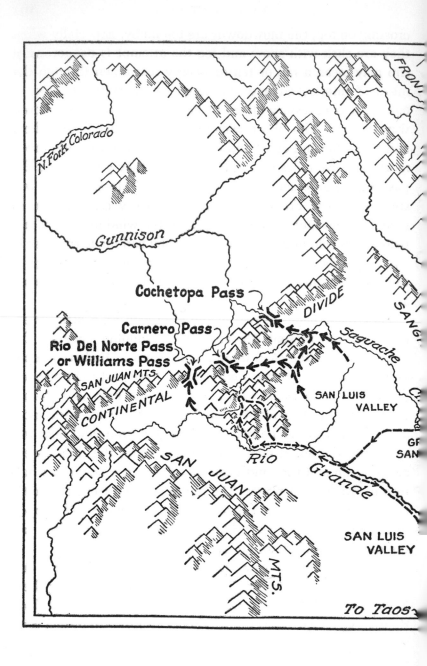

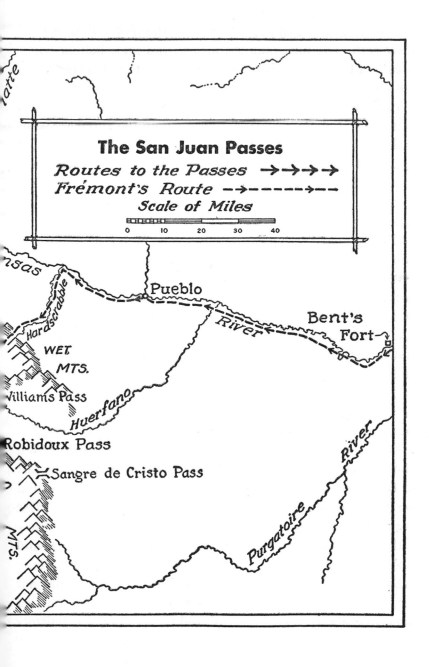

The San Juan Passes

Routes to the Passes →→→→
Frémont's Route -→------→--
Scale of Miles

0   10   20   30   40

cottonwoods and stripped off bark for the mules' dessert after their corn. The men huddled around the fires, behind windbreaks of tents and tarpaulins. The wind battered against these without cessation and it was clear a storm was descending.

In the morning they tried to go on again, but now the storm was at hand. A heavy fall of snow rode on the shrieking wind and the day was enveloped in a blizzard. They struggled against it for an hour or so and Frémont ordered them back to the shelter of the clump of trees in the camp they had just left. This was a moment of great danger for the mules. Since they had come down to the sand hills the temperature had hung below zero day and night. The mules, now thin and worn, could not have lasted long in such a cold in the open, during such a devouring storm. They were gathered in the cottonwoods and picketed in the smoke of the fires. Steam of sweat and breath settled in frost on their hides and each hair glittered with a tiny bead of ice. They bunched together, heads down, tails to the wind, snow settling and swirling away and settling again on their skeletal hip bones. The men, after seeing to the safety of the mules, put up their tents and windbreaks again. The men wore lashings of snow on their hat brims and epaulets of snow on their shoulders, and their whiskers and the ends of their long hair were, like the mules' hides, rimed white with frost. They made dough of some of the last of their flour and ate and were still ravenous, but there would be no game in weather like this in this naked country. Meat would have to wait until they got out of these sand hills, if they did, and reached fatter ground. They stitched up leggings and hoods of blanketing and made mittens and moccasins—those who were still wearing boots had discovered they would not do; if their stitching held together they threatened the feet with freezing by imprisoning air and perspiration. Fortunately their stitching did not hold together and boots had already been generally discarded, having fallen apart in the heavy go-

ing. The afternoon passed and by night the snow had banked
deep around the beds and tents and the men were warm and
could rest.

During the night the storm moved on into the high mountains and by morning it was clear, although colder still. They
packed up and traveled until about noon and found timber on
a creek and camped again. This was probably, and fittingly
enough, the present Cold Creek, which tumbles down from
the mountains to the sand hills just north of Williams Pass.
They were still moving between the sand hills and the Sangres
and on this day Colonel Frémont and Old Bill, Preuss, King,
and the botanist, Creutzfeldt, went exploring Williams Pass.
Everyone could see its gap in the mountains as they went by.

This little side excursion was a casual part of the work of
tedious observation and measurement that was the end objective of all the other work of the expedition and that must be
carried on without interruption as the expedition moved along.

A glimpse of this work is afforded by a description of the
business of making an astronomical observation during another
winter expedition: we "selected a level spot on the snow, and
prepared the artificial horizon. The thermometer indicated a
very great degree of cold; and standing almost up to our middle
in snow, Col. Frémont remained for hours making observations,
first with one star, then with another, until the occultation took
place. Our lantern was illuminated with a piece of sperm
candle. . . ."

Frémont's biographer, Allan Nevins, sums up these labors:
altitudes were determined by barometer, and "latitudes by de-
duction from a long series of astronomical observations of stars
to the north and south of the zenith; longitudes by telescopic
observation of the eclipses of the satellites of Jupiter, eclipses
of the sun, occultations of the planets and fixed stars by the
moon, and transits of the inferior planets over the sun's disc.
All these calculations were difficult, and some of them exceed-

ingly intricate. . . ." The survey was made by "taking the magnetic bearing of every point, estimating its distance, and then making a sketch or bird's eye view of the whole, this operation being constantly repeated as they moved forward."

At the several principal observation stations established on each expedition numerous observations would be taken, sextant observations of altitudes of a star or of the sun for time, and of Polaris or a southern star for latitude. This would also determine the setting of chronometer rates (two or three were usually carried to provide a mean, and their jolting on mule back was always a major problem). At such principal stations the expedition would be held in camp as many days and nights as were necessary to provide a sufficient number of careful sextant observations and barometer readings. One principal station on the third expedition had been at the Pueblo and it may be assumed that when the fourth expedition camped at the Pueblo, Frémont found time, after his talks with Hatcher and Old Bill and the other mountain men there, to make fresh astronomical observations and reduce them and check them against the table prepared from the data of the third expedition readings, thus establishing controls both for his instruments and his findings. A transit instrument with a two-foot telescope was used to fix longitude by moon culminations, "with an accuracy much more than sufficient for ordinary geographical purposes," to quote Joseph Stillman Hubbard, the brilliant young astronomer at the National Observatory in Washington, who calculated tables of latitudes and longitudes from Frémont's records of observation.

Along the line of march one daily or nightly series of observations might be taken, if seeing conditions permitted, as compared with the dozen or more logged at a principal station. The sperm-candle illumination described was necessary at night when in some way or other the dividing area of the sextant had to be lighted, and this, in a high wind such as that at the mouth of Robidoux Pass, could make a pretty problem in itself.

Measurement of the land they crawled across was one third of the purpose of such an expedition. The other two thirds was called by Frémont, in characteristic poetics, the study of "the flower and the rock," and told the story of soil and water and wind and weather and the life permitted thereby.

Dr. James Hall, of New York, the paleontologist, received and examined and reported upon the geological collections. John Torrey, the physician who was the leading American botanist of his day, studied and classified the botanical specimens from not only the Frémont expeditions but from nearly all the other principal western explorations of the epoch, although some of the botanical reports were prepared by Jacob Whitman Bailey, the West Point professor of geology who nevertheless shone brightest in botany. As an example of industry in this connection: on the second expedition some 1400 botanical specimens were collected, "many in regions not before explored by any botanist," as Dr. Torrey proudly stated. As an example of difficulties: more than half of them were ruined in the process of fording streams and packing and unpacking in Sierra blizzards before the expedition returned to place the collection in Dr. Torrey's hands. When Ned Kern went along on the third expedition Dr. Torrey was especially pleased, because Ned could make very fine botanical drawings. The fourth expedition went further still and took along its own botanist, Creutzfeldt, equipped with plenty of paper and other paraphernalia of collecting. Ned and Dick Kern also made sketches and notes, and their own botanical knowledge was somewhat more than a mere amateur interest. As for Doc Kern, his scientific bent ranged well beyond medicine, in the fashion of the time, when the walls of specialization were not high, and his learning in botany and ornithology surpassed that of his brothers.

Frémont's own botanical enthusiasm was at its best when he could find the spirit of Wordsworth frosted over the Sierra foothills in "the true English crimson-tipped daisy" or in the San Joaquin Valley in "Shakespeare's 'Love-in-idleness'" or "the little golden violets" that still in the spring splash such beauty over the green Kern River hills.

Frémont worked hard on his expeditions and he took his work very seriously. It was sufficient reward when the mighty Humboldt himself spoke of "Frémont's great hypsometrical investigations." Doubtless Frémont would have gladly changed the names of a dozen rivers in exchange for such praise. Frémont often pretended a stylish diffidence toward popular or political acclaim, but he frankly treasured this sort of recognition from men like Humboldt and from learned societies throughout the world.

But this work, the real work of an expedition, the measurement, observation, collecting, study, and notation, could only come after each day's routine work of keeping the expedition alive and in order and in progress, and this in itself was a highly demanding task.

Men would pick quarrels with each other, the gentlemanly technicians would resent being asked to do muleteers' work, the muleteers would resent the technicians' airs and their technical equipment, often hard to pack, and would slyly try to lose it along the way. The simplest item of daily routine, the roster for guard duty, was sure to be a source of arguments and complaints.

The American of that day, particularly the American gone West, was extremely sensitive on the matter of individual liberties. Volunteer regiments in the Mexican War elected their own officers, on the basis of rosy campaign promises, naturally, and retained the privilege of firing them from office and electing others any time they offended the electorate. Consequently, discipline among the volunteers was nonexistent.

Ruxton, used to the British Army caste system and flogging for impertinence, was astonished and revolted by the sight of rawboned, disheveled privates of the 1st Missouri Mounted Volunteers swearing at their officers and driving them away when their officers timidly ventured to interrupt their card games. Ruxton was even more astonished and rather puzzled at the beautiful way the 1st Missouri fought and marched.

Discipline among brigades of free trappers was, of course, also a sometime thing. The leader, wishing to go here, might be overruled by vote of the men and the party would go there. This happened even to iron Joe Walker. Trapping parties might split up at the drop of a wrong word and a trifling argument. Among the emigrant trains, parties separating from each other in wrath, or re-electing every few days a new set of wagon captains, was the rule rather than the exception. Trappers could separate and still go on trapping; emigrants could go their independent ways and still, maybe, get to Oregon; but if an expedition of exploration dispersed the expedition was ended. To keep the men together, to keep the piston working day after day, all its parts functioning in order, required constant care and watchfulness and an immense amount of tact. (The Navy's explorer of the Pacific Coast, Lieutenant Charles Wilkes, lacked sufficient tact and was court-martialed for using brutal disciplinary measures.)

It was important to select the right men in the first place, and it was important to have some real authority beyond the intangible authority of command. From Lewis and Clark on, the strongest implement in the hands of expedition leaders was the payroll. Men contracted for a stipulated journey and if they left before its completion their accrued pay was canceled. After the start of an expedition it was still possible to weed out the unfit and send them back from the first port of call, as the detachment of men found wanting for one reason or other were sent home from Bent's Fort on the third expedition. The rest, from here on, were expected to stay till the death, although in actual practice it was not rare for men to be released during the course of the expedition.

On the third expedition thirteen men left and went back the first day out, when Frémont read to them the articles of military law under which they would be governed. François des Montaignes, telling of this, gives a picture of Frémont the disciplinarian as seen through the eyes of an unspellbound follower. It seems a man on night guard duty had gone to sleep, and Frémont the next morning called a general meeting. "Martial law . . . was declared by our valiant commander-in-chief to be the law which should direct Him in governing his command. As to the drowsy headed fellow . . . he was formally pronounced to be no longer a member of the mule and packsaddle exploring expedition, but ordered to return as speedily as possible to the point whence none but an ill wind could have blown him. . . . Any one falling asleep hereafter, shall be shot after breakfast . . . the sanguinary oration of our warlike little Captain produced considerable of a sensation among the explorers . . . mostly a low grumbling and shaking of heads, but some unterrified, ten or a dozen, including several of the best men, presented themselves at the Captain's tent and throwing up their commissions and horsepistols chartered a conveyance which happened opportunely in camp and with a hearty hurrah were whirled swiftly over the rolling prairie in the direction of Westport. . . ."

The commonest punishment meted out by Frémont was to assign extra duty or make a man walk. In the habit of conscientious commanders he would sometimes appear in the middle of the night to check the guard, and if a man was found sleeping he might walk the next few days, leading his animal. This was supposed to give him a hint of how the going would be if, through his carelessness, Indians should steal the mules.

The charm of the romantic is a subjective thing: Trelawney

gave his devoted admiration to Shelley not so much because of what he saw in Shelley as what he saw of Trelawney mirrored in Shelley. Such charm has therefore for the objective view a certain cheapness, as of anything merely personal and egotistic. Not a cheap charm, even so, but a charming cheapness. Such charm is effective, with other romantics, to the degree to which it takes itself seriously. Frémont's was very effective. He easily inspired loyalty, frequently the sort of loyalty gone blind that is termed dedication. One emotional follower, writing of his "nobility and genius," clinched the argument by adding that "Col. Frémont never forgot he was a gentleman; not an oath, no boisterous ebullitions of temper, when, heaven knows, he had enough to excite it. . . . The greatest etiquette and deference were always paid to him, although he never ostensibly required it. Yet his reserved and unexceptionable deportment, demanded from us the same respect with which we were always treated, and which we ever took pleasure in reciprocating."

Frémont's discipline by knightly attitudes was part of his nature, but the utter absorption in his work that also impressed his followers was not. He had been in the beginning gay and impetuous, as much so as Godey himself, and the absorption had grown with responsibility.

There can be no question about Frémont's important achievements in exploration (which is seldom synonymous with pathfinding), and there are very few substantial achievements of any kind that are not built on hard work. Attitudinizing could account for only part of his absorption; in the greater part it was simply because the work of an expedition kept him extremely busy.

When he rode aside with Old Bill and Henry King and the botanist and topographer of the expedition to have a look into Williams Pass, Godey was left in charge of the day's march of the expedition. Godey, on foot, led the way through the sand hills "in a capital manner," as Doc Kern said. They marched up and down over the enormous dunes, sometimes floundering almost up to their necks in drifts of snow, and sometimes, from high points, getting glimpses of the valley floor and the mountains ringing its other edge that they would make for if they ever got out of the sand hills.

The day became brilliantly clear but the bone-cracking cold never relented. At the warmest hour of noontime the thermometer remained below zero. The steaming breath of mules and men was tranformed into clouds of frost that whitened heads and shoulders. Icicles clinging to mustaches steadily lengthened until they hung down from jaws and chins in wintry caricatures.

Old Bill and Frémont and the three men with them took five of the free mules for their excursion into the pass, but riding was worse than walking and when they returned some of them had to be helped from the saddles: their feet were frostbitten.

Straggling timber was found on Cold Creek, pine and cedar and cottonwood venturing into the sand dunes alongside the creek, and a stop was called here for camp less than an hour after noon. Fires were built, the mules were cared for, the men ate of their unsatisfying emergency rations and, probably, a few treasured scraps of jerky—there was still no meat from hunting, but maybe tomorrow they would get out into the valley and find game. Snow was kicked away and beds put down. The short day ended. The night was flooded with moonlight and the cold cracked in the trees and it was hard to get warm enough to sleep.

At last, after a few hours' march the next morning, they came out of the sand hills into the open plain of the valley. Now they could travel, and they made more than twenty miles, but there was no cover here, no timber, nothing but sagebrush and snow and the whipping northwest wind in their eyes. The mules kept trying to run from the wind back to the comparative shelter of the mountains and sand dunes they had left.

In the afternoon streaks of pencil gray clouds closed over the sky and snow fell again in swirling curtains flying down the wind.

But hunters had been sent ahead and this time game was found. Five deer were killed. Their camp that night was in the middle of the unprotected plain, with flaring fires of sagebrush and greasewood that burned as quickly as it was set aflame and would not serve to cook the supper. The deer meat was seared as well as could be and eaten raw. If the supper of fresh meat was a pleasure, the camp was a miserable one, completely open to the snow that blew over them during the night, by far the worst camping place yet, and extremely dangerous for the mules.

They had been heading fairly straight across the valley, but in the afternoon of the next day they raised the bend of the Rio Grande swinging up on their left hand and made a jog to the south to join the river, where they could see timber. They made a good camp on the frozen river, with plenty of wood for the fires, and the salvation of grass—when a couple of feet of snow was scraped away to disclose it—for the mules. The hunters found nothing, though, and that was a disappointment. It was thought the fierce storms had driven most of the game upriver, out of the exposed valley into the foothills of the mountains to the west. But those mountains were very near now. Surely the next day, or the next, they would find plenty of meat.

10

It was into the second week of December now. They were fourteen days out of Hardscrabble—there were eleven days of life remaining for the mules unless in that time they got over the Continental and found warm valleys and good grass.

The warnings about the winter had already been realized. The deep snow in the mountains and the days of solid and unbroken cold (the incredibly cold wind in the Sangres once drove the mercury in the thermometer entirely down into the bulb, McGehee wrote later, and maybe it did), and the storms, sudden and bitter and fierce, all these things were not to be expected in such severity so early in the winter. But this winter was to be a prodigious one. The Indians and trappers had said so, and it was clear by now they were right.

They had traveled from Hardscrabble perhaps 125 miles. There had been the day spent crossing the Wet Mountain pass, and the day lost at the entrance of Robidoux Pass, and the struggling two days getting through Robidoux Pass, and the entire day they had been held in camp during the blizzard in the sand dunes. They had been three full days getting out of the naked sand dunes, a distance of no more than fifteen or twenty miles.

Any optimistic estimate of fourteen days across the high mountains to the creeks of the Colorado River drainage had already been exceeded. The winter had seen to that. At least six of the days since they had left Hardscrabble had been days of short, halting, half-day marches, scurrying a few miles into the teeth of murderous weather or laborious country and quickly making camp again before mules or men should freeze or become too exhausted. And the big test, the pass of the Continental that was their great objective, still lay ahead. It was evident the timetable was going to be stretched to its limit. The mules' ration of corn was cut in half during the toiling passage of the Sangres, and cut in half again when the expedition was stopped in the snow and cold of the sand dunes. Now the mules were getting only a pint of corn at a feeding, once or twice a day.

In spite of the slow progress the expedition could be proud of its accomplishments so far. Not an animal had been lost, a tribute to skillful management. In this sort of weather, in this country, an error in judgment of an hour or two in extending a day's travel, a wrong guess in choosing a critical campsite, a little laxity in guarding the mules during a night of blizzard, and some of the animals, or most of them, or all of them, may have died; and now more than ever the expedition depended on the mules. If they died or were lost now the expedition was not only immediately finished but the men themselves, left on foot in this remote place, would face a hard fight to save their own lives.

A Santa Fe trader, James Collins, once compiled a record of some winter difficulties along the Santa Fe Trail for the information of the New Mexico territorial governor and legislature. The Trail was a much traveled road and not considered too hazardous for an occasional winter trip, certainly safe and easy in comparison with this mighty mountain country. But the menace of weather was always present nevertheless, and even on the familiar Trail, where places of wood and water and shelter were known, winter could strike with sudden disaster. In 1824 or 1825, Collins wrote, nearly all the horses and mules of a trading party were lost in a heavy snow; winter travel on the Trail was not popular for a long while after that, but in 1841 all the animals and two men of another party of traders were frozen to death "in a few hours" in a storm. The famous "Don Ant. Robidoux," as Collins called him, lost in one stormy winter night "over 400 mules and horses, and one or two men. . . ." Collins gave many other examples: 300 mules lost in a single night, one man dead and several others badly frozen; over a thousand head of animals lost in another storm; a train of twenty wagons caught by a blizzard in which all the cattle died "in a few hours."

And: "In 1848, Messrs Waldo, McCoy and Co., government freighters, on their return to Missouri lost nearly all their cattle, amounting to 800 or 900 head. The wagons were left on the plains until spring." This was the same storm the fourth expedition ran into November 3, on the prairie two weeks out from Westport, when Frémont cut short the day's march at noon and made camp and had the mules picketed in the smoke from huge campfires to keep them from freezing to death; and Carver and Doc Kern and Captain Henry King went buffalo hunting in the snow. Senator Benton, writing later of this incident, said Frémont was "not afraid of snows in the mountains where there are valleys and passes and wood. . . . He has been safe in his camp in a snowstorm which killed all animals on the prairies . . . while he . . . lost not an animal, and his men amused themselves in hunting and killing buffalo."

The feat of the fourth expedition in keeping its mules alive and working through the weather so far encountered was not, of course, to any one man's credit. Few trading caravans on the Santa Fe Trail were as rich in men of skill and experience as the fourth expedition. Besides Old Bill and Godey and Frémont himself, there were the old line professional arrieros or muleteers, Morin and Tabeau called Sorrel, and Manuel, Joaquin, and Gregorio, the young professional California vaqueros, and Taplin, a qualified trail boss in his own right, and such expert hands as Breckenridge and John Scott, and Raphael Proue bearing a cluster of graduate degrees gained through his long years on such expeditions.

The expedition had come through safely so far, in spite of the dangerous weather, because the men had spent recklessly of their strength and watchfulness. Their energy and knowledge were devoted to the well-being of the mules; all their skill and effort were thrown on the scales to maintain a balance that would keep the train moving as fast as possible and still conserve the stamina of the mules. If it was necessary to break a path through snowdrifts in the pass for the mules to follow, the men broke trail with their bodies, and a nice decision might be required at any moment to determine what depth of snow a mule could lunge through without too much risk of a strain, perhaps a rupture, and the consequent loss of the animal. Someone had to gauge and guess whether the mules could keep their footing on this slope or that, or whether they would need to go around another way. If the mules had to be watered with melted snow, the men worked at the kettles until the wet and tedious job was done. The men climbed cottonwoods and chopped down limbs and peeled the bark for feed for the mulada. Each night the guard stamped back and forth in the snow, watching the animals, and even so the mules, suffering with cold and hunger and frightened by their suffering, got away again and again and fled on the back trail, and had to be chased and caught. In the miserable sagebrush camp in the open valley the guards awoke the camp at three in the morning to give the alarm that the mules had broken away; it took four hours to hunt them down and bring them back, and by then it was morning and time to start on. (Tom Breckenridge remarked that no prayers were said when driving them back to camp.)

It was altogether against the mules' philosophy to keep

traveling into the cold gale wind they faced day after day.
At night they had to be tied, picketed, hobbled, guarded, and
on the road they often had to be herded along by men who
dodged about their heels and jabbed their flanks with rifles
and pointed sticks. In the best of times mules can drive a man's
patience to madness: during the night they will bellow to wake
the dead if they are unhappy, if they catch the scent of a
wolf—and wolves had been known to come close enough to
gnaw the mules' picket ropes—if their hobbles annoy them,
and quite reasonably they do—or they will merely bellow at
the moon or the wind or, if it comes to that, at nothing at all.
In the morning a man discovers his mule has hopped a mile
away or maybe two and then comes the comedy of catching
him up. A hobbled mule is comparatively easy, because at top
speed a man can run faster than the mule can crow-hop, but
the mule can whirl away with surprising speed and quickness
all the same. A mule who has pulled his picket and can run
with all his legs is something else—the man approaches, coax-
ingly, after his two-mile hike; the mule, standing in a flop-
eared doze, is apparently unaware of him; the man stoops to
grab the picket rope; the mule trots away. The man runs. The
mule runs faster. The man stops and swears. The mule stops
and dozes. The man creeps forward. The mule ambles ahead
of him. The man dives at the end of the picket rope, and the
mule gives his head a negligent little toss that flips the rope
clear. The man gets up out of the snow and screams cuss words
and dances on his hat. Eventually the mule is moved to pity
by his gibbering master and allows himself to be caught.
However, the mule still does not wish to return to camp and
don his pack. He plants his forefeet, stretches out his neck, and
stays there. The man gives up hauling at him and circles behind him and jabs him in the rump. The mule obediently jumps
around in a circle and is right back where he was, and then
he ducks his head and looks back at the man and demurely

tries to kick him in the chin. The mule may decide finally to return to camp because he sees most of the other mules packed and ready to start and he does not want to be left behind. Mules beat even Schopenhauer's porcupines in plaintive yearning for companionship. Or it may take two men to bring him in, one pulling on the tug rope and the other prodding from the rear.

But mules can even overcome their fear of being left behind if they feel they really need a rest. A note from Frémont's second expedition: "Men were sent back this evening in search of a wild mule with a valuable pack, which had managed (as they frequently do) to hide itself along the road."

It is not true that mules balk from sheer contrariness. Mules always have reasons for their behavior, although it may often take some penetration to figure them out. A mule will often balk to try to get out of going to work, but if he is in the habit of working that sort of balk is only a formality, a temporary delaying action; his heart isn't really in it because he knows by experience he can't win. A genuine balk comes when the mule faces something strange. This is eminently sensible. It is even human. Human beings, in fact, when faced with new and frightening situations sometimes dodge the question by retreating from reality altogether and are declared insane, but mules seldom go that far. A mule unaccustomed to fording streams may balk when asked to wade water. A mule thoroughly used to wading or swimming streams may balk at crossing ice; in such a case a lane can be chopped in the ice of a frozen stream so the mules can cross through familiar water. That's one way. Or a genuine balk can be overcome by a twitch—a loop passed around the mule's upper lip and twisted tight when pulled, a lead any mule will follow. At the first terrifying torture of the twitch, though, the mule is likely to sit down, squealing and rolling his eyes, and his pack promptly slides half off. He then bounds up, allows the twitch to lead

him while he shivers with panic until he is past whatever he
was balking at, and then closes the act by joyfully kicking the
remainder of his pack in all directions.

In view of these things it is strange that men should feel
an affection for their mules, but they do. When the balking is
over, when the train moves out and the mules take up their
steady, dainty, quick walk or jog, they will keep it up hour
upon hour, as long as it is asked of them, or until spasms of
fatigue stop them in their tracks and they are on the point of
death. They keep it up although starved for food until their
bones are almost protruding through their ragged coats. They
keep it up over any kind of going, sliding and scrambling over
rocks, climbing precariously on hairline footing up and down
veritable cliffs, plowing through snow that balls under their
feet until they are limping along on painful little frozen stilts;
they stand for their feet to be cleaned and then doggedly
hurry on. Their backs form raw sores from frostbite, lack of
food, and saddle gear frozen as hard as iron, until they flinch
and whimper with pain at each step, but they keep going on
as hardily as ever. They stumble in snow and fall and struggle
courageously to rise, although they know they can seldom
get back on their feet until their packs are first removed. At
the end of the day they are the epitome of exhaustion; they
huddle together on trembling legs through a starving night;
and the next day they are trotting on as bravely as before.
It's a mule's terrible persistence that wins affection. He doesn't
quit.

The ex-trapper and early American settler in California,
"Don Benito" Wilson, telling in his old age of killing his "faithful mule" for meat in starving times, said, "I feel sorry about
that mule yet, the killing of which occurred some forty-two
years ago."

And too the men had the mules to thank for all the equipment of each camp they made: their provisions and axes and

shovels and cooking pots and extra powder and shot, their spare dry clothes and the "India rubber blankets" they put down on the snow upon which to make their beds, and the bedrolls themselves. The mules literally carried the men's lives in their packs from march to march and it was only natural that the people of the expedition should feel, besides the sneaking sense of admiration, a certain gratitude.

Coming down from the Sangres, the expedition evidently swung north to cut across the northern section of the sand hills rather than circle down around them to the south. Today the only road into the sand hills, now the Great Sand Dunes National Monument, runs along the southern edge of the dunes and then heads up between the dunes and the mountains toward Mosca, or Robidoux, Pass, very much on the route of the old freight-wagon road down from the pass. Even the present-day trail from Williams' old pass, which descends into the sand hills considerably nearer their northern than their southern limits, turns to the south and makes its way down to join the Mosca road. But it may have been Old Bill's customary route from his pass to angle more directly across the northern reaches of the dunes, by way of Cold Creek and Sand Creek that almost cuts the dunes in two, rather than detour around them to the south.

The long day's march into the plain after leaving the sand hills was hard on both men and animals; a few more men were set to limping with the pain of frostbitten feet. They were doubling up their beds by now and sleeping two together for warmth. Doc Kern wrote that at the sagebrush camp he slept with Dick for the first time and "woke up covered with snow," indicating that the Kern boys were not bothering to put up their tent. They had raised it once, in the sand hills, the only time since Hardscrabble, and had probably found it more trouble in the wind than it was worth, and, worse, it would rob them of any warm blanket of new-fallen snow. They would

have learned by now how to make a bed in the snow: first a
layer of bark or brush or boughs, if such were to be had, then
one of the India rubber blankets, or tarpaulins, used in the
day as covers for the packs, then a set of blankets—it is important to have as much thickness underneath as on top—then
the sleepers, with another set of blankets over them and another India rubber blanket over the whole thing. Then if snow
fell, and it usually did, the new snow added still more warmth
and insulation against the cold outer air. In such a bed Doc
slept well, although McGehee later gave the temperature during the night at the sagebrush camp—maybe he looked at a
thermometer when he was roused to chase runaway mules—
as seventeen below zero.

The sagebrush camp may have been in the vicinity, perhaps
a few miles west, of the present little San Luis Valley community of Hooper. On this day's travel they had crossed some of
the reedy marshland formed by the sinking San Luis River.
Their first camp on the Rio Grande would have been very near
the spot where the present highway known as Gunbarrel Road
crosses the river, a couple of miles north of the city of Monte
Vista. Gunbarrel Road is a north-south highway in the valley,
so called because it runs as straight as a transit could shoot it.
The San Luis Valley as a whole still has today a desert look,
splotched here and there with alkali, the immense flats stippled
with dusty chico and sage and greasewood. But subirrigation,
possible here because the valley floor is so level, has painted
in widespread streaks and salients of green that are clustered
with rich farms and ranches, their fields bright with the elegant window dressing of clover and bees and purebred cattle.
The town of Monte Vista is a shipping point for the valley's
chief money crop—potatoes. Monte Vista is near the western
edge of the valley and the San Juans rise up close at hand,
and other mountains, washing out to horizon blue in the distance, ring the entire full circle of the land.

The expedition moved on up the river the next day. The wind ebbed and died and in the stillness the air was filled with myriad floating particles of frost, "speculae of ice," in Doc Kern's definition, that coated every man and mule a spectral white, and folded all the world about them in a drifting veil. The men were filled with awe. They spoke in hushed voices and the long file of men and animals moved through the snow as noiselessly as in a dream. The light of the sun was swallowed up in this curious frozen mist. In its shroud the wraiths of cottonwoods beside the silent river and the first sudden up-thrusts of the mountains they were entering were like the landscape of a dead planet.

Dick Kern, scribbling in his journal beside the campfire that night and recalling the effect of this scene, wrote, "Everything cold and ghostly. And as we moved along we seemed entirely out of place."

They crossed to the south bank of the river, where there was better timber for camp, hauling and driving the mules over the ice, and pulling them out when they broke through into the water. Their second camp on the river was made across from a landmark they called the Big Rock.

A town is there now, named Del Norte, and just outside of town the river first tells you it is going to cañon up, because the mountains are at hand. Little tan hills, with flat sides and square corners, more huge rocks than hills, rise up like gate-posts, and the river runs between them, and the farm lands and placid irrigation canals go roundabout and keep their distance.

The Big Rock north of the river is now known locally as Indian Head. It looks like a war bonnet. Its peak is serrated, and gives the impression of a spine of giant feathers running across its crown and down its back. It stands alone in the chico bush, apart from the other hills. It is four or five hundred feet high, and can be seen from far out in the valley.

Now they had reached the mountains and the snow was steadily deepening and there was still no game. But they had seen elk sign and in the morning Godey picked out five of the best hunters to go with him after meat. The rest of the men stayed in camp until noon, to give the hunters a chance. The hunt was a good one. Godey killed two elk, brought one in and hung up the other and it was left behind, a significant measure, an emergency cache of meat waiting for them if they failed in the attempted mountain crossing and had to come back that way. The camp made a short day's journey after the hunt, recrossing the river to the north bank, moving only five miles, and the elk gave them their first genuine dinner in many days.

They pushed on up the river the next morning, eleven miles. Now the mountains closed in on either hand in high sharp buttes and steep timbered slopes that swept up to the sky, and a winding way had to be found among swelling hills and the first incipient walls of rock. Ahead, the river valley seemed to bend to the south and lose itself in tiers of white clashing peaks.

They passed, within the first couple of miles, the mouth of Embargo Creek, running down to the river from the mountains on their right hand. They went on to another creek, eight and a half miles beyond, today called Alder Creek, and here made camp.

They traveled through snow up to the mules' bellies, but this happened to be a beautiful day. The cold wind had returned, but the sun was bright and there were wisps and scarves of cirrus in a deep blue sky, and each green piñon on the snow-covered foothills cast a pool of turquoise shadow. Looking back down the cañon of the river they could see the Sangres, far away across the valley they had left, toy mountains carved of white jade, shimmering with distant color.

The next day they turned up Alder Creek and began climbing into the mountains that had been on their right.

Later, Ned Kern wrote in a letter to Antoine Robidoux, "We continued a couple of days up the Del Norte, and then turned up what Williams called your pass on to the Compadne. In this he was evidently mistaken. . . ."

11

On his second expedition, at the mountain man hangout of St. Vrain's Fort, Frémont had asked about information concerning central passes through the mountains, and wrote afterward, "I had been able to obtain no certain information in regard to the character of the passes in this portion of the Rockies. . . . It is singular that, immediately at the foot of the mountains, I could find no one sufficiently acquainted with them to guide us to the plains at their western base; but the race of trappers who formerly lived in their recesses has almost entirely disappeared—dwindled to a few scattered individuals—some one or two of whom are regularly killed in the course of each year by Indians."

This seems odd at first glance, this complaint of lack of expert information, when it is understood that Frémont had with him on that second expedition two of the most famous leaders of that race of trappers, Tom Fitzpatrick and Kit Carson. It has for so long been customary to say of such renowned mountain men that "they knew every foot of the West" that the phrase, a rhetorical liberty, has come to be taken rather literally. But the West is, of course, somewhat too large for any one man to know all of it, or even much of it, with any intimacy.

The best of the brigade leaders among the trappers developed a matchless trail sense: they photographed a country with a look and kept the picture clear for many years. Frémont writes of Kit Carson's recognizing landmarks in California he had seen only once fourteen years before. They became so learned in the ways of slopes and streams and the life of trees and flowers they bore that even in a strange country they could never be quite lost—only confused for a time, as the old back-woods expression has it. Bill Williams, leading a trapping party into an unexplored mountain range, pointed out a place where "from the run of the country" there would be water, and there was.

A man might be able to keep his direction even on a star-less night from the very trending of the earth beneath his feet, the shifting of the breeze and the smell of the woods, the feel of the leaves of any of the various "compass" plants which tend to direct their radical leaves north and south (while the flower heads of most plants are bent in the early nighttime toward the west, if there has been afternoon sun). He will find his way by "instinct," and follow a faint trail made plain to him by a thousand stimuli acting on his knowledge and experience.

Reading the "sign" that enters into such trail judgment, made up of countless variegated fragments of real evidence though it may be, must remain one part sign to ten parts judg-ment. The minute clues of sign are observed, in the words of a more modern authority on such matters, Horace Kephart, "as infallibly, and with as little conscious effort, as a woman notices the crumbs and lint on her neighbor's carpet," and are then processed through the intricate works of a judgment based on years of experience. The mountain men habitually staked their lives on this educated judgment. It had to be good. The real masters of the trade filed it to an edge of remarkable precision. One mountain man, guiding troops in chase of In-dians on the edge of the San Luis Valley, told the commander after several days of trailing that on this day, at such and such an hour, they would overtake the Indians; the commander was skeptical and bet a hat he couldn't be that accurate. The guide won the hat.

But all this applies to generalities. A skilled man could track and travel and keep his bearings and stay alive in a country known only sketchily or doubtfully or even known only by hearsay. But an exact exploration of useful passes needed something more. It needed a guide with a creek-to-creek knowledge of the country. It was to Carson's and Fitzpatrick's credit that they admitted they were not specialists enough in east-west travel through the central Colorado Rockies to pilot such a route. In that region the beaver hunters had more generally moved north and south from the Bayou Salade, and the main routes of travel to the west happened to start from north or south of those central mountains, either up north via trails bearing to South Pass or the Green River rendezvous country or down to the south at Abiquiu and the other New Mexican settlements, and so were split around much of what is now the mountain state of Colorado.

But there were specialists who knew the east-west roads through those mountains. There were native New Mexican traders who came up that way to do business with the Ute, whose home was in the mountains. And there were some French and American traders and trappers who had gone that way for years. Among these the three reputed to know the country best were Antoine Robidoux, who had not only traveled back and forth many times to his trading posts on the western slope but had regularly taken wagons through—although sometimes strewing a few along the way to pick up when he came back—and Antoine Leroux, and Old Bill Williams, who knew the country not only as its oldest trapper but also as a naturalized citizen among the people who had always lived there, the Ute.

These men were experts, consulting specialists who could

be expected to take under advisement a problem of routing, match it with the maps they unfolded in their minds, and come up with an accurate solution. When Frémont met one of these three men, Old Bill, on his third expedition, he saw Old Bill perform his specialty with admirable precision, leading the way through the mountains from the head of the Arkansas.

Probably at this same time he told Frémont of good passes that lay still farther south, as far south as the headwaters of the Rio Grande. This was the region "where the information of the mountain men," in Benton's words, led Frémont "to expect to find the best Pass."

In this area three principal passes were known to the mountain men, the Cochetopa, the Carnero, and the Pass of the Rio del Norte. The Cochetopa Pass was the best of these, the lowest in altitude, and suitable for wagons. Carnero Pass was said to be almost equally easy and was a little shorter for travelers going west from the San Luis Valley: it would carry you from the center of the valley to the westward-flowing rivers, the Grand, the Uncompahgre, the Green, the Colorado, a day quicker than the Cochetopa. The Pass of the Rio del Norte crossed the Continental Divide directly from the Rio Grande and was steeper and rougher and higher than the other two but shorter still: a day faster than Carnero Pass, two days faster than the Cochetopa. It was the hardest of the three for winter travel and would hardly come highly recommended as a railroad prospect, while the Carnero and particularly the Cochetopa would sound extremely promising for this purpose.

Cochetopa Pass ran out of the northwestern corner of the San Luis Valley, through the broken country now known as the Cochetopa Hills. It crossed the Continental Divide and fell on a creek called Cochetopa Creek, a tributary of the river now named the Gunnison, which flows west and northwest to join the Colorado. This pass was not high (at slightly more than 10,000-feet altitude it remains still one of the lowest passes of the Continental in Colorado) and was broad and level and made for easy travel, although the road on west along the Gunnison was through exceedingly rough country for many days, with frequent crossings of steep-cañoned streams that fed into the river. Captain Gunnison, whose name stuck to the river that was called by the mountain men the Grand, spoke of the route beyond the Cochetopa as being "the roughest, most hilly, and most cut up" he had ever seen. "Hills with flat tops, hills with round tops, and hills with knife edges and points, and deep chasms on every side."

The Cochetopa Pass (familiarly called the Cocheto by the ranchers around the present-day cowtown of Saguache) was well known to the Indians and the trappers, and to wild animals: its name is said to signify in a Ute tongue "Buffalo Gate." By the time of the fourth expedition Old Bill Williams had known the region of the Cocheto for at least twenty years; certainly he had had occasion to know it in winter as well as summer.

There were various approaches to the region of the Cochetopa from the floor of the San Luis Valley. From the northern end of the valley the most direct route was via a creek called the Saguache, quartering down from the mountains that cup around the valley's upper shoulder. Some twenty-five miles south down the angling wall of the western mountains another stream, Carnero Creek, furnished a well-known approach, serving as a short cut to the Cochetopa road from farther down in the valley.

There's a highway over Cochetopa Pass today, and another road today travels up Carnero Creek to cross the mountain spur separating it from the Cochetopa road, joining that road a dozen miles before the pass is reached. This is that same Carnero Creek short cut, still in use today, and still the shortest approach to Cochetopa Pass from any place in the central valley, as it was the shortest approach then.

But the mountain men also sometimes used a complete and separate pass beginning on Carnero Creek and bearing left into the mountains to avoid the Cocheto altogether, a pass route running roughly parallel with the Cochetopa trail but keeping south of it all the way across the Continental and to at least forty miles beyond. This was Carnero Pass. This pass has been utterly forgotten today.

Carnero Creek tumbles down to the plain some ten miles north of the great gap of the Rio Grande. Theoretically, still another approach to upper Carnero Creek could be made by entering the cañon of the Rio Grande for a few miles and then swinging up over the intervening arm of the mountains to join the upper Carnero Forks. Traders may have had reasons for using such an approach in mild weather, reasons of grass or gradients, of easier stream crossings or fewer obstructing rocks and timber. Oral tradition says they sometimes did. But it would seem to be a highly unlikely alternative to entering Carnero Creek directly, only one day's march away, back out of the cañon of the river and up the edge of the plain.

The Rio Grande itself appears to offer a tempting highway into the mountains and so it does, for twenty or thirty miles. Then the cañon cleaved by the river begins to writhe and turn as the mountains crowd in upon it and the river can only be followed at intervals and scrambling passage must be found among the mountains beside it, and at length the head of the river is reached in a cul-de-sac of high mountain lakes and trickling creeks that spring from the throat of the Continental.

At various places along the cañon of the river, though, the mountains bordering the river on the north can be crossed. One such crossing was known to the mountain men as the Pass of the Rio del Norte. This road, now forgotten, was located some thirty-five miles up the cañon of the river. It took off above the present town of Creede and crossed directly over the Continental Divide, which has slanted down from the northeast here to meet the river and run along the mountains of its northern wall. This pass was accurately described by Antoine Leroux to Dick Kern, who drew it from his description on the map reproduced in the end papers of this book and gave it Leroux's name. However, another explorer of the time mentioned that this Pass of the Rio del Norte was sometimes called by Americans "Williams Pass, in honor of Old Bill Williams, who discovered it."

This crossing is high, although not particularly hard to travel once the first steep pitch of ascent to the upper "flats" or plateaus has been managed. Nevertheless, it is probable such a crossing was considered by the early trappers and traders as chiefly for summer use.

It is necessary to understand that what the trappers and traders spoke of as "roads," such as the Cochetopa road and the Carnero road, were by no means fixed and sharply identifiable places. A specific area, the low saddle in the mountains that contained the region of the pass, was the only fixed point about any such trail. This low place could be reached by any of numerous approaches. In some cases, where the pass was an extensive low area strewn among hills and peaks, as is the case with the Cochetopa, rather than a single suitable cañon, the pass itself might contain various and separate trails. Much early travel over the Cocheto, for example, was via Pass Creek, but the present motor highway falls on Archuleta Creek, five miles south.

The mountain men who traveled these passes quite naturally varied their routes, sometimes seeking better trails, sometimes dodging Indian trouble, sometimes forced into new paths by flooded streams or winter snow. They would have thought of the principal roads of the Cochetopa or the Carnero as the focal points for a number of trails leading into them, branching back and forth between them, and still other trails swinging up into them from the cañon of the Rio Grande hanging parallel on the south.

The question for Old Bill was which of these trails, or which combination of them, if any, might conceivably be passable in winter, and a hard winter; which might be best for mules and men and feed and weather; which would be best worth Frémont's study as a possible railroad pass and would deviate least from his cherished line in the neighborhood of the thirty-eighth parallel.

Old Bill's problem on the fourth expedition was infinitely more difficult than the usual routine performance of his mountain-crossing specialty, such as on the third expedition, because it was winter and because Frémont, ridden by his passion to restore himself after the court-martial, was a different man.

Travel in mountain country where there are no marked trails is usually along the ridges, whenever possible, thus escaping the hard, brushy going of the creek bottoms, and on the ridges the various divides are visible and you can see your way and better avoid the chance of bearing down the wrong fork. The creek-to-creek, ridge-to-ridge knowledge of the expert tells him when to swing down from the ridge, when to cross the divide from this fork to the next to miss an impassable cliff or gorge or bog ahead, when to drop down to the creek and ford to the other side, and when to climb and follow the ridge again. Without this knowledge progress is a halting business of probing ahead, turning back, seeking blindly from ridge to ridge. But in the winter the windswept ridges are too cold and inhospitable to be traveled, and when they must be topped they are crossed immediately and shelter sought again below their upper reaches. The creek bottoms also are generally closed, being choked with deep drifts of snow. Passage must be found, for the most part, by traversing the slopes and finding paths along the sides of the cañon walls, and now the ridge-to-ridge knowledge needs to be close to perfection, for the

winter paths are often entirely different from the summer
paths, in some cases finding footing on drifted slopes that could
not be climbed at all in summer when bare of snow; and the
advantage of steering a course from the crests of divides is
gone with the winter wind.

But these were still only the minor difficulties of a winter
crossing. The really critical decisions would always relate to
the winter itself, to the weather at a given moment. A route
entirely feasible in summer, perhaps passable by different paths
in a mild winter or in a mild interval in a heavy winter, might
be absolutely closed off after the weather passed a certain
point. Factors such as the condition of animals and men, provisions, the country that lay beyond the immediate passage
in question, all had to be balanced and considered by the guide
and weighed against what he could see and predict of the
weather.

This was one half of the handicap Old Bill carried on his
bent back. The other half was Frémont's relentless determination. Frederick Dellenbaugh, experienced in the strategy and
tactics of exploration in the West, wrote, "Lines of progress
across a country are determined for any intelligent explorer
by the topography, and he heeds the great obstacles to progress, unless he has a special reason for not doing so." Frémont,
of course, had a special reason for not doing so: the whole
purpose of the expedition was to find a pass located not too
far off the straight line that had been drawn in Senator Benton's study in Washington City and to drive through that pass
against the odds of winter. And if the odds became too heavy?
Then Frémont had a special reason to continue to ignore them,
the special reason rooted in his iron state of mind: defeat, this
time, could not be tolerated; he could not allow the slightest
crack in his thoughts to admit its shadow; it was much easier
to continue to demand the impossible toward victory than to
submit to the possibility of defeat.

The Cochetopa, the Carnero, not to mention the tough Pass of the Rio del Norte—all of those passes ahead led through tremendous mountains, a land of savage storms and dizzying cliffs, locked in snow and bitter cold. Good passes were there, to be sure, and the Cochetopa was even excellent; they were passes feasible in an ordinary winter, but not in this winter. In a winter such as this the wisest and safest route west from the San Luis Valley was to travel south all the way down the valley to the vicinity of the New Mexican settlements, more than a hundred miles, and turn the southern flank of the San Juan Mountains, picking up the old Spanish Trail that ran from Abiquiu in New Mexico to Los Angeles in California. This route detoured around the main body of the high mountains ahead, rather than through them or over them.

And first Old Bill suggested taking this safe route south out of the San Luis Valley, down around the tail of the San Juans to the Spanish Trail. Tom Breckenridge, as an old man, remembering, said, "In camp there was a disagreement between Colonel Frémont and Williams. Williams was a man that said but little, but he was a long time with Frémont that night, and when he turned in (we bunked together), he said that they disagreed in regard to the route we should follow. He said the snow was deeper and the weather more severe than he had ever known it to be before. He said he had advised a route out of our difficulties, to go south around the San Juan mountains. . . ." Micajah McGehee quotes a remark held on very tenuous evidence to come from a notebook kept by Old Bill: "I wanted to go one way and Frémont will go another, and right here our troubles will commence." Wherever it comes from, the remark has an authentic ring. It will strike a familiar note to any guide who has ever guided an opinionated hunter, or to any hunter who has ever traveled with an opinionated guide.

The look of the winter, now definitely setting itself for a

record breaker; the condition of the mules; the snow in the mountains; and the mountains beyond the mountains, days upon days of the hardest kind of travel waiting after, and if, they got over the principal pass—all these things told Old Bill to swing south and dodge the worst of the winter and the worst of the mountains.

But this would also be dodging the great objective of the expedition, which was to force a passage through the mountains in the face of winter's heaviest artillery. It would be giving up the battle at the first look of the enemy's array, and before a shot had been fired. And Frémont was in no mood to be timid or even reasonably cautious.

Old Bill saw Frémont's point and accepted it, although, certainly, with the gravest kind of warnings. He had told Frémont what he should do, and quoted the odds on the mountains ahead, and Frémont had elected to venture the mountains. Well, the more fool he, do 'ee hyar, and right there their troubles would commence, but if the others had the nerve to try it Old Bill had the nerve to try to lead them. It was foolhardy to drive straight on and offer battle against this winter, but, even so, there was always a thread of a chance of winning until the last mule died. Frémont had picked a bad man to dare. Old Bill wasn't noted for a lack of boldness.

There were later stories of an open breach between Frémont and Old Bill, which had Frémont in effect dismissing the old mountain man from his position as guide and plunging ahead on an intuitive route of his own choosing. These stories were invented from hearsay distortions for contemporary political use and are of course worthy of no credence.* But they do reveal, born as they were from a germ of truth contained in reports of Old Bill's warnings, that a number of the people of the expedition were aware of Old Bill's Jeremiac misgivings

* See Notes: A Note on the Trails.

even as they marched across the valley toward their critical assault on the west-wall mountains.

From the sand hills, where the expedition entered the San Luis Valley, the Cochetopa Pass lies cater-cornered across the valley to the northwest. The gap of the Rio Grande lies fairly straight across the valley due west, with Carnero Creek slicing into the mountains just above it.

Certainly, in camp in the Sangres and in the sand hills, Frémont and Old Bill, and doubtless Godey with them, stood in the snow and discussed the valley before their eyes and the westward passes out of it and the various approaches to them in the greatest possible detail.

Saguache Creek, across at that upper corner, took you into the Cochetopa by an easy grade, but you were a long time in the unsheltered plain getting up to that corner. If you went straight across to the western wall of mountains and then north along them to Saguache Creek, you were carried out of your way, because the mountains did not run straight north and south but slanted northeast and you had to swing out in an oxbow around them to pick up the Saguache and follow it into Cochetopa Pass. That was why the traders generally struck straight into the mountains up Carnero Creek, the shortest way into the Cochetopa Pass and the entrance to Carnero Pass as well, if you wanted to follow that instead.

Or you could enter the gap of the Rio Grande and follow up the cañon of the river to the steep pass of the Rio del Norte, bypassing both the Cochetopa and the Carnero. This pass could have had an appeal for Frémont as the shortest and quickest, but it is hard to believe he heard anything in its description to make it sound worthy of an examination as a railroad pass over the magnificent Cochetopa—or the Carnero, which lay almost exactly along the desired route of the thirty-eighth parallel.

It can only be guessed how much of the course may have

been decided before the expedition started across the valley from the sand hills. They lined out fairly straight across the valley, apparently with the intention of heading for the mouth of Carnero Creek, but in the afternoon of the second day on the plains, after the dangerous and wretched night in the sage-brush camp, sudden decision appears to have been made to swing aside to follow the Rio Grande, then curving up parallel with them less than two hours away on the south, its timber visible and highly attractive to men wanting a timbered camp-ing place ("at last" they turned toward it, Doc Kern wrote), and wanting hunting and grass and protection for the mules. Once on the Rio Grande, talk may have first come up of using one of the pass approaches that mounted directly from the river; the longer they stayed in the timber along the river the safer it would be for the mules. (And the mules had now been out from Hardscrabble fifteen days, with only ten days of life expectancy left unless they found some decent pasture; and so by now every hour counted for the mules.) The route may have been decided in camp on the eastern wall of the valley, or it may have been decided by the pressure of this expediency or that as they crossed the valley and entered the mountains; the best of these trails would be monstrously hard to travel in this winter and the difference in choice between them would be only in the degree of the compromise between the winter and Frémont.

All that is definitely known is that the expedition crossed the valley and entered the gap of the Rio Grande and turned up a creek that Old Bill said was the route of Robidoux's pass. And that Old Bill, out of his vast experience, had the gravest doubts that they could push on through the pass against this enormous winter. And that the men of the expedition were aware of his doubts.

Nevertheless they followed up into the mountains, the old voyageurs and the young greenhorns, the mountain boys, the

hunters and ex-trappers, the three limber young Indian cow-
boys, the Negro servant, the scientific corps, the young tubercular Andrews, the British gentleman, Cathcart, the recent
bridegroom, King, the settled family man, Rohrer the mill-
wright, and found themselves almost immediately in a narrow
cañon rougher than anything they had yet seen. On the left
a vertical wall of layers of rock reached up to fill half the
sky, and on the right a mountainside rose in bounds of but-
tresses and ledges, feathered with clinging aspen and pine.
The floor of the cañon was piled with rocks and overgrown
with thickets of high brush half concealed in the snow. The
long file of mules plowing or springing through the drifts could
not find passageway except by crossing from side to side of
the creek to take advantage of every level stretch at the foot
of the cañon walls.

At places the stream was iced over and at places it was
open rushing water. It ran twisting among rocks and there
was seldom a comfortable ford where the mules could be given
a whack or two and cross with a couple of splashing jumps.
More often the men had to wade the numbing water and fight
the mules across. At the last crossing whole groups of the mules
had to be worked across one by one with twitches, and after
that they took to the mountainside on their right, picking a
winding way upward in uneasy footholds in the frozen snow.
This was hard, exhausting going, and here the first mule was
lost, collapsed from fatigue. More and more frequently the
tired mules slipped and fell on the slanting rock and had to
be laboriously and precariously rescued and stripped and
helped to their feet again. Camp for the night was made in
the midst of an expanse of slope so sharply angled it was hard
for the mules and men to keep their balance during the work
of unpacking. Spruce logs and brush were banked up in the
snow to make level beds. They were "at an immense height,"

Dick Kern wrote, and, still an artist, he added, "Had two very fine views down and up the cañon."

The sense of beauty that in most men responds to mountains may be in some part subtly allied to fear, or more properly to the enjoyment of being awed. The beauty of mountains is in more than the composition of their patterns of pinnacles and peaks and sweeping cliffs of tumbled color; it is in part in the simple elemental immensity of height as well. It is also present in the fact that, as a cowhand said it, they sure are quiet for their size. This is the spirit of majesty and that too is beautiful. The feeling of immense and plunging height wrapped in silence is the ecstasy of mountains, and so the most stirring of the magnificences of any mountain view.

The next day it was snowing. The party continued to climb. The worn-out mules found it very hard to make the grade, struggling upward through the snow, gathering their legs under them to scramble across jutting rock, having to stop to be breathed or to wait for trail to be broken above through the drifts: they worked their way at a rate of 200 yards an hour. At noon they stopped to rest and in the afternoon the going leveled off. They had reached the high flats that make up the shoulders of the mountains and they camped that night in a mountain meadow, a park, a vast scooped-out clearing surrounded by ranks of blue green spruce, each tree hung with a mantle of new snow.

These high mountain parks are among nature's more winged works. They may be several miles across, deep with grass in summer, spired around by the topmost upthrusts of the mountains, the veritable peaks, trailing plumes of clouds. They are great amphitheaters made apparently only for deer and elk to graze in. There seems to be some mystery as to their creation: the high mountain forests march up to their borders and stop, although there appears to be no good reason why they should stop. An open area left by a burn is covered with new growth within a very few years, but the parks stay unchanged through the centuries. (Since one guess is as good as another, one guess might be that ancient beaver ponds maintained undisturbed for many generations had something to do with their formation; and another guess might be that some kindly Indian god set them there to show his people what the happy hunting grounds were really supposed to look like.) The expedition made a good camp here. There were big fires to warm the mules and dry out wet and frozen leggings and thaw frostbitten feet and hands, and small twinkling cooking fires to make the supper of macaroni and bacon and perhaps a few treasured scraps of elk meat still hoarded from the elk camp down on the river.

They were up the next morning long before daylight, gathering the mules and packing to move on—the job took hours. The little corn remaining was being rationed even more carefully now and the mules were slipping across the border from constant hunger to starvation, and the poisons set up by fatigue and unrestored tissue in their dying bodies would put in motion the same circle of endogenous toxicity that starving human beings would experience, with the habit of moral decision swept away (mules too conduct their behavior upon fixed morality patterns) and accompanied, perhaps, by mulish hallucinations. Eyesight would be failing, training and obedience forgotten. They moved on at last and in the afternoon of this day they emerged above timberline to look about from what was almost the top of a world of snowy mountains, with the great white bowl of the San Luis Valley floating off to the east. They were now at very near 12,000 feet. They were standing in the shadow of a summit that is called today Pool Table Mountain.

The mountaintops of the Garitas are, in part, as smooth as the prairies of Kansas. They swell in giant rounded knolls that are blanketed with sheep fescue in summer, giving them a neat barbered look, but with here and there an unexpected precipice dropping five hundred or a thousand feet and here and there giant rockslides in almost vertical slopes. The extreme headwaters of the various creeks form in rincons here, cornices set against soaring walls, with only the uttermost peaks of the mountains above them.

The expedition moved around Pool Table Mountain and slid several hundred feet down its precipitous backside to make camp in an embryonic cañon, where fingers of spruce reached up from the forests held at bay below these naked mountain-tops.

The last of the men and mules made their way into this camp long after dark.

The next ridge beyond was the head of this high draw in which they were camped. It was no more than three miles away, up a long curving open slope broken only by scattered knots of spruce and gnarled wind timber, most of this then buried in massive drifts of snow. This ridge represented the top of the wall of mountains bordering the Rio Grande—but not the Continental Divide. Across this ridge creeks could be picked up that could be followed, theoretically at least, to Carnero Pass over the Continental—some twenty miles more of mountain travel—or, theoretically, all the way to Cochetopa Pass—some thirty miles more of mountain travel. They were still only on the first step to either of these passes. The people of the expedition did not realize this, but they did not need to realize this to feel that they had missed their way.

For the suspicion was growing by now, at least among some of them, that Old Bill was lost. The most experienced had felt it almost as soon as they had turned up from the river. They had to hunt their way, Frémont wrote to Jessie, when they entered the mountain cañons. And Ned Kern wrote of Old Bill's road: ". . . he was evidently mistaken, for a worse road I never saw."

Some hint of this suspicion among the more experienced would have seeped through to even the least experienced. Nevertheless they kept on. To take fright at this suspicion and turn back would be defeat, immediately, since the mules would certainly never last to go back to the river and try any other route. Frémont, in spite of the suspicion, seems never to have thought of turning back. And if this suspicion, added to the menace of the winter and the mountains, gave birth to any spirit of hopelessness among the tired men, this is not evident.

On the first day of the attack on the mountains, forcing a way up the narrow cañon and climbing on its wall, they made seven or eight miles. On the second day, going up and over the shoulders of the mountains through new-falling snow, perhaps seven. On the third day, to the camp in the high head of the draw beyond Pool Table Mountain, perhaps five. And now, moving up the long open slope to the mountaintop ridge ahead, the men worked constantly in relays with mauls and broke way for the mules through snow that curled in streaming crests high over their heads, and now the days were no longer counted by so many miles but by stages that are an hour's walk apart, or a twenty-minute walk, or a ten-minute walk, on a fine summer day; or by stages that earned no progress at all, as when an entire day was spent fighting the wind and snow of the storms that scoured these exposed peaks with no distance gained from the resting place of the night before.

No greater tribute was ever paid Frémont's peculiarly romantic hold on the imaginations of men who followed him. He was moody, erratic, obsessed, desperate to dare the devil, and the people of the expedition recognized all this (by observation and on the authority of Old Bill Williams) and answered it with a sustained effort of blind courage and what can only be called gallantry.

But it was not all Frémont's spell upon them, of course. Each man warmed his hands at the spark of his own spirit before he went forward to grapple with the winter here in the storming, drumming heart of the winter's stronghold. This was, in a sense, what each one had come for, what he had been born for, what his age had bred and created him for. This was consummation, culmination, and fulfillment, and if it was futile, if his age was culminating in nothing but a gesture, then the grandeur of the mere gesture itself would be made to express his meaning.

12

Mortality in exploration in the romantic age ran high.

In 1848, the year of the fourth expedition, Friedrich Wilhelm Ludwig Leichhardt, a German scientist and the foremost explorer of Australia, began a daring journey from east to west across the Australian continent. He disappeared in the Never Never Land of the interior with his entire party, and their fate is still unknown.

In 1848, the last members of Sir John Franklin's great arctic expedition fell down and died as they staggered across the northern ice fields. Sir John Franklin was one of the most celebrated arctic explorers of his time and this, his third expedition, fitted out with two ships and stores expected to last for three years (wrongly expected: some of the suppliers furnished food that rotted), was the most grandiose attempt yet made to hunt down the Northwest Passage, object of a search for 400 years and with a price on its head for 70 years of £20,-000 offered by the British Admiralty.

Thirty-eight relief expeditions from various countries went into the arctic during the next ten years (Ned Beale was once approached about heading one of them) before the remains and records of the Franklin expedition were found. The records proved that the expedition had indeed discovered the complete route of the Northwest Passage, even though none of them had lived to sail all the way through it, and a statue to Sir John was duly erected back home giving him the credit.

The romantic age was unique in accepting seriously the belief that mankind and his works were susceptible of perfection, thus freeing the period from the limiting skepticism of other ages. This belief had been a plaything for the encyclopedists of the preceding century; the romantic Utopians earnestly made of it an axis on which to spin the world as Will and Idea. Divinity came down from the sky to reside in the frontal lobes. This introspective demigod engrossed in exploring the perfectible within showed a remarkable loss of compassion for the temporal without, and Malthus and Ricardo were eagerly reworked by whole shoals of thinkers to prove many times over that distant perfection was to be approached by keeping present wages at a minimum subsistence level.

Force, that is, the essential concept of energy, was stripped of its mystery and presented as a tool, bedazzling in its might and splendor. In 1847 Hermann Ludwig Ferdinand von Helmholtz, a young man of twenty-six who had been born a hydrocephalic and became, after an operation, one of the half-dozen most brilliant prodigies in all the history of science, published news of the tremendous revelation that force could be neither created nor annihilated; and another young man, Herbert Spencer, immediately set to work to apply this thought to philosophy, concluding within fifteen years a system containing a principle called Force, which formed and guided all organization and change in the entire universe.

It was not a total coincidence that in 1848 two other young men, Karl Marx and Friedrich Engels, published the *Communist Manifesto*, without, incidentally, splashing up even a ripple of excitement. The doctrine of perfectibility having been accepted, the imagination had license to range where it would regarding means and resources and transient objectives. The Second Republic of France, born among the bloody barricades of the 1848 revolution, was attractive to its more radical members, even in the brightest hour of their brief triumph, only as a vestibule to a still brighter and more perfect future.

The age in its attitudes threatened to withdraw from the present into the future, an inner-world future where anything was possible, because the Will was limitless. To bite off more than they could chew was the common practice of ambitious men moved by this faith. To die in the name of this future was recognized with simple earnestness and without any em barrassment or prudish cynicism as the highest form of life, just as to probe tormentingly deep into the inarticulate quick of this inner world was acclaimed as the highest form of art. Due to the coincidental culmination of a series of great conflicts, between science and religion, industry and the individual and the social being, the age was awakened to an extraordinary awareness of its transitional nature, one facet of which emerged in the sense of historical importance previously remarked upon. The romantic age quite openly marched under the banner with the strange device, and elevated to the highest point the ideal of striving up the face of tomorrow.

From all this came the hero. In 1840 Thomas Carlyle delivered his lectures on "Heroes, Hero-Worship, and the Heroic in History," exhibiting the power and the glory of the ideal of heroic attainment. In our present time Thomas Huxley's grandson has said ironically, "My dear young friend, civilization has absolutely no need of nobility or heroism. These things are symptoms of political inefficiency." But "these things" were the chief distillations of the romantic age. The hero, being universally announced, did in fact come resoundingly to life.

Each day, as the fourth expedition mounted higher in the mountains, the snow deepened. It was three to four feet deep in the cañon of Alder Creek when they turned up from the river. The next day, climbing over the cañon wall, they encountered fifteen-foot drifts, and the following day, passing

Pool Table Mountain, it was necessary to break a road much of the way for the mules, the average depth of the snow being a foot or two above the backs of the mules, so that when an animal would flounder off the beaten trail he would bury himself in snow until only his frantic nose would appear. From beyond Pool Table the men moved on up foot by foot, through gigantic waves and billows of snow. They cut mauls from spruce limbs and used these as well as shovels to beat down a trail. The cold and the high altitude took the breath from the mouths of the laboring men, and they bled at the nose. The mules, when they were driven on up this trail, found the snow still so deep that it took all their strength to struggle through it. Seven of the mules, including Godey's favorite saddle mule (named Dick), gave out this day and fell in their tracks. By the time of the setting of the winter sun they had traveled most of the three miles to the backbone of the dividing ridge ahead. Not far below this ridge there was an island of thin woods, a few straggling, stunted trees that could furnish wood for fires, and here they made a camp.

Until now the weather had remained mostly clear and cold, with occasional flurrying snowstorms. But now, even so, the mountains were no longer silent: during the night they could hear, above the crying of the mules, the terrifying roar of snowslides. Up here, above the cover of timber, was the land of thundering avalanches. And during the night a storm struck.

Ned Kern later wrote his sister, Mary, back in Philadelphia, "You can have no conception of the way it storms here." The mountaintops reach up to meet storms face to face. In summer, in thunderstorms, it is as though the heavens wrap around them and explode. Screaming winds reach fantastic velocities, driving seemingly solid sheets of rain and hail. The lightning appears to strike from only arm's length, like a triphammer fist, usually in blows of three at a time in rapid-fire bursts, and the thunder echoes and re-echoes from the cañons below in a

deafening and incessant cannonade. The electricity in the air
may be felt upon the skin, a ghostly substance from which the
nerve ends recoil. In winter life can not long exist on the
summits in such a storm.

But in the morning they moved out from their camp in the
snow and tried to continue breaking a road ahead into the
teeth of the storm, an astonishing effort. There is something
hypnotic in the spectacle, something at the same time noble
and horrible, since in at least some part they were now acting
in blind automatism. The machine of the expedition was still
in motion, the piston still driving, the rods oiled and shining
no longer but nevertheless still inexorably at work. There is
a curious term used to describe a boxer who is beaten into
blind insensibility but somehow has not lost his equilibrium
and fallen and keeps moving around the ring, mindlessly,
wearily, continuing the practiced gestures of dodging and
weaving, blocking and jabbing: it is said he is staying on nothing but heart. And the wise insiders say it is condition, all
conditioning. Possibly the two together are the answer, and
it is conditioning of the heart.

They reached the top of the ridge, an altitude of a trifle under 12,300 feet; it took them something more than three
hours. The distance was perhaps 500 yards from their camp
if they moved direct to the summit, perhaps a mile if they
angled in a traverse. The snow was swept away from a narrow
space along the top of this ridge and the men could stand on
nearly bare rock, and having reached this, where there was no
snow to assault, and the wind hurled its full power upon them
and they were completely swallowed up in clouds of whirling
snow, the machine faltered. The men sank down on the rocks
to rest and were within a few minutes on the point of freezing
to death without realizing it. Those still on their feet, aware of
the danger, knowing this was cold that could not be borne,
forced their companions to their feet and led and drove them

back to the camp they had left below the ridge; some of them could suddenly not move without help and others had as suddenly gone temporarily blind. Old Bill rode his mule up on the ridge and tried to follow the ridge a little distance, undoubtedly to try to see the way ahead, but no one could see the way ahead through this gale of driving snow, this "pouderie," as Frémont called it. The cold clamped its grip on Old Bill and he fell over the saddle horn unconscious. Someone got his mule back down to the camp below the ridge and the old man was pulled from the saddle and brought back to life.

The next day the storm had lulled, for a time. The wind was still singing across the ridge but the sky was clear. The temperature was twenty below zero. They broke way for the mules once more and crossed the ridge, no traversing, no winding, the shortest way up and over. On the other side they could see a little creek that began in two forks and dropped down to timberline and curved away to the northward down cañons furred with snowy spruce. They made camp in a grove of spruce between the two forks, the first timber they came to, a mile beyond the spine of the ridge. They brought the mules over, and now a mule's shivering legs gave way every few yards and he fell and it was necessary to unpack him, with numb and bleeding fingers, and help him up again. The mules moved over a trail ditched through ten feet or more of snow. By now they were skeletal creatures made of heaving flanks and yellow teeth, with mucus frozen at their eyes and nostrils and frozen scabs of sores hanging from their coats, but they would have moved on still with quick and dainty quivering steps past the work parties of hollow-eyed men resting against the banks of the trail.

The mules were now closing the twenty-second day of the twenty-five days of life allotted to them after Hardscrabble. A few had already died. A few more, weak from starvation, froze that night. During those twenty-two days the men had

had game three times; the rest of the time they had lived on jerky and staple rations. There had been a few cases of frostbite, and accumulated weariness was a constant companion, but there had been no serious illness. There had not been time for it. There had been time for nothing during all those days except the sustained occupation of moving on. It had filled each day, from rising in the dark to the evening meal briefly devoured, again in the dark, while hands trembled and heads nodded, and then those not on mule guard fell asleep at once, or as soon as they could burrow under blankets and get warm enough. They slept in their clothes. At such a time even the trivial business of washing face and hands became a luxury not to be attained for days in succession. The important matters, in their order of importance, were protecting the mules, moving on, keeping warm, food, and, at the bottom of the list, rest.

At the new camp across the ridge the mules were unpacked at last and then moved on to a knoll beyond, where the snow had drifted away to expose the tops of a few clumps of browse.

The next morning the men turned out as usual, picked up mauls and shovels, and began working a trail onward, down the little valley of the creek. It had snowed heavily during the night, and while the men worked at the new trail another storm struck, worse than the one two days before, and they retreated to their camp, where the storm enveloped them for the rest of the day. Someone made his way to a dead mule and butchered it up, and mule meat was eaten that evening for supper, for the first time.

The storm continued that night and the next day and the next. In the camp, each mess of five or six or seven men lived around its fire. Some messes dug fire pits in the snow and engineered drainage so surrounding snow, melted by the fire, would not flood the floors of the pits. Other messes let the fire melt down through the snow and the snow water run where it would, occasionally dragging their beds out of the worst of it. Some trees were chopped down and burned where they fell. Each mess slept together, putting down one of the 14-by-16-foot rubber pack covers, spreading their blankets over that, and another tarpaulin on top. The walls of snow around each fire were too high to see over. The men crouched at the bottoms of the pits and the smoke from the fires blackened their faces and irritated and inflamed their eyes. When the inflammation became acute enough a painful blindness resulted.

They waited, quite helpless, while the time passed and each man in his own way prepared himself for defeat. Doc Kern's crisis came early. He gave himself up to "horror desolation despair" while Dick Kern calmly made new moccasins. Others assigned themselves the job of butchering the dead mules. First the mules that had frozen had to be found and dug out of the snow, a considerable task in the storm. The work of butchering itself was a barehanded affair, exquisitely painful in this cold. Mittens were in the way. But if skin touched the metal of a knife or ax the skin came off, and if the blood of the animal still ran it soaked clothes and hands and immediately froze.

In the face of their own difficulties the hearts of the men could still be moved by the plight of their mules. Young Micajah McGehee wrote, "Poor mules, pitiable!"

At night the crying of the starving mules could be heard above the crash of snowslides, at every lull in the roaring of the storm. The mules ate bits of halter rope, blankets if they could get them, pads off the pack saddles. They ate each other's manes and tails entirely bare, even into the flesh. They would somehow make their way to the fire holes and try to eat the blankets off the sleeping men, or even their clothing. They did eat, among other items, Ned Kern's "woolen comfortable." On the bare knoll where most of them died they could move about, and in the worst of the storm, when panic of death would overtake them, they would charge madly off the knoll in bunches, dive deep in the snow, and as frantically struggle back again, leaving one here or there to sink in the snow, Tom Martin said, and the snow would drive smooth over him without so much as a mound, but if you found the place soon enough there was a little hole in the snow that "showed their resting place, perhaps fifty feet below." (But perhaps Thomas Salathiel is at it again, and tacking on a few feet. The accounts written on the spot mention a great deal of snow but the snow deepens thereafter in fairly direct ratio to the time elapsed since; so Tom Martin remembers, thirty years later, an estimated 150 feet of snow in the deepest drifts in the cañons.)

For the most part the mules died where they stood, faced away from the storm, heads gradually sinking lower. Death was a simple matter of a spasm shaking the leg muscles, a contraction of the barrel as if the mule humped himself for one last kick, and then the body surrendered, swayed, and fell on its side.

On the second day of the storm the men climbed out of their fire holes and made another attempt to drive a trail onward, and again were driven back. This was the twenty-fifth day out from Hardscrabble, and on the evening of this day Dick Kern counted the mules still alive: there were fifty-nine, or somewhat less than half of the original mulada.

The next day the men tried once more to make a trail to a better campsite, and once more were thrown back.

And with this the long unequal battle came to an end. That evening, while the storm cleared away, leaving a rushing tide of wind and a tremendous cold, Frémont decided to turn back. The expedition was defeated.

The incipient creek, beyond the ridge on which they camped through these five days of storm and these repeated stubborn futile efforts to move on, is called Wannamaker Creek today and is the southernmost headwater of Saguache Creek. Some thirty years afterward, Albert Pfeiffer, the son of Colonel Albert H. Pfeiffer, frontiersman and long-time friend of Kit Carson, was trailing a wounded deer through this high country and came on the Wannamaker Creek camp of the expedition. There were numerous stumps chopped off high (the lowest four to five feet above the ground), indicating a considerable depth of snow, and the charred sites of the campfires of the various messes. Their camp for two nights, back over the ridge, from which they assaulted and at last crossed the ridge, has recently been located in a thin patch of timber, which at some time since has burned, probably in a lightning fire, and the dead trees lie scattered in ghostly sticks over the bare slope. Among them, though, a few similar high-chopped stumps, seared by the burn, may be found, the ax marks still visible. Below this point the expedition's route into the mountains from the Rio Grande can only be deduced from the circumstantial evidence of agreement with description, direction, and distance.

Doubtless it entered at Alder Creek, just across the Rio Grande from the present village of South Fork, climbed up to Pool Table Mountain, and on around this summit to the next ridge beyond, which was the dividing ridge, and across this ridge to the head of Wannamaker Creek. The exact route took some cliff-hanging detours to miss the deepest snow that would be hard and dangerous to follow in the summer, but the general route of the ascent is pleasant and easy in the fine-weather season. Columbine of shades from pink to royal purple blooms in clusters among the milk-white trunks of quaking aspen. The bark of the "quakeys" is blazed here and there at head height where elk have shredded the velvet from their antlers. There are endless cool forests of pine and spruce and fir. Rabbits and chipmunks—the speedball little one that carries his tail like a radio aerial, and the clumsier big one known by the rhythmic name of picket-pin gopher—clown around the tent like characters out of a Disney film. Along the stream a water ousel may be heard, but unless you hold a card in the

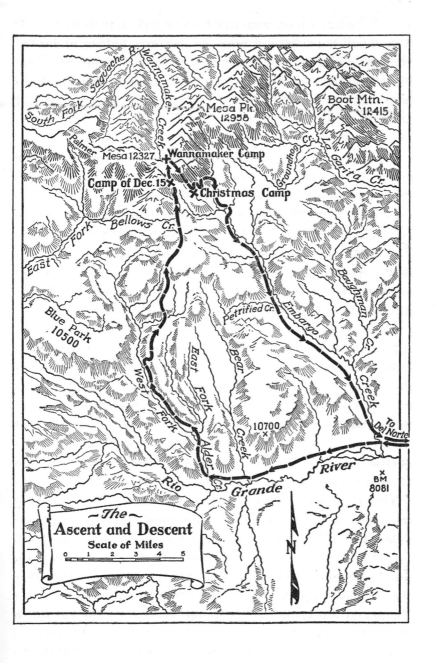

The
Ascent and Descent
Scale of Miles

Ornithological Union you won't be expert enough to find its nest, a delicate sphere of moss, so they say, hidden under the spray behind a cascade. The edges of the high sunlit parks are filled with the song and dash of birds, among them the dusty blue camp robber that tumbles contentedly about your feet and will steal the bacon out of the frying pan. Deer graze in the parks in the misty early morning, or they may disappear and a mountain lion, head up and searching, trot across the arena. Above timberline the mountains and valleys and desert of a considerable slice of the Southwest are mapped before your eyes, and the surroundings near at hand are on such a huge scale that a hundred-foot cliff looks like a garden wall. Tiny arctic flowers bloom against a summer snowbank, and on the rockslides mantling the swelling peaks a cony leaps up every ten feet or so to whistle like a traffic cop. Dots in the distance are a band of feeding elk; if you're on horseback you can ride up to them.

Pleasant though it may be in summer, nothing about this high route appears to recommend it as an approach to any of the passes. Nevertheless there may conceivably have been a way up Alder Creek and across to Carnero Pass that was sometimes used by early traders. It is a trifle more conceivable that there may have been an occasional approach up one of the nearby creeks to the east, passed when traveling up the Rio Grande before Alder is reached.

That there was a customary or at least occasional crossing someplace in this immediate vicinity must remain a possibility unless Old Bill was entirely and unaccountably off his bearings. Ned Kern wrote that Old Bill said they were entering a usual pass, and Thomas Salathiel Martin said years later that they followed up the Rio Grande "until we reached a point where Old Bill Williams said he had crossed for the last thirty years." Thomas Salathiel, incidentally, is indulging his propensity for slight exaggeration again here, for even Old Bill hadn't been in the Rockies quite that long. Unquestionably Old Bill thought he knew where he was going. Frémont wrote, ". . . having still great confidence in this man's knowledge, we pressed onwards with fatal resolution. . . ." An error in memory leading him up the wrong one of several neighboring creeks may be credited easily enough, but it is not easy to understand how he could have been wholly outside the neighborhood of a known approach to one of the passes.

But the evidence shows that the people of the expedition thought the ridge they reached and crossed was the Continental Divide, that they thought they were passing directly from the Rio Grande to the watershed of the Colorado. Doc and Ned Kern and Frémont himself expressed this belief clearly (clearly still believing it as they wrote) in letters and journal entries written at the time or a few weeks afterward. This could only mean they thought they were taking the Pass of the Rio del Norte, Williams Pass, the hard high pass farther up the river that ascended from the Rio Grande to cross the Continental immediately. That Frémont had decided to try this pass, perhaps swayed by the thought that it was the shortest and most direct and would keep them for the longest possible time in the shelter of the river, would point up the vehemency of Old Bill's obections and warnings—any of the three passes would be bad enough in such a winter, but this one would be the worst. But nothing would help to explain why, when they started for this pass, Old Bill missed it by some twenty-five miles.

Unmistakable landmarks, such as the narrows of the river cañon known today as Wagon Wheel Gap, lie between the creek they turned up and the pass they were evidently seeking. How could Old Bill have gone that far wrong?

But the strongest probability must remain that they were indeed aiming for the Pass of the Rio del Norte, and that he was that far wrong.

It goes against all our traditions to admit it, it almost seems unpatriotic, but the mountains were after all bigger than any of the mountain men who tilted with them; the locution has been used that these men tamed the mountains, but it is not so, they are not tame yet today, any more than the Alps of Europe that have casually shaken their avalanches on generations of civilization, and never will be until they are at last melted away by the waters into dying hills. The most cautious and dependable of the mountain men could go wrong in them: Antoine Leroux, guiding another exploring expedition, lost his course in this same country under conditions far easier than those facing Old Bill with Frémont, in the summertime under no pressure from lack of feed and a desperate commander. (The leader of that expedition wrote, "For the second time our guide returned to camp last night ill at ease, and it was evident that his two morning's examination of the route ahead . . . had quite surprised his memory.")

Perhaps to Old Bill the South Fork of the Rio Grande, bending away through the glimmering snow-covered mountains, became the sharp southerly bend of the river at the place of the Pass of the Rio del Norte. Perhaps after the events of the last few months, the shattering betrayal of his Utes that would have left an uglier scar than the one in his shattered arm, and the monumental drunk to end all monumental drunks, to be followed by the monumental hardships of this winter journey (that could vividly recall so many hardships of so many past years), perhaps now a time had come when his memory and his eyes were playing tricks, when in the flying snow the mountains subtly changed and he believed he saw what he only remembered.

But the creek when they entered it was not the same, and the mountains when they climbed high in them were not the same, and the old man's mountaineer instinct to get up on the ridge and fix his position when off the known trail made him ride his mule along the backbone of the mountain in the driving storm, where a man could not live thirty minutes, Ned Kern said, and where Old Bill pushed the time limit to its edge, staying there and trying to see until he lost consciousness from the cold.

However, it cannot be assumed that the expedition was defeated because Old Bill missed the pass. The error of choosing Alder Creek instead of the true route into the Pass of the Rio del Norte is not really of great significance in the final decision. The conclusion is inescapable that regardless of which route might have been taken up from the river, or westward into the mountains from the San Luis Valley, the expedition could not have gotten through in this region against the winter of that year. No doubt the error in the route contributed to stopping the expedition a little short of a point that might have been reached by different trails, but on any other westward road, the Pass of the Del Norte or Carnero or Cochetopa Pass via whatever approach, the winter would as certainly have brought it to a halt sooner or later. The expedition, with its little remaining supply of corn, and facing many days of hard mountain travel after getting through any of those passes, could not have survived.

The extraordinary ferocity of the winter described in the various accounts left by the people of the expedition is the single point on which they all agree. "Even along the river bottoms," Frémont wrote, "the snow was already breast deep for the mules, and falling frequently in the valleys and almost constantly on the mountains. The cold was extraordinary. At the warmest hours of the day . . . the thermometer . . . stood, in the shade of a tree trunk, at *zero;* and that was a favorable day, the sun shining and a moderate breeze. Judge of the nights and the storms!" Of the mountains Frémont said: "Along these naked heights it storms all winter, and the raging winds sweep across them with remorseless fury." In the storms of such a winter there could be no traffic over the mountains. Life came to a standstill. Indians stayed close in winter quarters, living on food made during the summer, and if that ran out dying from one of the frequent famines that haunted their way of life. In the storms of such a winter even today, with highways and railroads running the passes and powerful snow-clearing equipment available to use on them, there is no traffic over the mountains. (Cochetopa Pass, low as it is, is not usually kept open in the winters for highway travel.) Communities may be isolated by week-long storms, trucks and cars brought to a standstill and held imprisoned day after day, buried in snow, and trains stopped in their tracks while rotary snowplows labor upward day and night, yard by yard, and dynamite is used to break a way into the drifts.

It happened that in October, 1848, Secretary of War W. L. Marcy handed dispatches to Edward Fitzgerald Beale, the ex-commander of boats, then in Washington, to be carried post-haste to Santa Fe and California. Doubtless these included the emergency orders to the military in California designed to offset the effect of Benton's fiery letter to the people of California that Frémont was bearing with him; Secretary of State Buchanan's letter opposing it was sent by another courier, a Post Office agent going to California. Ned Beale started across country with an escort of seventeen mounted men, "all raw recruits and a few adventurers." Very sensibly, he avoided the central Rockies altogether. He went to Santa Fe over the much traveled Raton Pass, very low (under 8000 feet) and usually thought of as easy going, and went on west by the southern route of the Gila Trail, considered the safest of winter routes, far removed from the sort of winter the fourth expedition was fighting in the mountains more than 300 miles to the north. Ned Beale's journey gives a view of the winter of that year seen from the relatively mild edges of its periphery.

On December 3, the day the fourth expedition emerged from

the Sangres and camped in the sand hills, Ned Beale was in camp at Big Timbers, among the "thousands of Indians" wintering there. A snowstorm was raging on the plains. Not long before, in Chester, Pennsylvania, Ned had met a girl named Mary Edwards. In time to come he married her. At the moment he was writing a letter to her young brother Harry, which, naturally, Mary would read too.

He wrote: "The weather here is most cruelly, bitterly cold, it is snowing and freezing. You may form some idea of the severity of it when I tell you that a trader who passed some sixty miles to the southward of me lost in one snowstorm *ninety* mules frozen to death in a single night. I counted in one day myself, seventy-two animals dead and dying, belonging to a large company returning to the United States. In this weather we have sometimes at night after travelling all day to cross the river filled with floating masses of drift-ice to get wood, and bring it over again to camp and this where the river is from three to five or six hundred yards in width. I mean no disparagement of your manhood, Harry, but I do not really think you could stand what I am doing, nor could I endure it but that I am constantly buoyed up by the hope of returning to you all once more."

Having thus obliquely cast a tragic eye at Mary, Ned continued:

"I get from the traders here most discouraging accounts of the Raton Mountains, which I am just now about to cross. It is said they are impassable but I have passed *impassable* places before. They tell me also to tie my hair on before starting, as every party ahead of me has been attacked and defeated by the Apaches. . . .

". . . I write in great haste and a snowstorm is no place for letter writing. . . .

"Ned"

If this letter consigned Mary to agonies of worry as well as admiration, such are the ways of the Life Force in scheming for recognition. That Ned was not drawing on imaginary ammunition is indicated in the further record of the trip. Many of the mules were frozen and a number of men disabled by frostbite in crossing Raton Pass. At Santa Fe seven men dropped out and eight new men were enlisted. In the Mimbres Mountains in southern New Mexico they ran into heavy snowstorms and a number of mules were "frozen to death at night even under tents and covered with blankets." A sergeant and six privates deserted and, Ned thought, may have perished on their way back to the settlements.

In view of these experiences it would seem that even if Frémont had taken Old Bill's original advice to travel south and skirt the tall mountains the fourth expedition might still have had a rough passage, although to be sure it was not made up of all raw recruits and a few adventurers.

Any day after entering Robidoux Pass through the Sangres could have provided the moment of catastrophe. A sudden blizzard, the mule guard momentarily relaxed, and their animals the next morning might have been frozen carcasses scattered in the snow. Any day could have provided the equally fatal catastrophe of the death of spirit. Since crossing the Sangres, when the corn ration for the mules was grimly cut to its minimum and the stock of flour for the men approached exhaustion, discouragement had piled upon discouragement, in the storms of the seemingly endless sand hills, in the sagebrush camp, in the snows and ominous enveloping mists of the river, in the rock walls and gigantic drifts of the false pass. They had thought there would be an "abundance of game . . . as well as plenty of grass for the stock," as Tom Breckenridge remembered it, in the valleys and the river bottoms—there was only snow and below-zero gales. Breckenridge said, "We were continually looking for something better, and the conditions were growing daily worse." But the mules were kept alive until the last of the corn was gone and the spirit remained stubbornly and rather unreasonably alive (long after the conditions might reasonably have pronounced it dead) until at last, in the days of storm on the mountaintops, each successive attack on the ten-foot snows ahead was repulsed and any further progress was physically impossible and, after the mules were gone, useless.

The impressive point is not that the expedition was eventually stopped when it tried to go ahead and make a fight of it against the center of this winter, but that it got as far as it did.

When defeat arrived, during the five days of storm in the Wannamaker Creek camp, Frémont made plans to recross the ridge and work back down toward the Rio Grande, and while the men were moving the baggage along this march he would send a detachment to Taos for more animals and further provisions.

There were then on hand as provisions, Tom Breckenridge calculated in his memory, "probably fifty pounds of sugar and about as much coffee, and a small quantity of macaroni and candles. . . . Our staff of life consisted of frozen mule meat." Frémont wrote that the provisions consisted of a "store which I had reserved for a hard day, macaroni and bacon." He estimated that "with economy, and after we should leave the mules, we had not two weeks' provisions in the camp."

The day after the storm ended men made a trail back across the ridge, or a trench through the snow, as Frémont called it. They did not go back across it the way they had originally come over but trended eastward, to aim a descent through the mountains that would bring them out on the river nearer the open country of the San Luis Valley. A place for a new camp was found at the edge of timberline on the other side of the ridge, at the head of Embargo Creek, two miles from the Wannamaker Creek camp.

The new camp was spoken of as Camp Hope. The Wanna-maker Creek camp was by now named Camp Desolation.

Four days were spent moving the baggage and the few mules still alive—there may have been a half dozen or so, and Tom Martin said most of these died on the way back over the ridge—to the new camp. These gaunt survivors were not taken along as pack animals but as meat on the hoof, to be killed and butchered from day to day.

The trenched trail was wide at the top, narrowing down to no more than a foot or two in width at the bottom. Through this the men moved one by one, dragging or packing baggage to the opening on the summit of the ridge, where the snow was swept fairly clean by the wind for a space of several yards. The baggage was then pushed sliding down the opposite trail to the new camp. Spruce logs were squared off and carpentered into a sled, but it was cumbersome and the snow was not right for it, so it was of little use.

Other than the men and the last of the mules there was no sign of life on the mountains. Except for the occasional cracking of a tree down at the edge of the timber or the occasional rumble of a distant snowslide (like the boom of heavy artillery, Tom Breckenridge thought) there was absolute silence.

The way between the two camps became littered with dead mules and remnants of abandoned baggage, as the men worked back and forth in trip after trip. Each man carried sixty or seventy pounds on his back, as much of a load as could be managed at that altitude.

Captain Cathcart, during this work, found enough breath to make some observation on the adventure his hunting trip had brought him. Whatever it was he said it amused young McGehee, who processed it through his Mississippi ears and later quoted his words as, "Who'd a thought it? A captain in the 11th Prince Albert's Huzzars eating mule meat and packing his baggage amongst the snow of the Rocky Mountains?" Possibly the remark lost something in translation.

On the third day of moving, the Kerns settled their mess (Alexis Godey, presiding chef), in the new camp, among frosted spruce trees in six or seven feet of snow. A new fire hole was dug out, kitchen equipment set up, books and papers and personal belongings and bird-skin collections and drawings and medical supplies and instruments stowed away, and beds put down. No one among them (hunkered at the smoky fire, strips of blanket wrapped around feet and legs and strips of blanket hooded over black and bearded faces and tied under the chin) seems to have made much of it, but that night was Christmas Eve.

The weather was fine on Christmas Day. This was the time to bring out hoarded treasures, a little elk meat saved from the elk camp on the river, a serving of rice from the colonel's emergency store, and even, here and there, the makings of a hot toddy; and there were mule-meat pies for all.

Frémont, thinking of a future career after the court-martial, had somewhat unenthusiastically decided to read law when he got to California and had lugged along a set of books, which had been undoubtedly damned over all the long miles by the mules and arrieros. He wrote Jessie: "You remember the volumes of Blackstone which I took from your father's library . . . ? They made my Christmas amusements. I read them to pass the heavy time and forget what was around me. . . ." This was his first law lesson and his last, since Blackstone was abandoned not long after, and notions of the law along with it.

The site of the Christmas camp, Camp Hope, was also stumbled upon by young Albert Pfeiffer some thirty years afterward. He found many stumps standing which had been cut off as much as seven or eight feet above the ground, and he came upon not one but two old handmade sleds, one about four feet long and the other some six feet in length. A number of the campfire sites are still evident among the high chopped stumps. A belt buckle and a mule's foot shod with an ox shoe were happened upon in 1928 at the Wannamaker Creek camp, where a much weathered bit of wood still identifiable as a spool was kicked up out of the spruce needles in 1951 (maybe the spool of thread Dick Kern used in making moccasins there). There were and still are numerous bones around the Wannamaker camp, where the mules died. Both of these campsites are extraordinarily well preserved: the sites, being on the top of the world, are too high to be disturbed by flood runoff; for most of each year they are enclosed in snow and kept in a deep freeze; and there are seldom passers-by up here. Brush back the layer of needles that have sifted down in the century since, and the ashes of the fires, it may be imagined, look very much as they looked when the spring of 1849 disclosed them. In the summer of 1951 the Forest Service posted markers at the Christmas camp on Embargo Creek.

Sheepherders, living on the mountaintops in summers, have long been curious about these "old camps with the high stumps." For many years they have camped regularly nearby the Wannamaker Creek camp, but they rather carefully avoid camping on the site itself, due to an innate good taste about such matters and a respect for the mountain's memories. There are other mementos those who travel in the back rooms of the mountains have seen in the vicinity: a shovel (the handle rotted away) grown up in an aspen, a packsaddle hanging high in another quakey—these trees, of course, had grown up bearing these things in their branches—a cap-and-ball pistol found beside a stream.

On Christmas Day the relief party was preparing to set out for the New Mexican settlements to get animals and supplies for the stranded expedition.

Tom Breckenridge, reminiscing, said Colonel Frémont sent

for him and said, "Breckenridge, we have been in many tight places together, and I know you are one of the hardest and toughest men I have. . . . We must get aid, and a small party can travel faster than a large one. . . . I have concluded to send yourself, Kreutzfeldt and Bill Williams, under King, down the river for relief. King, Kreutzfeldt and Williams have volunteered—now will you go?" Breckenridge, naturally, replied, "I will go. . . ."

Frederick Creutzfeldt, the botanist, must have been a pretty good man to have been picked for this mission. Frémont considered Captain Henry King his most dependable lieutenant, next to Godey. Old Bill was, of course, the logical man to pilot the relief party out to the settlements. Mountain boy Tom Breckenridge would make a very capable fourth.

They would travel down the Rio Grande to the nearest place where animals and provisions could be found. That might be the Red River settlements in New Mexico, about 130 miles away, or it might be Taos, 160 miles. They were to be allowed sixteen days to go and return. For mounted men in summer the round trip would take no more than a week.

The four men left Camp Hope on the morning after Christmas. Tom Breckenridge wrote: "On account of the depth of the snow we planned to carry as little weight as possible with us. We took one blanket apiece, a few pounds of frozen mule meat, about one pound of sugar, a little macaroni, and a few candles. We had three Hawkins rifles for defense against the Indians, about fifty bullets, and one pound of powder. We also had one shotgun."

Godey went partway down toward the river with them, to look for a route down from the mountains the rest of the expedition could travel with the baggage. The companions they were leaving behind emerged from the snow to see them off and shout heartfelt wishes for a fast trip.

Even Doc Kern climbed up from the fire to wish them a

"successful journey and speedy succour." On Christmas night Doc had fallen sick. He was shaken with nausea and vomiting, and left so weak he could not move from beside the campfire for the next two days. It may have been the Christmas dinner that upset him. It may have been the climax of his spiritual wrestling with the immense fear that had descended upon him eight days before when he had wakened in the blizzard in the Wannamaker Creek camp, "peeped out and told Dick the expedition was destroyed."

Part Four

THE DEFEAT

13

Embargo Creek is an idealized picture of a trout stream, cold and swift and rushing over many stones that rub together and make a soft pattern of sound like mumbling speech beneath the laughter of the water. From the mountaintops above timberline, above the springs and rincons that are the first beginnings of the creek, its deep valley can be seen like a jagged knife cut ripped down to the river. It has the look of a direct and easy road and the river can be glimpsed, flat and placid, at its foot. But the cañons of the creek's upper forks, startlingly beautiful cañons laced among the remote high places of the mountains, are steep and savage and bitterly hard to travel.

Still today they are hard to work a way through, even in summer, these hidden jewels of upper cañons down which the lost expedition struggled, and from one year to the next are only seen by the Forest Ranger and an occasional rider from a mountain cow camp and a still more occasional hunter.

The men of the expedition traveled between fifteen and twenty miles descending along this creek from the tops of the mountains to the Rio Grande. It took exactly twenty days for all of them to reach the river.

In this twenty days the four men sent for relief, including Bill Williams, master trapper, one of the best men the Rocky Mountains ever saw, made only seventy miles or so toward the New Mexico settlements—a little more than halfway.

Advancing into the winter and the mountains these same men had conquered as much ground day by day, against the greatest difficulties, as they could now cover retreating week by week.

Something happens in defeat. It may be impossible for any man to fully admit defeat (with no inner self-justifying reservations) and remain the whole man he was before. It may be that to the strongest, proud of his strength, defeat is absolutely intolerable, and utter disintegration the inevitable result if the reality of defeat is finally forced upon him. The bigger they come the harder they fall may apply to courage as well as to poundage.

Mankind is driven by many forces: the quasi-mystical need for recognition that moves all life, that makes a bird sing, a child cry, a tree unfold; the need for survival in order to strive for this recognition; the need for life in order to strive for survival; and behind all these forces the always lurking fear of their defeat. Harnessed by hope and bitted by courage, this force of fear, tautly kept in its place as an accessory, works wonders and moves mountains. But escaped and running wild it rains down ruin and destroys souls.

These forces live in the deeps of those subtle sensations that can not be put in words, that are felt as fleeting points of contact between thought and being. Only the wind-tossed spray above them can be caught and examined in the conscious emotions. On this conscious level courage and hope and fear are quite obviously bound up and balanced together. Courage and fear are not opposites and one merely the absence of the other, for a man with the instincts of a coward may still be very brave indeed and the most heroic heart has fathered bastard fears. From the earliest epochs of thought it has been realized that in every man there lives a hero and a coward, and either one may be called to the threshold under certain conditions. Courage without fear is an absurdity, of course, since without fear there is no call for courage. And hope, which gives dimension to courage, is equally essential to fear. The Spanish have a proverb, *quien espera desespera:* who hopes, fears; and likewise there can be no fear without hope; when the child is dead you no longer fear for its life. These values, courage and hope and fear, are as close together as the fingers in a fist, each intricately organized of its complex of joints and nerves and muscles.

The fourth expedition gambled itself against the most slender hope of success, and sacrificed itself in an effort shining with courage. Then hope, stretched too far, was distorted and the fist was distorted until it cast the shadow of a claw and fear sprang out unbound ("It is impossible," Tom Breckenridge wrote, "to imagine the state of terror we were in. . . .") and the men were distorted in its spell—the same men who had climbed so high as heroes descended headlong into darknesses where courage became ruthlessness and skill and gallantry, cruelty and cunning.

It was not sudden. Defeat came upon the expedition suddenly enough, on the stormy ridges above timberline, but the people of the expedition did not simultaneously accept it, by any means. It approached them singly, stealthily here, with a rush there, and one by one in the days that followed the men gave up and surrendered to its fears, each in his own way. To some, defeat in itself was only incidental to the fear of death; and to the god of that fear all the immaculate qualities of their humanity, honesty, compassion, resolution, even skills and reason, were submitted one by one. To others, to whom life was customarily something to spend, not save, the fear of death was incidental to the fear of defeat itself and anything at hand, however precious, was willingly risked in twisting and turning to elude it.

Thus Frémont clung to the last to the unreal hope that he could still be saved, at whatever cost, from the obliteration of bowing to unconditional surrender, that somehow this defeat could be circumvented and things could be as things had been before. Time and strength were risked on working the baggage down to the river at once, so as little time as possible would be lost in moving on when the relief animals arrived, while the last of the few provisions ran out and the lives of the men became irrevocably staked on the success of the detachment sent for relief—four exhausted men on foot against 160 miles of winter.

Camp Hope gave way to Camp Disappointment, and with Godey leading a way down the upper cañons of Embargo Creek the men left their fire holes and toiled in relays to move the baggage (eighty mule loads left, let us say, which would be three hundred man loads, and twenty-nine men and a boy— Godey's nephew, Theodore—to transport it).

They carried also their saddles and packsaddles, to equip the animals the relief party would be bringing up the river. Frémont may have been still so far from giving even a distant nod to defeat at this time as to entertain a fantastic hope of trying again to attack the high mountains, when the relief animals appeared. Micajah McGehee understood that Frémont planned to take the expedition on across the mountains "by a different direction," and "still pursue a westerly course on the 38th degree." Frémont himself, however, later wrote to Jessie that he intended to use the relief animals "to transport our baggage to Taos," from where the expedition would go on by a southerly detour around the mountains.

On the way down to the river the last of the emergency provisions were distributed, and the men entered by twos and threes into that nebulous and forbidding land called by the trappers starving times. They began boiling up rawhide tug ropes and parfleches for something to eat. (By parfleches they commonly meant in this instance rawhide bags and panniers.) The last of the mules were killed and eaten during the trip

down the creek and the rest of the frozen mules had been left
buried in snow on the mountaintops. No mention is made by
anyone of the elk that had been cached down on the river
against just such an eventuality as this. The four men of the
relief party would have had the first chance at it, but if anyone
got it the fact was suppressed in later recollection.

Disintegration began with the group, with the machine as a
whole. Later it extended to the several parts, and later to separate individuals. The expedition broke into fragments on the
way down Embargo Creek. Frémont's mess was in the lead,
with Godey. Others straggled along Embargo in different
camps, as they labored with the baggage. The Kerns, with more
personal belongings than most, seem to have fallen well toward
the rear. The Kern splinter party was now made up of the
three brothers, Captain Cathcart, and the three Indian boys,
Manuel and Joaquin and Gregorio. After only a week Frémont's mess camped on the Rio Grande; the rest of the men
were strung up and down the creek behind him for more than
ten miles.

From Camp Hope they descended into the head of a cañon,
down a very steep pitch that in summer is an almost vertical
rockslide, but Godey, exploring on down this cañon, found
that it was practically impassable, as it still is today, narrow,
cascaded, and choked with great boulders. So this became
Camp Disappointment and they climbed up out of it by the
opposite wall and went on to the next main fork east of it.
They made their way down this fork, sometimes dropping
down into its cañon, sometimes keeping high on the divide
above it. This happens to be one of the most magnificent little
cañons in the West, its majestic rock walls like folds of gilded
drapery, and Dick Kern, artist becoming westerner, was not
too much occupied with dragging bales of baggage through
the snow to be unaware of its beauty. Another fork passed
on the way down the creek has a cañon of extraordinary

grandeur; it's called Cathedral Creek nowadays, and veritably looks it.

The weather was fine for a week after Christmas. The extreme cold gave way to bright sunny days, blinding in the snow but warming and cheerful. Life emerged: little flocks of juncos appeared chirping in the trees, and when fire holes broke through the tunnels of mouse runways deep in the snow the mice came out and scoured for forage, and Doc Kern wrote that he looked at them with a hungry eye. The men, endlessly shuttling the baggage along through these pretty days, were sometimes almost in high spirits, sliding the baggage down the braes, even jumping aboard a bale to catch a ride. But sometimes, crawling on hands and knees up a slope while blood ran from the nose, or pulling in after dark to crouch wearily by the fire of wet wood and cook a supper of macaroni and mule soup, they were plunged into fits of despondency, and then they took turns cheering each other up.

One of the last of the surviving mules to be butchered was a saddle mule that had been part of Doc Kern's professional fee from the Arapaho at Big Timbers. Apparently Doc had become fond of this mule in spite of the number of times it had thrown him, for others killed the mule while Doc was away from the camp, possibly to spare his feelings. On New Year's Eve the Kerns' mess, all alone several miles behind the other camps, sang songs and Dick read poetry aloud: Thomas Hood. Some of the humorous selections, no doubt; "The Bridge of Sighs" would not have been a felicitous choice. The new year of 1849 came in with snow flurries and signs of a new storm. Ned Kern made mincemeat for the New Year's Day dinner out of mule and some buffalo jerky and pemmican saved for the occasion. Snow fell off and on that night and all the next day. A heavy storm was unquestionably building up; the skies remained gray, gusts of wind whipped the spruce and aspen, and the air grew steadily colder.

On New Year's Day the Kerns moved down the creek below the junction of the upper forks and made a camp only seven miles distant from the river. Here Cathcart and Dick Kern built a lean-to for shelter against the approaching storm.

This site, in a draw grown with aspen and willow, lies in flood bottom bordering Embargo Creek and so no evidence remains of this camp where the Kern boys and Cathcart and the three California Indians and Proue, who had fallen back to camp with them, lived for ten days. Here they eventually gathered all their baggage they thought worth saving, and here they eventually left at least most of it cached. An exceedingly interesting part of this baggage was the important collection of records and documents dealing with the California conquest, gathered during Ned's stewardship at Fort Sutter, that Ned was carrying back to California with him.

Most of the other people of the expedition had settled in a camp called the Cottonwoods, one mile below the Kerns. The grove of narrow leaf cottonwoods, some very large and correspondingly old, is still standing. The snow here was not deep, but as little as two feet in the shallowest stretches. Baggage was still strewn along the back trail for five or six miles above the Kerns' Seven Mile Camp, and each day the men worked back and moved a little more baggage down to their two main camps.

The day after New Year's Frémont and his striker, Saunders Jackson, the faithful Mr. Preuss, Godey, and Godey's fourteen-year-old nephew camped on the river.

Below the point where the upper forks join to form the main stream of Embargo Creek, the mountains begin to open out and fall back from the creek, and timber thins out to islands and peninsulas, and bleak hills, ribbed with dike rock and crowned with bristling piñon, roll away to the river. The Kerns' Seven Mile Camp and the camp of the Cottonwoods were separated from the river by a half-dozen miles of barren flats along the creek. Winter can lash unhindered this bare flank cleaved in the coat of the mountains. The barns of the little ranches that today spring up beside the creek here are placed like dugouts in the earth and their roofs battened down with sod. The expedition was scattered in these camps when the new storm struck.

The storm spent several days in preparation, days of sluggish wet snowfalls interspersed with clear, cold, brilliant nights, and burst in a blizzard of wind and heavy snow. It lasted four or five days at its height. The men stayed close to their camps. There was little to feed on but their thoughts. They grew morose, and would sit for hours at a time in silence, with bowed heads and vacant eyes. They lived inside themselves, engrossed with the occupation of measuring their strength. They thought daily that they felt weaker and less able to resist the cold and endure the storm. Fewer, day by day, assigned themselves the thankless job of trying to revive and entertain the almost jealously secluded spirits of their companions. They looked to each other, as Doc said of Proue, "weakly and melancholy." Once Dick played his flute "to cheer us up." Doc also wrote in his diary: "Washed my feet hands and face. . . ." This was his last entry.

Early in the storm young George Hubbard killed a "goat" (probably a mountain sheep), the only game of any kind mentioned along the creek. The men shot at the juncos. Cathcart, the big-game hunter, later on hit one.

When the storm began to let up Proue tried to take a pack to the river, over the half-dozen miles of open flats where the cold, McGehee said, was "perfectly unbearable." Lorenzo Vincenthaler, from the Cottonwoods, started later the same day to pack a load to the river and came on Proue lying in the trail. Proue said his legs were frozen. Vincenthaler wrapped blankets around him. When he came back from the river Proue was dead.

McGehee wrote, "We passed and repassed his lifeless body,

not daring to stop long enough in the intense cold to perform the useless rite of burial."

Frémont was rather clearly infuriated by this death of Proue, his most constant follower, member of all his expeditions, for death after all implied a certain admission. Frémont said accusingly, "In a sunshiny day, and having with him the means to make a fire, he threw his blanket down on the trail, laid down upon it, and laid there till he froze to death!"

This does not take into account the fact that in the open stretch where Proue fell it is unlikely there was firewood at hand. It would seem Vincenthaler might have brought wood to him but maybe the cold was too strong to allow him to delay. But even so Proue's death was, more clearly than most of the others, a death that worked from the inside out. Raphael Proue, "a Frenchman and old mountaineer," as Tom Martin described him, perhaps gave his heart to defeat a little sooner than some of the others more because of what he knew from his long experience than in spite of it. In the long battle on the mountaintops above, Proue had endured far more than the comparatively calm rigors of that sunshiny day, as they all had. But then they had been trying to win, and now they knew they had lost.

Proue died on January 9. Two days later, January 11, was the date on which Old Bill and his men were due to return with relief. But they did not appear.

Old Bill, King, Breckenridge, and Creutzfeldt had gotten down to the river in three days. On the way an important part of the rations they had with them—their sugar—"was tipped over in the snow and lost—to us a very great misfortune," in Tom Breckenridge's words. The provisions they had carried with them were almost gone when they reached the river, Breckenridge said. They ate the last of them, two tallow candles, for lunch; later that day he records that he killed a small hawk, which made their supper. He says nothing of the elk left cached on the river.

They followed the river out into the plains of the San Luis Valley. Traveling constantly, without sufficient food and without sufficient equipment to make a decent camp at nights, and with their resistance increasingly lowered by fatigue, they were at the mercy of the cold. Their feet became badly frostbitten and progress was painfully slow. Blood clotted in the frostbite blisters, which then burst, leaving raw sores. The men could not bear to walk in leather and took off their moccasins and tore strips of their blankets to tie around their feet (an act which probably saved their feet and legs from progressive coagulation and stoppage of circulation). They ate their footgear. They seared and ate their belts and knife scabbards. One day the body of a dead otter was found on the ice of the river, but there was no other food.

Out in the valley, the four men struck off across the snow-covered plains to short-cut the great bend the Rio Grande makes to the south.

Breckenridge wrote that they left the river because Old Bill saw the smoke of an Indian fire ahead. The Indians were Utes, Old Bill said, and the others were jubilant because they knew Old Bill was a blood brother of the Utes and they thought he could get help from them. But Old Bill said he would have to swing away from the river and dodge them instead, and he told what had happened the previous summer, when in his "drunken spree" he had first spent the Utes' money and then led soldiers against them. "It was the meanest act of my life. For my treachery every Ute Indian rightly seeks my scalp."

However, Thomas Salathiel Martin was told later that they left the river because Old Bill wanted "to reach a small town on Rabbit Creek called Socorro." In the 1830's a number of New Mexican families had founded a settlement on the Conejos (Rabbit) River, a few miles north of the present New Mexico line and some fifteen miles west of the Rio Grande. The Utes harassed them and the attempt was finally abandoned until 1854, when New Mexican settlers tried again and established the first of the villages that are clustered there today. It is supposed the earliest settlements had been definitely given up by the time of the Mexican War; this was later a moot point in the lengthy legal proceedings in which rights to the extensive Conejos Grant were denied the earliest settlers on the grounds that their settlement had been too long abandoned. Tom Martin's remark is a somewhat surprising hint that Old Bill may have heard mountain talk of a settlement still there as late as 1848. If there was any chance of getting help at any such place as this Socorro (the word means succour) on the Conejos, it would be considerably nearer than the Red River settlements or Taos or Abiquiu, which otherwise were the nearest settled places to the scene of the expedition's disaster. And the shortest way to the site of this place would indeed be across country, swinging south into the plains away from the bend of the river. Someone told Tom Martin this was what they had tried but that "the snow storm drove them back" to the timber along the river.

In the open plains of the valley, off the course of the river and so with no wood for a fire, "we would pack down the snow and make a hole," Breckenridge recalled. "In this we would spread a blanket; then sitting in a circle, our feet together, we would draw the remaining parts of the blanket over our heads to shelter us from the piercing night wind. Every day our blankets grew smaller. Those around our feet would wear out, and we were obliged to tear off new strips to protect them. . . . We talked but little and suffered in silence."

Their eyes became inflamed and swollen from snow blindness. There was no sign of game, but it is questionable if they could have done anything about it if there'd been any.

Breckenridge said, "It is an utter impossibility to describe the agony of those days."

This was their condition when January 11 arrived, the date they were expected to return to the expedition with relief.

Now appears a little mystery.

This detachment of four men was under the technical command of Henry King, the bridegroom, Frémont's trusted lieutenant, an earnest and probably inspired young man. King kept a journal, and the last entry in it read: "This morning, as usual, I have had a quarrel with Bill Williams. Nothing to eat. We travelled one mile and a half today." This is on the testimony of Charles Taplin, who had evidently seen the journal. Taplin explained that the "cause of the difficulty with Williams was the latter's daily increasing weakness, and his inability to proceed. King endeavored by remonstrances to urge him forward."

Someplace, presumably, Taplin got this picture. Presumably from Creutzfeldt, the fourth man, since the picture of the situation Tom Breckenridge remembered does not fit in with it.

When they were almost to the end of the short cut traversing the great bend of the river, according to the Breckenridge account, when they were within a quarter mile of reaching once more the lifesaving timber along the river, Henry King said, "I can go no further, I am sorry, but I am tired out, and will sit here until I am rested. You three leave me and push on to the river and make your camp. When I am a little rested, I will follow."

Breckenridge and Old Bill and Creutzfeldt went on to the river—it took them two hours to make the quarter of a mile, crawling and rising to their feet to fall and crawl again—and built a fire of driftwood. Creutzfeldt then went back for King and found him dead.

Creutzfeldt now, Breckenridge said, became "very despondent. His mind seemed to dwell upon the poor fellow's death.

When he had approached King he thought the latter was
asleep, and was much startled at finding his old companion
dead. I could see that the shock was affecting his mind. He
could talk of nothing else."

In any case, whether he had been the weakest or the strongest and whether Crcutzfcldt did or did not go back to him on
a trip that would apparently have been a two-hour Calvary
each way, King was dead, and with this the three survivors
yielded up the last of their will to the finality of defeat.

Breckenridge remembered, "In the morning we broke camp
and started down the river not caring if we were not alive by
night."

Frémont had spun up the hope of relief until he had con-
vinced himself it was a certainty. On the basis of that certainty
he had gambled the last margin of safety for the rest of his
men—time, strength, and the final stocks of emergency provisions—on the laborious disposition of the baggage so that when
the relief came the expedition would be intact and in order
and ready to go on and the defeat only the briefest of delays
after all. Evidently he did not allow himself to think of what
would happen if the relief should not arrive. His mind refused
to consider a possibility that the relief party might be stopped
by the winter. He wrote Jessie later that he "could imagine
no other accident" to them than that they might be "cut off
by Indians." Any suspicion of that finality of defeat was un-
speakable and could not be tolerated.

He had so far fenced with the winter with all his skill at
every step, saving the expedition and the mules a dozen times
when another commander might have lost them; he had allowed a lavish excess of time with those twenty-five days of
corn; he had likewise allowed a lavish excess of time for the
relief party; surely there must some time be an end to the
chain of events "so signally disastrous as absolutely to astonish
me with a persistence of misfortune, which no precaution has

been adequate on my part to avert," as he wrote to Jessie. The relief must arrive. And so he assured himself and busied himself with nothing more than waiting for it, and his men, still working the baggage through the relay points of their camps six and seven miles above the river, were at the gray gate of their ordeal of starving times and one of them, his oldest follower, was already dead in the snow.

But hope again had carried boldness too far. The relief did not arrive on the appointed day. The membrane broke. Frémont immediately divided the last of the remaining provisions, taking about half for himself and the four men with him and leaving about half for the twenty-four other men, and that same day set off down the river himself for relief, accompanied by Saunders Jackson and Preuss, the boy Theodore, and Alexis Godey. He left the rest of the expedition under the command of Lorenzo Vincenthaler, with orders to get all the baggage to the river and then follow down the river until they were met with relief.

McGehee wrote that Frémont started off, "taking just enough provision before it was all exhausted to do them down the river. . . . He left an order that we scarce knew how to interpret, to the effect that we must finish packing the baggage to the river and hasten on down as speedily as possible to the Mouth of Rabbit River" (a trifle more than halfway to the Red River settlements) "where we would meet relief, and that if we wished to see him we must be in a hurry as he was going on to California. By this time, being forced to abandon his projected route, he had determined to proceed to California by a Southern route."

Frémont wrote in his letter to Jessie, "We carried our arms and provisions for 2 or 3 days. In the camp the messes had provisions for two or three meals more or less; and about five pounds of sugar to each man. Failing to meet King, my intention was to make the Red River settlement about twenty-five miles north of Taos, and send back the speediest relief possible. My instructions to the camp were that if they did not hear from me within a stated time they were to follow down the Del Norte."

On the day the relief was expected Cathcart and the Kerns, as certain as Frémont that the relief would appear on schedule, left their camp early in the morning to go to the river and welcome the relief, "meet and hurry the mules," as Dick Kern put it in his diary. Before they reached the river they learned the relief had not come and that, instead, Frémont himself was leaving. At this they stopped and camped where they were beside the creek, perhaps because of discouragement, perhaps because they were too weak to make the whole seven miles to the river in one day. Doc and Ned Kern met Stepperfeldt and Carver and camped with them in a grove of willows. Dick Kern and Cathcart fell in with Midshipman Andrews and young McGehee and camped overnight with them under a cave. (This cave is four and a half miles up Embargo Creek from the river, one of several in a rocky escarpment.) Piñon logs were rolled down from the hillside above and a fire built. The "last morsel" of their provisions, McGehee wrote, was a cupful of boiled macaroni and a cup of sugar to each man, and this Andrews happened to upset into the fire. The four huddled among the rocks throughout a snowy, stormy night. McGehee said some dry bones were found in an old wolf den and these were pounded to pieces and boiled. In the morning for breakfast they boiled up parfleche and rawhide rope.

The next day the Kerns and Cathcart returned to their Seven Mile camp, where they waited until the next day, resting, and then broke trail through new snow down to the river. For a couple of days after Frémont's departure men continued to trek back and forth between the upper camps and the river, but McGehee wrote that not all the baggage was transported to the river as per Frémont's instructions. The Kerns especially do not appear to have troubled to move all their possessions down to the river camp; they brought only their bedding and arms.

The river camp would seem to have been at the U in the river below a present-day bridge known as the Granger Bridge, midway between the towns of Del Norte and South Fork and some eight miles down the river from the point where the expedition had turned off to climb into the mountains. The Rio Grande is serene and handsome here, and big and handsome trout lurk in its shaded ripples.

Within four days after Frémont had gone all the rest of the men were gathered in the river camp, under gaunt trees hung with beards of thick white frost. Some still had a little sugar and coffee, some had a few candles left. The rest were living on parfleche and lash rope. Some were stronger than the others; some were already too weak to travel; a few were suffering from severe cases of frostbite.

The process of disintegration continued. The two old engagés, Morin and Tableau, the two old men of metal, started away down the river on their own. The Kerns began to quarrel with Sergeant-Captain Vincenthaler, who had been left in command by Frémont. Frémont's choice of Lorenzo Vincenthaler is a puzzling one. In making it Frémont passed over not only Ned Kern and a number of other older hands such as the hunter John Scott, but also the greatly experienced and trustworthy Captain Charles Van Linneus Taplin. The Kerns implied afterward that Vincenthaler flattered his way to this position, so maybe his eagerness in chasing all those runaway mules earlier in the trip paid off after all.

The quarrel between the Kerns and Vincenthaler was an elemental one. It concerned survival. But the point at issue was a principle. Vincenthaler's theory was that he should take those who were now the strongest and best equipped and leave those who were weaker and those with raw and frostbitten feet who would have trouble keeping up. The Kerns and Cathcart and Taplin took the stand that all should stay together and help each other along the way.

Ned Kern, writing the story to Antoine Robidoux, said, "The company had for its head Vincut Hatter, about as contemptible and cowardly a fellow as ever walked. . . ." Which was typical of the repeated, and heated, observations the Kern boys made of acting-captain Vincenthaler.

Thus wrangling, and tending to divide into hostile camps separated by the bitterest enmity, the last remnants of the broken expedition started down the river, five days after Frémont had left. Morin and Tabeau being someplace ahead, there were twenty-two men left in all, hairy and skeletal, bundled in ragged blankets, their eyes bloodshot and their faces black from the smoke of the fires. Any scratch or cut became a running sore that did not heal. Their teeth were loose in their mouths. Their hands were withered and clumsy, sometimes unaccountably numb and helpless. They moved along in small groups or one by one. Cathcart and the Kerns lagged behind with the three California Indians. The eldest of the Indian boys, Manuel, was in very bad shape. His feet had been frozen and the flesh had rotted until the soles of his feet had fallen off. Wise, another invalid, stumbled along with them, very weak, all intent on keeping up with the simple business of the march. During the day Carver dropped back with them. Carver was preoccupied with his hunger. He was flashing-eyed and talkative and trembling on the edge of delirium.

Within a short while Manuel called Vincenthaler and begged him, as commander, to shoot him. Manuel could see that he could not totter along fast enough to keep up and he dreaded being left alone. Vincenthaler would not kill him. Manuel then said his farewells to the others and made his way back to the brush lodge at the river camp they had just left. His friends Joaquin and Gregorio helped him back to the brush lodge. When they got him there they worked up a pile of firewood to keep him warm as long as he should live, and stayed with him overnight.

The rest of the men made about two miles on this first day's march, and camped near the site of the elk camp of their upriver journey.

On this day Frémont and his little detachment, moving down the Rio Grande a number of miles ahead, came on an Indian youth. They had picked up the trail of a Ute family group—two lodges—their second day out. The sign said the Indians were traveling downriver also, and Frémont had hurried on in the hope of overtaking them. They managed to approach the Indian youth without frightening him, made friends, and went on with him to the Indian camp. The boy was "an Utah, son of a Grand River chief we had formerly known," Frémont wrote. A later story was appended by Jessie that Frémont had once spared the life of the boy's father, the chief; numerous grace notes about the tale give it quite an air of composition, although it may be founded on the fact that Frémont was indeed known to these Indians, and that his name among them was good.

Frémont had always tried to give himself a favorable reputation among the Indians, because it helped him on his way, it was the prescribed romantic-chivalric behavior, and it was his wish to perform for his expanding country a faithful service by leaving "no heritage of enmity for those who would follow," as Jessie put it. Often he had failed in living up to this code; more often he had succeeded. It is possible the Utes found on the river would have known him by reputation even though Frémont may never have had occasion to spare their chief's life. And too, the Utes would later remember this interesting meeting itself: for some years afterward the Utes were said to have circulated and recited verses about "the American general lost in the snow."

Before coming up with the Indians, Frémont and his men had run out of provisions. The only game they had been able to kill was a hawk, all "bone and skin and feather." Now they camped overnight near the two Ute lodges, gave presents of blankets—Frémont gave the only blankets he had with him, two, and left himself without any—a rifle, and "a very large four bladed knife," and presumably got something to eat and also prevailed upon the Indian youth to go with them as a guide and take along four of the Indians' horses. These were wretchedly poor, Frémont said, could only travel at a slow walk, and were wanted "principally to carry our little baggage."

The next day, provided with the Ute guide and his four horses, Frémont and his men traveled on down the river and at a point that must have been not far beyond the junction of the Conejos River they saw the smoke of a camp, went to it, and found Old Bill Williams, Breckenridge, and Creutzfeldt. Frémont wrote, "They had been starving." He said they were "the most miserable objects I have ever seen. I did not recognize Creutzfeld's features when Brackenridge brought him up to me and mentioned his name. . . . King had starved to death a few days before. His remains were some six or eight miles above, near the river."

After King's death Breckenridge and Old Bill and the botanist Creutzfeldt had trailed on down the river, frequently crawling on their hands and knees. Flesh was beginning to come off their feet, Breckenridge recalled, leaving "horrible sores," which could only be dressed with scraps of their woolen blankets. It was impossible to walk more than a few steps at a time. Creutzfeldt collapsed and was near death when, Breckenridge relates, he luckily killed a deer (first holding snow to his eyes until he could clear his vision). The smell of the kill revived Creutzfeldt, and Old Bill "came and took the meat in his long bony hands and began tearing off great mouthsful of the raw flesh, like a savage animal." They feasted on deer meat the next day, Breckenridge said, and the day after that "we saw a party of four coming on horseback from the river. On the instant all was excitement. It was natural for us to suppose they were Indians and if so it meant a fight. . . . Williams remarked that when the fight would be over the Indians 'would have more hair or we more blankets.' Suddenly . . . watching . . . Williams rose to his feet and swinging his gun in the air shouted with all the strength of his lungs. At the head of the party was Frémont himself. At first he did not recognize us, so changed and emaciated were we. . . ."

The feet and legs of these men had been exposed to continued effects of frostbite for many days. Some of them were reported later to be frozen as high as their hips.

In the expedition as a whole there were numerous cases of acute frostbite; Doc Kern and Frémont usually speak of them all indiscriminately as cases of "frozen" feet, frozen hands, frozen faces. Frémont recorded ten or twelve such casualties in one day—on the first attempt to get over the top of the mountain during the "pouderie." Undoubtedly conditions of clothing and activity were such that capillary permeability was not paralyzed for any length of time and affected red cells retained or frequently resumed their discreteness. Otherwise the frostbitten members would have become mummified and indubitably lost, even disregarding the further likelihood of thrombosis and gangrene. It may have been that the onset of the deep shock sometimes accompanying severe frostbite accounted for some of the collapses and deaths, although with the exception of Proue the men who died were said to have died of "starvation," which of course merely means the widening of the threshold to permit death to enter from any direction it chooses.

But among the survivors, after long and constant exposure
to frostbite, there was not noted the amputation of so much
as a finger.

Frostbite has the precise effect on tissue of a burn. These
men suffered repeatedly from such burns, complicated by the
effects of starvation and massive fatigue, but recovered the use
of their limbs after no more than a few days' to, at the most,
a few weeks' rest in bed. The only treatment mentioned was
bathing the wounds with juniper tea. (Modern treatment of
acute frostbite includes transfusion of blood and plasma, lum-
bar blocks, penicillin, sterile dressings, use of anticoagulant
agents; hospitalization may be from a few weeks to many
months.) Most of the survivors resumed normal activity after
less than a week of recuperation. Old Bill Williams, sixty-two
years of age, hospitalized six months before with a bullet-
shattered arm, was on his way back to the mountains within
a month after his ordeal on the river.

For Frémont, the discovery of the wreckage of the King-
Williams mission meant at last the ultimate wreckage of his
tattered web of hope. He retreated to the deepest corners of
self-deception and built up his last-ditch defense against defeat with excuses that willingly sacrificed values he had always
held most precious: truth and loyalty and honor. He set aside
the memory of Old Bill's warning of the winter ahead and
advice as to a safe route and said the disaster was Old Bill's
fault; the guide had blundered. He set aside the memory of
the magnificent effort and blind loyalty his men had shown—
the men who had marched to meet immolation and patiently
awaited immolation under his orders and were undergoing
the anguish of that immolation even as he wrote—and said
the disaster was the fault of the men; their spirits had failed
too easily. "In fact, I have never seen men so soon discouraged
by misfortune as we were on this occasion; but as you know
the party was not constituted like the former ones." The fourth

expedition, as has been seen, was constituted principally of men of previous expeditions, veterans now who had been greenhorns then. Jessie Frémont wrote on another occasion: "Many of the men had been with Colonel Frémont before, and he knew the power of the party, numerically so small." But this was the first experience of any Frémont expedition with defeat.

These excuses, hurled up in rage and desperation, represent one of the sudden chasms cleaved in Frémont's life and are in every way unworthy of the man and his precepts, idealistic if literary. To the unfortunate romantic when he fails as he must to live up to his imaginative ideals the world becomes all a despised place, and only fit for unworthiness. Very likely unrealistic romantic ideals have tripped up far more lives than have difficult realities. They play a strange role in the drama of human happiness, such ideals, forever lifting up and hurling down, Lucifer's fall re-enacted in continuous performance. It might be they are the gentleman himself.

Thus Frémont met defeat. But even so it was not to be wholly admitted. He would go on to California by the southern route, and he wrote, "The survey has been uninterrupted up to this point, and I shall carry it on consecutively." And a few months later he summed up the railroad-pass exploration achievement of the fourth expedition: "The result was entirely satisfactory."

When he found Old Bill and Breckenridge and Creutzfeldt he loaded them aboard the Indian horses and took them on to the settlements at the Rio Colorado.

And here occurs a revealing contradiction. Tom Breckenridge, dictating his account many years later when all the others were dead, was urged by some ancient memory of bitter guilt to relate that Frémont only stopped long enough with him and Williams and Creutzfeldt to eat some of their venison and then pushed on, leaving the three to crawl on their hands and knees the forty remaining miles to the nearest settlements, those on the Rio Grande. ("Only forty miles! . . . we felt strong.") He said it took them ten days. But Frémont wrote that "by aid of the horses, we carried these three men with us to Red River settlement."

The case would appear to rest on no more than a choice of which witness to believe, although Breckenridge's testimony is weakened by the fact that before ten days they would have been met by Godey returning with relief.

However, corroboration for Frémont is furnished in a letter written by Ned Kern to his sister upon his arrival in Taos: ". . . the relief party sent under King . . . were picked up by the Col on his way down. King was dead and the rest in a most horrid state of starvation." Elsewhere in the letter Ned remarks that he has not yet seen Frémont, so his information was not from that source; furthermore Ned was not in a mood at the time to hold any brief for Frémont, if the point was in any controversy.

McGehee, likewise, writes that Godey and Frémont found the three men "in a weak and emaciated condition . . . more or less frozen from their hips down . . . and nearly dead, with intellect shaken and scarcely any hearing, sight, or sense left, and half deranged and nearly sightless they took them along upon the Indian horses into the little outer settlement of the Rio Colorado."

Breckenridge's false indictment displays a startling malice, after so long a time, almost fifty years after the event. (Frémont wrote that when he found the stranded men, Breckenridge said "he would rather have seen me than his father. He felt himself safe.") Only a deep and terrible sense of guilt can account for such a malicious resentment, that draws on fantasy for support, gravely presenting a distortion of facts so bizarre that on examination they are wholly ludicrous—presenting a picture of not only Frémont but the kindly Mr. Preuss and the knightly Godey and the colored servant, Saunders, and Godey's young nephew and the friendly Indian youth all coldly observing these three almost sightless, frozen, starving men, helping themselves to their venison, and then callously riding on, leaving them jubilant because they only had forty miles more to crawl to the settlements.

But what guilt? Perhaps the guilt of having failed in the mission of relief. But there is another stronger reason for resentment, and possibly for a deeper and more secret guilt.

Frémont told Jessie that when he found Old Bill and Breckenridge and Creutzfeldt they gave confused answers to questions about King, said he had "wandered out of camp, they did not know where he was. But they could not in their enfeebled state long conceal the fact and the remains of King's body were found in another camp where he had died of starvation, and starving the other three had utilized him to sustain life."

This story of cannibalism was told over Taos when Frémont and his little detachment reached there. All the first reports of the expedition's disaster mention it as tragic fact, that in the extremity to which King's companions were driven they "were forced to eat a part of his body." Taplin mentioned it several months later: "A dire necessity had left them no choice, and it was done in self-protection." Senator Benton repeated the story years later in his autobiography: that Frémont found young King "dead and horribly devoured."

This, then, might explain the nature of the malice preying on Tom Breckenridge's mind for so many years afterward— whether the story was true or not; and preying all the more relentlessly if it was true. (Breckenridge does his cause harm in his account by going to some lengths to state a defense against the never-mentioned charge of cannibalism, until the feeling comes that he protests too much. He makes a point of the deer he providentially killed, yet none of the others who, at the time, describe the condition of the three men when

found by Frémont speak of it. He tells of a raven circling and
settling over the dying King as they leave him, which would
account for any statement that King's body was found par-
tially devoured, but the question arises as to why the three
starving men did not then shoot the raven for food—they had
shot a hawk and eaten a dead otter found on the ice. But too
it is not impossible that during his starving time Breckenridge
left the white frozen world of reality about him and entered
the pleasanter world of a dream, and that in this world a buck
sprang up and fell to his rifle, and that in this world strips of
flesh cut from King's body and brought to their camp were
magically washed as clean as venison, and that all that remained later of revulsion was the vivid memory of Old Bill
taking the meat in his long bony hands and tearing off great
mouthfuls like a savage animal.)

But while considering bizarre fantasy in these excuses and
accounts and the depths of guilt and resentment and defeat
they reveal—excuses being always more revealing than the
simple truth—it is necessary to look at Frémont's own story
of his trip down the river for relief. He emphasizes suspiciously
(as suspiciously as Breckenridge with his deer) the fact that
the four Indian horses were of negligible help in making the
journey. They could move no faster than a slow walk; they
were wanted principally to carry their little baggage. He
states explicitly that he and his party made it to the Red River
settlements "on foot." And they made it in ten days, while
Old Bill and his detachment had not made much more than
half the distance in twenty-two days by the time Frémont
picked them up, and the rest of the men struggling along the
river farther up were doing no better if as well. This states
the claim that Frémont, accompanied by three men and a
boy (even though one of them was Godey), averaged some
thirteen miles a day on foot through the snow while none of
the others (even though one of them was Old Bill Williams)

could average better than two or four or at the most six. Obviously the Indian horses were the salvation of Frémont's march down the river, but obviously he preferred the fantasy that they were not, implying thereby that any of his lost men should have been able to do as well, and exhibiting thereby what a simple admission of truth could never have illuminated so piercingly, how he was haunted by their ghosts.

The Frémont party reached the Red River settlements—the neighborhood of the present Questa, New Mexico—four days after picking up Old Bill and his companions. The others were left in the care of the Mexicans there and Godey and Frémont, hunting horses and supplies, rode on alone to Taos. There Godey rounded up thirty some horses and mules and four Mexican packers and a stock of food and was back at Red River leading this outfit the following evening, a round trip of fifty to sixty miles and the formation and take-off of the relief party accomplished in two days, a lightning-fast piece of driving of which Godey was justifiably proud.

Frémont stayed in Taos. The first newspaper reports from Taos had it that Frémont himself, "though much emaciated, and in feeble health," led the relief expedition that started back up the river for his men. However, Godey took the relief alone. Frémont explained to Jessie that "it was not necessary for me to go back with him, and it was necessary for me to remain and prepare the means of resuming the expedition to California as soon as he returns with the men left behind."

When Frémont arrived in Taos in the evening he went to Don Carlos Beaubien's store; Kit Carson and Dick Owens were there. Frémont limped up to them, ragged and drawn; they did not recognize him until he spoke to them. They took him to Carson's house and put him to bed.

14

On the day that Frémont came upon Old Bill and the ruins
of his party, the rest of the expedition up the river was going
hunting. Rather, the best hunter—John Scott—had been sent
out to hunt while the others stayed quiet, to give him an opportunity at undisturbed game, if there was any game. All
were now starving and they had to have food. But panic would
not permit patience, and before Scott could have had a chance
for a reasonable hunt the restless Vincenthaler gave the command to move on.

They traveled a half-dozen miles and camped close on the
site of another of their camps on the way in (thirty-nine days
ago, now), below the Big Rock, Indian Head, in the vicinity
of the present town of Del Norte.

Henry Wise could not finish this day's march. He threw
away his blanket and rifle, staggered on a little way farther,
and then fell and could not get up, and presently was dead.
The others went on. The two Indian boys, coming along from
the river camp where they had left Manuel that morning,
found Wise's body. He had fallen on the surface of the frozen
river—the men walked on the ice of the river to avoid the
deeper snow along the banks—and Juan and Gregorio carried
his body over to the bank, scooped out a grave in the snow,
and covered him with brush.

Tabeau and Morin, the two old voyageurs who had started

on ahead from the river camp, fell back to join the main party, probably at the camp made at the end of this day's march. The two old men of metal had worn themselves out in the first day or two of their frantic dash to escape the winter. It is one thing for defeat to overthrow spiritual subtleties of courage and humanity, but it is perhaps more wonderful still that it can stun skill and the practiced behavior of experience, so that these two "old Voyageurs who had spent a life time amid such scenes," as Ned Kern described them, did not rate themselves, conserve their strength, use all the artifices of their knowledge and experience, but instead merely turned and fled headlong until their strength was gone.

And in this camp Carver went wholly out of his mind and raved throughout the night, and those around him were afraid and stayed awake to watch him. He said he had received an inspiration by which they could all be saved and tried to convince the others that he could lead them to safety. The next morning, still delirious, he went away by himself to return to the mountains and was not seen again.

On this day Vincenthaler asked the camp to remain quiet while several of the stronger men again tried to hunt. He went ahead hunting with Tom Martin and young Hubbard and John Scott and a few others. One of them struck it rich and killed a deer. Instead of taking the deer back to the waiting camp, Vincenthaler and Tom Martin and perhaps a few others of his hunting companions made off with it down the river. John Scott and Hubbard and young Ducatel either accompanied them or overtook them before evening and got a share of the kill, and the next day the rest of the camp, hurrying after them, caught them. By then the share remaining for grudging distribution to the Kerns and Cathcart and the Indian boys and four others in their group was a fore-shoulder blade.

Dick Kern wrote in his journal, "It was the intention of Mr. L. D. Vinsonhaler . . . to have said nothing about the deer

but to have taken it and the strong men and pushed on . . .
and left the rest of us to perish. Our share of the meat was so
unjustly small that it did us no good." But again, with this
incident, the colors of the picture are best brought out by another fantasy, possibly the most bizarre of all, soberly presented by Thomas Salathiel Martin. Thomas Salathiel himself
killed the deer, he said, and "We then waited 4 days until the
rest of the Company should come up. When they arrived we
divided the deer with them. . . ."

It was clear by now that the march down the river was a
contest. The contest was between the strong and the weak, a
grim game of hide-and-seek. Vincenthaler, Tom Martin, and
a few others who were in better condition—"who had plenty,"
as Dick Kern put it—wished to leave those who were weaker.
The weak, too blind and unsteady to hunt, did not wish to
be left. Their chief hope was to be at hand to get a share of
any game the stronger ones might be lucky enough to kill.

Once again the surviving men were all together. Requests
to Vincenthaler to hold the entire camp a day for rest and
hunting were denied. Sergeant-Captain Vincenthaler was "too
big a coward," Dick Kern wrote in helpless fury, "and cared
for self alone." He moved his mess on and the others had no
recourse but to move with him.

At this time Vincenthaler, McGehee wrote, "spoke up and
told us [that he] then and there threw up all authority . . .
he looked upon our condition as hopeless, but he would sug-
gest . . . that we break up into small parties and, hunting
along, make the best of our way down separately."

The contest was therefore in the open, it was every man
for himself, and Dick Kern scrawled in his journal that it was
"a piece of rascality almost without parallel."

Vincenthaler immediately put the new order of things into
effect by making a long march, the longest day yet, following
the Rio Grande down the middle of the great snowy valley

to about the neighborhood of the present town of Alamosa, a day's travel of some fifteen or sixteen miles.

Tom Martin wrote, ". . . at midnight when they were all asleep, Capt Haler, Scott, Duketel, Hubbard, Billy Bacon, and I crept out of camp and started. . . ." The weaker faction could keep up if it was able.

The old Frenchman, Tabeau called Sorrel, could not keep up. He had taken a violent fit the night before, McGehee wrote, which "resulted in an entire prostration. . . . At the same time, he was almost totally snowblind. Speaking to R. Kern of our situation, he said, 'Oh, Kern, this is a *mise Dieu* (a visitation from God) and we can't avoid it.' Poor fellow, the next day he travelled as long as his strength would allow, and then, telling us we would have to leave him, that he could go no farther, blind with snow, he lay down on the river bank to die." Doc and Ned Kern stopped to smoke a pipe with him and urge him to keep on but Sorrel would have none of it. He told them he was finished. Later Morin asked them if they had seen Sorrel and when they told him Morin put down his pack and went back up the river. He found Sorrel and built a fire and stayed with him until they died.

Vincenthaler's party on the day of the long march was made up of Vincenthaler, Martin, Scott, Ducatel, Hubbard, Bacon, Rohrer, and the two California Indian boys. Kern's group, the weaker faction, included the three Kerns, Andrews, McGehee, Stepperfeldt, and Cathcart. Captain Taplin also stuck with them. Ferguson and Beadle split off together in a little camp of their own.

The Kern party was able to trail along and keep the others in sight for this one day, but the pace was too much. This was the last day all the various splinter parties were together.

And on this day Godey and Frémont reached Taos.

In the morning the Vincenthaler party went on, "determined to leave us," Dick Kern wrote, "to get along as well as we could or perish." The Kern party again tried to follow along, made only three or four painful miles, and had to stop. The long march of the day before had been too much.

Of the end of this day McGehee wrote, "Dr. Kern came up so exhausted that he fell down, almost senseless, and remained in this torpid state a whole day. After a while Andrews came up; arriving within several hundred yards of camp, he raised a faint call and fell down, completely exhausted and senseless so that two or three of us had to go and pack him in. . . . Soon Rohrer came up. Vincenthaler's party, to which he belonged, was ahead of us; being too weak to proceed farther, he stopped with us."

Ferguson and Beadle made even less distance than this and camped a couple of miles behind them on the river.

The Vincenthaler faction went on and disappeared.

On the evening of this day Godey was back at the Red River settlements, some eighty miles away, with the hastily organized relief. Most of the provisions and animals, including some horses recently captured from the Utes, had been furnished him by the Army and the government commissary agent at Taos. On the way to Red River he picked up eight or ten more army horses.

In the Kern camp there was no longer any question of moving on. Taplin, no older than Doc Kern but seasoned by many years, half his young life, as a frontiersman, was the only man even able to move about and make some motions at hunting.

It is likely that Taplin voluntarily threw in with the weaker faction to give what help he could, abandoning his better chances with the stronger group ahead. In any case, Taplin still had more strength, evidently, than many of the people of the so-called stronger party. Taplin and Stepperfeldt were the remnants of another mess that joined the Kern mess, and Ned Kern wrote, "To this junction we owe our lives."

It has been remarked that hope gives definition to courage,

and the hope of survival that drove on the Vincenthaler party being a very real thing to all concerned at the time, it lends considerable shine to Taplin's humble act of courage. We commonly think of courage as containing the element of self-sacrifice for an ideal or a principle, something at any rate outside the self, but only in its most rarefied reaches sacrifice for that most inarticulate sort of stirring, compassion. Taplin and the others in the Kern camp made a pact with one another to stay together and help each other "while life lasted," as McGehee said it. Vincenthaler and his men traveled onward with the understanding that as any man weakened and could not keep up he would be summarily left behind.

For those who accused him of cowardly desertion, Vincenthaler had a countercharge: he accused them of cannibalism. In his report to Frémont he excused his conduct in abrogating his responsibility and leaving the weaker to perish by saying it was necessary to split up to keep the men from feeding on each other. It is difficult to see how he hoped to effect this laudable end by withholding from those most starved any game his least starved group might get. He represented the weaker group as hanging on his flanks rather like jackals waiting to snatch and devour those of the stronger party as they should fall, leaving those of the stronger party no honorable recourse but to flee. Thus the stronger based their action on the remarkable assumption that the weaker would outlast them with vulturous intent, and thus to prevent cannibalism the stronger ones abandoned all the dying group to those among them of alleged cannibalistic intent; and thus another, bizarrerie, and a particularly ugly one.

Vincenthaler got to the ear of Frémont some time ahead of the other survivors. Certainly cannibalism had been mentioned, thought of, discussed, and even tentatively proposed—and on the word of McGehee rejected—during the time of starvation on the river. But it is possible that the excuse in all its phosphorescent hues occurred to Vincenthaler when he first heard the story of King, before he talked to Frémont.

However, beyond all this, a concern with cannibalism was one of the whims of the age. The nineteenth century treasured a number of very odd curios of which cannibalism was a particular favorite. London applauded Little Billee and Gilbert's elderly naval man who was all at the same time captain and cook and mate and crew of the *Nancy* brig. At the time of the fourth expedition Bostonians were shivering delightedly over the long pig people in Melville's *Typee*. The enterprising century poked European noses into many savage far-off places and nearly all those places, so it seemed, were inhabited by cannibals. Among the less informed of the public, cannibal became a synonym for primitive man anyplace, whether in Africa or the South Seas or the American West. General Kearny's topographer on the way to California in 1846, Lieutenant W. H. Emory, supposed that even Navajos were cannibals. And the West had its full quota of stories of cannibalism among trappers and emigrants.

Tom Martin said of King's fate that Old Bill and his two companions brought "his body into where they camped and it is supposed that they lived on it, although they never would acknowledge it." But backing up Vincenthaler in his campaign against their particular opposition, he affirmed, "I know positively that the men we left behind lived on those of their companions who gave out, as I had it from some of the same men." This is the only evidence supporting Vincenthaler's charge. It may be worth noting that it comes from Vincenthaler's chief lieutenant. Taplin is quoted by Frémont as testifying to the existence of intention of cannibalism, but at the time Frémont wrote Taplin had not yet arrived in Taos and so he is necessarily still quoting only Vincenthaler. Doc Kern, obviously unaware of similar rumors about his own party, innocently related the horrifying story of King in a letter home. The two Indian boys,

Joaquin and Gregorio, were said to have left the Kerns' mess and joined Vincenthaler through fear of being eaten—this was said by Vincenthaler, who may have introduced that fear into their minds, since Joaquin and Gregorio were still relatively strong and active and would be an asset to whichever party they chose. McGehee knew of this or heard of it later, but Doc Kern only writes in his letter home that "The stronger party containing the hunters enticed away our two Indian boys and deserted us."

These alleged instances of cannibalism or intention of cannibalism can neither be proved nor disproved. That isolated, perhaps secret and stealthy, acts of cannibalism took place would not be unreasonable among men more or less insane from hunger. Weighing all the evidence, it is extremely doubtful that any cannibalism in the Kern party, if it existed at all, came to anything more than this. Weighing all the evidence, the charge of premeditated intention of cannibalism leveled by Vincenthaler appears to be false.

George Bernard Shaw says someplace: ". . . the only real tragedy in life is the being used by personally minded men for purposes which you recognize to be base." Surely cannibalism would appear to be this tragedy in its bluntest form. On reflection, though, the false accusation of cannibalism, for the base purpose of relieving the conscience of the accuser, might surpass it. But a decision in any such conflict between the physically detestable and the morally despicable is of no moment. The imposing fact is that the defeat and the hounding winter brought such a conflict into being. The men of the fourth expedition had descended a long way into the abysses, from their time of glory and valor on the high peaks, from the sparkling heights to which they had marched like heroes.

In the Kern camp, now stationary, Midshipman Andrews, who had never recovered from his exhaustion after the long march, was unconscious and near death. Rohrer was very weak and unable to move from his blankets. Most of the others huddled listlessly around the fire. Some of them had accepted the idea that they were going to die and were merely waiting for the time to come. Some still tried to put up a wall of passive resistance. Taplin went hunting. He shot two prairie chickens. They were divided scrupulously, down to the entrails and pin feathers, among the nine men. Taplin found a dead wolf on the river and brought it in; it was the leaving of other scavenging animals or birds. It had been mostly eaten but the skin was divided and roasted, and soup made over and over again from the bones and at last the bones themselves were eaten. A day passed and Andrews died in the night.

The weather had been snowy for much of the time on the way down the river, although out here in the valley the snow was not too deep. Now the winter brought a novelty, a cold rain that instantly froze, freezing the men to the ground as they lay in their blankets and holding them sheathed in sleet until the next day's sun appeared.

Most of those in the camp were now too weak to move more than a few feet at a time. Firewood became a problem. Some of the men crawled from one log of driftwood to another, kindling a fresh fire at each. Some fed the fires with scraps of their clothing and blankets.

For the first time since the start from Westport, blank days appeared in Dick Kern's diary, and consequently it is impossible to determine the date of the deaths that occurred. McGehee writes that Andrews died in the camp (an entry in Dick Kern's diary implies that neither Andrews nor Rohrer made it to this last camp, but they may have come up after this entry was written) and that the next day Rohrer was seized by a delirium of panic. The others talked to him of his wife and children back in Georgetown to try to rekindle his will to live, but Rohrer remained out of his mind and raving and died that night.

Here is found the only mention of the subject of cannibalism from the side of any of the accused.

McGehee wrote, "As we sat waiting for him to die, ―――― came over to the fire where Taplin, Stepperfeldt and I were sitting, and in a sad tone, said, 'Men, I have come to make a proposition.'" The unnamed man, who would necessarily have been one of the Kerns or Cathcart, then proposed making use of Rohrer's body for food. The body of the dying man, he said, would "'become the prey of wild beasts. Now I propose instead that we make use of it to save life. It is horrible, I know, but I will undertake to do the butchery, as you may call it, and you need have nothing to do with that part; you need not even see it done. . . .' All sat in silence; then several of us objected. I spoke up and said that for my part I had no conscientious scruples against such a procedure. I knew that early prejudice and conventional opinion founded on prejudice were at the bottom of our objections to it, but these existed, and it was a horrible proposition to entertain. I fully appreciated our situation but I thought that by making up our minds to it and remaining quiet, we could hold out three days longer, by which time, after finding that we could not possibly bear up longer, it would be soon enough to think of adopting so horrible an alternative. . . . 'But by that time,' he said, 'we will be too weak and too far gone ever to recover. You see what they have come to, and you see what you will come to.' 'I can't help it,' I said: 'I am determined to risk it at the peril of my life;' and so saying, I walked over to the other fire. They talked about it for a few minutes, but were unwilling to follow such a course unless all united in it. . . ."

Another day passed. Doc Kern was overcome with weakness and was unable to move. The others thought he was dying and wrapped him in extra blankets. He crawled to a little piece of rope, soaked it in a "spoonful of sweet oil" found in his pocket, and ate it. The attack was evidently one of nerves more than of muscle fiber, since later on Doc grew stronger again.

They ate the soles of their moccasins. They found some rosebuds along the river, and these were carefully divided among the seven men and eaten. Doc Kern found some water bugs on the river where the ice was broken. They scraped away the snow and dug in the frozen ground for roots.

Some of them dreamed constantly of food. McGehee wrote that he kept himself from madness by working mathematical problems in his mind.

In the little camp farther up the river, Beadle was dying. Ferguson sat by the fire alone.

In the Vincenthaler contingent, Hubbard was the first man to give out. They built a fire for him and left him, "without turning their heads," Vincenthaler told Frémont. John Scott was next. (Frémont said to Jessie: ". . . Scott—you remember Scott—who used to shoot birds for you at the frontier. . . .") They left him and went on. For a day or two they had kept on, to make possibly twenty miles below the Kern camp, and then they too were brought to a stop. They were able to kill a little meat, an occasional hawk, raven, or prairie chicken, and found the remains of a dead horse. Eventually the two Indian boys left the Vincenthaler camp and went on ahead by themselves, either because they were by now the only ones still able to travel or because, having had fears of cannibalism once planted in their minds, they didn't feel easy about any companions at all.

Godey, pushing up the river, overtook two Mexicans with mules bearing bread and flour and cornmeal, bound out to trade with the Utes. He added them and their provisions to his relief party.

In Taos, Frémont rested in bed in Kit Carson's house. He was beginning his letter to Jessie (". . . the mind turns from the scenes I have witnessed and the sufferings we have endured . . .”). But rage still contested with torment, and in this period his brooding thoughts hit on another explanation for this thing that had happened, this defeat: Old Bill had deliberately misled the expedition, deliberately lost it in the snow, with the intention of later making off with the riches of the abandoned baggage.

Jessie later wrote that it was from Kit Carson at this time that “Col Frémont first heard what others subsequently confirmed of Bill Williams’ evil character.” (Kit said, Jessie related, “In starving times no man who knew him ever walked in front of Bill Williams.”) This revelation of Williams’ evil character would seem to be somewhat tardy, since Frémont had been in the mountains hearing the gossip of the mountain men for years and had previously hired Old Bill himself as a guide. With this ignoble theory of being the victim of a deliberate double cross, Frémont at last sounded the rock bottom of the crevasse that had been opened in his soul.

There remains a bare possibility that this plot lifted from an Italian novella came later from Jessie’s imagination rather than from Frémont’s own. Jessie quite frankly threw away any rule book when it came to protecting or comforting her husband. In our curiously asymmetrical sense of the rightness of things, which persists in weighing the act against the purpose, it may seem almost admirable for her to do so but the opposite for Frémont to do the same thing to protect or comfort himself.

Godey came on the two Indian boys in the evening of probably his third day out from Red River, having covered some sixty miles searching his way up the river, firing signal shots at intervals. Joaquin and Gregorio said Vincenthaler’s camp was not far behind them. Godey provisioned the two boys and went on the next morning and found the Vincenthaler camp and the four men remaining there, Vincenthaler and Martin and Bacon and young Ducatel. Vincenthaler later told Fré-

mont that they all cried together like children. Vincenthaler
went on up the river with Godey to where they had left
Scott—Scott was still living. They went on to where they had
left Hubbard. He was dead. His body was still warm.

It would have taken another day's travel for Godey to reach
the vicinity of the Kern camp and here Godey, short-cutting
a bend in the river, missed the Kern camp and came on Ferguson, camped farther up. Ferguson's companion, Beadle, had
died only the night before. Ferguson insisted the Kern camp
was below him and Godey coursed back down the river in
search.

By now the Kerns, Cathcart, McGehee, Stepperfeldt, and
Taplin, become skeletons with wild eyes almost blind and mat-
ted hair and beards, were beginning the sixth day in their
stationary camp. Oddly enough, McGehee, writing his account
not long afterward, remembered it as only three days.

Doc Kern wrote in his letter home: ". . . during a snow
storm as we all sat silently around our little willow fire Taplin
suddenly exclaimed By God there is a halloo. Tis but a wolf
again we said. Rising to his feet he said Christ there's a man on
horseback over the river, we gave a shout you may be sure,
almost in an instant Alexis Godey was with us. Well boys I
am damned glad to find you alive. He then pulled some bread
from his pocket. Oh he has bread we cried and some of us
trembled with joy at the sight of it. Yes boys and there is a
mare you may kill. . . ."

This was January 28, the thirty-third day after the King
party had started for relief from Camp Hope.

Ned Kern wrote, "Here ended our troubles."

Godey left them with food and horses and one of his Taos
muleteers to stay with them and take care of them and went
on up the river. He found the bodies of the old Frenchmen,
Morin and Tabeau called Sorrel: "One lying by the side of a
little fire the other sitting against the bank as if he had been

looking at his friend." He kept on to the river camp at Embargo Creek, only some fifty miles back up the river from the Kern camp. Here in the brush lodge he found Manuel, the Cosumne Indian, still living. Manuel said Carver had come back, out of his mind, and headed into the mountains up Embargo Creek, and Manuel had not seen him again.

Godey tried to get up Embargo with his animals to the Cottonwoods and Seven Mile Camp to recover the baggage cached there, but had several mules frozen and had to give up. He packed aboard a little baggage from the river camp, principally a trunk of Frémont's, and came back down the river, bringing Manuel along, and picking up the other survivors along the way. He arrived back in Taos on February 11, having made the round trip of some 320 miles, hunted down and cared for the survivors, and made his try to get through the snow up Embargo Creek, all in twenty days.

One story has it that when Godey found the Kern camp and the rescued men were telling him a special providence had brought him at that moment because one more day would have been too late for most of them, Godey grinned and said, "Providence, hell. 'Twas good management."

Postscript

By the time Godey had returned with the last of the survivors Frémont had borrowed money to refit what was left of the expedition. Two days later he set out, with those of his men who wanted to go on with him, to travel westward by the Gila route, or even south of that if need be to escape the winter. The Kerns, Taplin, Cathcart, and Stepperfeldt stayed behind. The Kerns at least parted from Frémont in bitterness. The quarrel appears to have had no single cause. Perhaps the principal reason was that the Kerns had lost all their possessions and were left absolutely penniless in a strange land and Frémont did not make good any of their loss, although both sides make it clear that he offered to mount any of the survivors who wanted to go on to California with him. Perhaps general criticism of Frémont's conduct of the expedition was the chief cause of trouble. Undoubtedly the aftermath of the conflict on the river with Vincenthaler, who remained in favor with Frémont, was a factor. Young McGehee was the only survivor of the Kern camp who continued on with Frémont.

Cathcart, after recuperating, went back to England. The Kerns, without any means whatever, found it necessary to borrow a little money from him to live on. Stepperfeldt, while convalescing, went temporarily insane and wandered out on the desert and disappeared. He was later picked up and brought in safely and eventually, Dick Kern wrote to Cathcart, "published Frémont." Taplin went back to Missouri.

No more than two weeks after the Kerns had been brought into Taos, Doc got Old Bill Williams to join him and with Mexican packers and a train of mules went back up the river to the mountains, intending to try to bring down the Kerns' baggage from the camp on Embargo Creek. They never returned.

Tradition holds that they were killed by Utes. One investigating army officer formed the opinion they were killed by Jicarilla Apaches under the bloodthirsty Chico Velasquez, who was said to wear a necklace made of the finger bones of his victims. After their disappearance some of the Mexicans who had been with them were found wearing clothes belonging to Doc and Old Bill, leading to a theory they might have been murdered and robbed by their packers. Certain Ute spokesmen later admitted their people had picked up and distributed the abandoned baggage of the expedition. Nothing definite was ever learned, although Ned and Dick kept various investigations alive for several years.

Dick and Ned stayed in the West and together or separately served as topographers and artists with various exploring expeditions during the next five years. Ned returned to Philadelphia for a year or two in 1851, and sailed for three years with a U.S. Navy surveying and exploring expedition to the North Pacific and the China seas in June 1853 (thus running the westward trail all the way to the Far East), while Dick was setting out with the Gunnison expedition of 1853 to explore the central railroad route that had been the objective of the fourth expedition. The Gunnison expedition made a summer passage of Cochetopa Pass, and in October, Gunnison and a small detachment including Dick Kern and the expedition's botanist, who was Frederick Creutzfeldt, were killed by Paiutes near Sevier Lake, Utah. Captain Charles Taplin had been the wagon master of the Gunnison expedition as far as the San Luis Valley, but ill health had forced him to drop out. Possibly he had never fully recovered from the fourth expedition. He died only two years later.

In 1858 Ned sailed with another Navy expedition, charting a steamship route between San Francisco and the China Coast, and was shipwrecked in a typhoon on the coast of Japan the following year. He came home in 1860 on a Japanese Navy steamship, the first Japanese ship to visit the United States.

Some time during these years Ned and Frémont had become reconciled and Ned served under him once more, as a captain of topographical engineers during Frémont's brief command at St. Louis in the early days of the Civil War. In 1863 Ned, then forty years old, died suddenly in Philadelphia.

On a wartime pass, under the listing of peculiarities, Ned wrote, "Brilliant."

On February 7, 1849, while Godey was bringing in the last survivors from the river, Benton made a speech in the Senate introducing a bill for a "National Road to the Pacific," and took occasion to point with pride to the Frémont fourth expedition, which he assumed had by then gone successfully through to California. On February 21, while Frémont was traveling south down the Rio Grande below Albuquerque, a public meeting was held in St. Louis to acclaim the notion of the National Road to the Pacific, and adopted a resolution of thanks to Frémont for his explorations in the Rockies. It was the presumption of this meeting that the fourth expedition had gone through as scheduled.

It is probably as well that Frémont knew nothing of these praises at the time. The fourth expedition had not found its central pass. The losses of the expedition were ten lives and ten thousand dollars. Instead of restoring himself after the court-martial, he was left deeply in debt and quite possibly his public career was now shattered beyond repair.

But in Taos there was verified news of the discovery of gold in California. On the Gila the Frémont party fell in with a crowd of Mexicans bound from Sonora to the fabulous California gold fields.

The vast, worthless mountain ranch in California, the Mariposas, which Larkin had bought for him instead of the seaside ranch Frémont had wanted, was found to be rich with gold. Later at the Mariposas, after placer mining had already yielded fortunes, Godey made, it was said, the first discovery of gold in the rock in the Mother Lode country.

Eighteen months later Frémont was a millionaire and California's first U.S. senator.

But before this the blot of the court-martial was at least partly effaced, Frémont thought, when the newly elected President, Zachary Taylor, appointed him to serve on the Mexican Boundary Commission (upon which ex-Kearny man Emory, chief astronomer of the Commission, immediately offered his resignation). Frémont wrote: "I regarded that commission as a disavowal on the part of the President of the proceedings recently held against me." Jessie said it represented an official expression of Taylor's expressed opinion at the time of the trial ". . . that it was an outrage." President Taylor was intimately acquainted with the record of the trial, inasmuch as his brother, Colonel J. P. Taylor, had been a member of the court. Frémont accepted the position as a formality for a short time and then resigned.

The rush of population to California made Benton's letter to the Californians, and Buchanan's letter answering it, obsolete documents. There was no longer any question of a fight for territorial status, although as a matter of fact public meetings did spring up demanding that the people take the initiative and establish territorial government without waiting any longer for federal action; these ceased with a proclamation from the military governor in August, 1849, calling for a state constitutional convention. California acquired statehood the next year.

Saunders Jackson was given permission to go up to the Mariposas and wash out enough dirt to buy his family's freedom. Jessie said he accumulated the necessary $1700 in gold dust within a few days.

There were reports in 1849 that Frémont, on entering California, bought the great Rancho Santa Ana del Chino (near Los Angeles) for $200,000. If any such negotiations were begun, he must of course have been acting in the name and on the credit of an eastern investor, since he had no money of his own at that time. Thomas Salathiel Martin, who left the Frémont party here, said he understood Frémont bought this ranch and left Vincenthaler in charge of it.

Cathcart, in England, rejoined the Army for service in the Crimean War, and became Major Cathcart (rejoining too late to accompany his old regiment, the 11th Hussars, in a celebrated blunder at Balaclava known, since Tennyson, as the Charge of the Light Brigade. Before this time he had sent Frémont from London a handsome presentation sword.

In 1853, at last, Frémont made a final effort to expunge the defeat of the fourth expedition. This was his fifth expedition, also in the winter, also over the central Rockies, and without any guide except Frémont himself. This expedition went through Cochetopa Pass and succeeded. This time he met a mild, open winter; the first snowfall was encountered at the summit of the Cochetopa, and until then the valleys and lowlands had been as free of snow as the weather free of storms. Even with this advantage the fifth expedition made it on to Utah only at the cost of great struggle and privation, the death of one man, the loss of the animals, and, finally, the caching of the equipment along the way.

On January 22, 1889, the day after Frémont's seventy-sixth birthday, Jessie wrote to him from Los Angeles (he was in the East on business):

"Dear Heart,

"I would not send you this notice of Godey's death on your birthday."

She related the details of Godey's illness and death, that he had been brought from his home at Bakersfield to Sisters Hospital in Los Angeles at the insistence of ranchers and cattlemen and "millionaire friends," and that his two rooms at the hospital were beautiful.

"I had a surprise in meeting his *widow*. Maybe you knew he was married again? . . . This time to a really uncommonly pretty little thing and a genuine Californian but of a delicate variety. . . . Lil and I were glad he had had a kittenish young life around about his. . . . She is very childish—says 'he left her a good house and she has many silk dresses.' She is so pretty. . . . Only twenty now but already six years' 'casada.' . . ."

This was Godey's fifth wife.

"She was prim and intending to be quite correctly a 'mourner,' but her eyes danced over 'mi casa.' She knew—vaguely—of you, that 'es el Señor que tenga una casa . . . muy grande.' . . ." And Jessie, with obvious delight, quoted the young widow's Spanish to the effect that in this house of Frémont's in Los Angeles there was a room always ready for Godey, when he came to the city. "So you can see Alexis felt sure that what was yours was his to command."

And Jessie said, "I left it at that."

Notes

A NOTE ON THE POEM

The original of this poem, a holograph first draft, is among the Frémont papers at the Southwest Museum, Highland Park, Los Angeles. A later note by Frémont's daughter Lilly guesses the date of composition as 1875.

The exact date is not important. The circumstances of composition are implicit in the poem itself: a distinguished old gentleman, considerably down on his luck, a passenger in a westbound train of sooty parlor cars and diamond-stack locomotive climbing the Continental Divide, is remembering a young man who once passed by here in somewhat different circumstances. And so we have a sentimental journey inside young Lieutenant Frémont personally conducted by white-haired General Frémont, his troubled ghost.

The score of horsemen referred to means the first expedition.

Written on Recrossing the Rocky Mountains
in Winter, after Many Years

Long years ago I wandered here,
In the midsummer of the year,
    Life's summer too.
A score of horsemen here we rode,
The mountain world its glories showed,
    All fair to view.

These scenes in glowing colors drest
Mirrored the life within my breast,
        Its world of hope.
The whispering woods and fragrant breeze
That stirred the grass in verdant seas,
        On billowy slope;

And glistening crag in sunlit sky,
Mid snowy clouds piled mountain high,
        Were joys to me.
My path was o'er the prairie wide,
Or here on grander mountain side,
        To choose all free.

The rose that waved in morning air,
And spread its dewy fragrance there
        In careless bloom
Gave to my heart its (   ) hue
O'er my glad life its color threw
        And sweet perfume.

Now changed the scene and changed the eyes
That here once looked on glowing skies
        When summer smiled.
These riven trees and windswept plain
Now shew the winter's dread domain
        Its fury wild.

The rocks rise black from storm packed snow,
All checked the river's pleasant flow,
        Vanished the bloom.
These dreary wastes of frozen plain
Reflect my bosom's life again
        Now lonesome gloom.

The buoyant hopes and busy life
Have ended all in hateful strife
    And baffled aim.
The world's rude contact killed the rose
No more its shining radiance shows
    False roads to fame.

But here thick clouds the mountains hide
The dim horizon bleak and wide
    No pathway shews.
And rising gusts and darkening sky
Tell of the night that draweth nigh
    The brief day's close.

Where still some grand peaks mark the way
Touched by the light of parting day
    And memory's sun,
Backward amid the twilight glow
Some lingering spots yet brightly show
    On roads hard won.

A NOTE ON THE TRIAL

From Frémont's *Defence before the Court Martial*, published after the trial in a pamphlet of seventy-eight pages: [1]

"In the winter of 1845-6 I approached the settled parts of
Upper California with a party of sixty-two men and about two
hundred horses, in my third expedition of discovery and topographical survey in the remote regions of the great west. . . .

[1] Frémont, *Defence of Lieut. Col. J. C. Frémont before the Military
Court Martial, Washington, January, 1848.*

"I had left the United States in May, 1845—a year before the war with Mexico broke out; but I was aware of the actual state of affairs between the two countries, and being determined to give no cause of offence to the Mexican authorities in California, I left my command at the distance of about two hundred miles from Monterey, and proceeded, almost alone, to the nearest military station, that of New Helvetia (or Suter's Fort) and obtained a passport . . . for myself and attendants to proceed to Monterey, the residence of the commandant general or deputy governor, General Castro.

"Arrived at Monterey, I called upon the commandant and other authorities, in company with the United States consul. . . . Leave was granted [to winter], and also leave to continue my explorations south to the region of the Rio Colorado and of the Rio Gila.

"In the last days of February, I commenced the march south, crossing the valley of the Salinas, or Buenaventura, and soon received a notification to depart, with information that Gen. Castro was assembling troops with a view to attack us. . . . I took a position on the Sierra, called the Hawk's Peak. . . .

". . . after remaining in the position from the 7th to the 10th of March, and seeing that we were not to be attacked in it . . . I quit the position, gave up all thoughts of prosecuting my researches in that direction, and turned north towards Oregon. . . .

". . . We were now at the north end of the Greater Tlamath lake, in the territory of Oregon, when on the morning of the 9th [of May] I was surprised to find ride up to our camp two men—one turned out to be Samuel Neal, formerly of my topographical party, and his companion, who quickly informed me that a United States officer was on my trail, with despatches for me, but he doubted whether he would ever reach me; that he and his companion had only escaped the Indians by the goodness of their horses; and that he had left the officer, with three men, two days behind.

"Upon the spot I took nine men, four of them Delaware Indians, coasted the western shore of the lake for sixty miles, and met the party.

"The officer was Lieutenant Gillespie. He brought me a letter of introduction from the Secretary of State (Mr. Buchanan), and letters and papers from Senator Benton and his family. The letter from the Secretary imported nothing beyond the introduction, and was directed to me in my private or citizen capacity. The outside envelope of a packet from Senator Benton was directed in the same way, and one of the letters from him, while apparently of mere friendship and family details, contained passages enigmatical and obscure, but which I studied out, and made the meaning to be that I was required by the government to find out any foreign schemes in relation to the Californias, and to counteract them. Lieutenant Gillespie was bearer of despatches to the United States consul at Monterey, and was directed to find me wherever I might be; and he had, in fact, travelled above six hundred miles from Monterey, and through great dangers, to reach me.

". . . The arrival of this officer, his letter of introduction, some things which he told me, and the letter from Senator Benton, had a decided influence on my next movement. . . ."

Which was his return to California and, shortly afterward, participation with the American settlers there in an open war against Mexican authority.

These quotations tell less than they leave untold, but they nevertheless contain the clearest statement I have been able to find of Frémont's own explanation of two puzzling matters: the Hawk's Peak episode, and the more important and more intriguing question of what instructions, if any, Lieutenant Gillespie brought to Frémont from Benton.

In his *Memoirs* Frémont describes one foreign scheme in relation to California of the sort that Benton so much feared: the plan of one Father MacNamara to colonize California with Irishmen—Ireland was then suffering the terrible desolation of the potato famines. Frémont states that a grant of some thirteen million acres was approved by the Mexican government for Father MacNamara on July 7, 1846, but on the morning of that day the American flag was raised at Monterey, ending Mexican authority. Frémont also quotes the English Admiral Seymour, arriving in Monterey Bay in July a few days after the vacillating Commodore Sloat had raised the American flag there, as saying, "Sloat, if your flag was not flying on shore I should have hoisted mine there." Father Mac-Namara, after the wreck of his hopes, left California in Admiral Seymour's flagship, the *Collingwood*.[2]

But Benton's "instructions" to Frémont would undoubtedly have been limited to counteracting foreign schemes, for Benton was opposed to an aggressive war of conquest against Mexico.[3]

Commodore Stockton sailed for the Pacific with orders, dated in October 1845, to proceed to the Sandwich Islands and accomplish certain duties and then join Commodore Sloat's squadron off California.

On July 12, 1846, the war with Mexico now being under

[2] Frémont, *Memoirs of My Life*, Vol. 1 (Chicago and New York: 1887).

[3] James K. Polk, *Diaries*, M. M. Quaife, ed. (Chicago: 1910), "Monday, 11 May 1846: Col. Benton called . . . and I gave him the copy of the message [to Congress, demanding declaration of war] and he retired to an adjoining room to read it. . . . I found he did not approve of it in all its parts. He was willing to vote men and money for defence of our territory, but was not prepared to make aggressive war on Mexico. He disapproved the marching of the army from Corpus Christi to the left Bank of the Rio del Norte, but said he had never said so to the public. I had a full conversation with him, and he left without satisfying me that I could rely upon his support of the measures recommended by the message, further than the mere defence of our territory."

way, Secretary of the Navy George Bancroft sent the following orders to Commodore Sloat:

". . . The object of the United States is, under its rights as a belligerent nation, to possess itself entirely of Upper California.

". . . This will bring with it the necessity of a civil administration. Such a government should be established, under your protection. . . ." [4]

In July, when Stockton arrived at Monterey, Commodore Sloat turned the command over to him and went home. In August, Stockton wrote to Secretary Bancroft:

"You have already been informed of my having, on the 23d of July, assumed the command of the United States forces on the west coast of Mexico. I have now the honor to inform you that the flag of the United States is flying from every commanding position in the territory of California, and that this rich and beautiful country belongs to the United States, and is forever free from Mexican dominion.

"On the day after I took this command I organized the California battalion of mounted riflemen, by the appointment of all the necessary officers, and received them as volunteers into the service of the United States; Captain Frémont was appointed major, and Lieutenant Gillespie, captain of the battalion. . . .

". . . in less than a month after I assumed the command of the United States forces in California, we have chased the Mexican army more than 300 miles along the coast; pursued them 30 miles in the interior of their own country; routed and dispersed them, and secured the territory to the United States; ended the war; restored peace and harmony among the people, and put a civil government into successful operation.

[4] *Proceedings of the Court Martial in the Trial of Lt. Col. Frémont* (Senate Exec. Doc. No. 33, 30th Congress, 1st Session, April 7, 1848).

". . . having almost finished my work here, I will sail in the *Congress* as soon as the store-ship arrives. . . .

"When I leave the territory, I will appoint Major Frémont to be governor. . . ."[5]

This jubilant news was sent East overland in the hands of Kit Carson. The same news was received in Mexico, in official communications from General Castro, the Mexican commander in California, who fled without giving battle, and the Mexican government announced, on October 16: "The loss of the Californias is consummated."[6]

In the meantime, in Washington, an army regiment of mounted rifles had been organized, of which Frémont was named lieutenant colonel. Previously, Frémont had held his commissions in the Corps of Topographical Engineers, which was not a Regular Army unit and was officered with both Regular Army men and technicians, such as Frémont, appointed to it from civil life.[7]

Doubtless his skyrocket rise to fame had already created certain envies within the Topographical Corps itself. His selection for this elite Regular Army lieutenant colonelcy of the new mounted rifles, over West Point men who regarded him as little more than a son-of-a-politician civilian, would have created a very natural bitterness in still other quarters. Captain Philip St. George Cooke, of the 1st Dragoons, apparently applied in person in Washington for the lieutenant colonelcy of this new

[5] *Ibid.*, letter from Stockton to Bancroft, Ciudad de Los Angeles, August 28, 1846.

[6] *Ibid.*, Report of Secretary of War Marcy, December 5, 1846.

[7] Frémont's commission in the Topographical Corps, dated July 9, 1838, came soon after a reorganization of the corps which provided that half the corps should be taken from the civil service. His status in the corps led Frémont to state in his *Defence before the Court Martial* that at the start of his third expedition, "I was then brevet captain in the corps of topographical engineers, and had no rank in the army, nor did an officer or soldier of the United States army accompany me. . . ."

regiment, and was refused it.[8] Captain Cooke was later promoted to major of the 2d Dragoons but did not learn of this for some time, being then with General Kearny's Army of the West. Under Kearny he commanded the battalion of Mormon volunteers, and was given an appointment as lieutenant colonel from Kearny.

Late in June, while the Bear Flag revolt was under way in California, Colonel Kearny, freshly brevetted brigadier, left Fort Leavenworth with his Army of the West. His orders, from Secretary of War W. L. Marcy, dated in June, read:

"Should you conquer and take possession of New Mexico and Upper California, or considerable places in either, you will establish temporary civil governments therein. . . ."[9]

Further orders, dated a few days later, spoke of additional forces, a regiment of New York volunteers being sent to California by sea, and stated: "These troops and such as may be organized in California, will be under your command."[10]

Kearny also had a letter from his old friend, Senator Benton, telling him he was to be the civil and military governor of the territory of California.[11]

The conquest of New Mexico by Kearny was even more bloodless than the conquest of California by Stockton, and took place about the same time, in August.

Kearny then marched for California with a force of 300 dragoons, leaving the rest of his army in New Mexico. Eleven days and 150 miles out of Santa Fe, Kearny met Kit Carson and party, twenty-six days and 800 miles out of Los Angeles. Carson was en route East with Stockton's word of victory in California. Kearny, at this news, trimmed his escort down to only 100 dragoons, sent Carson's dispatches on East by an-

[8] *Proceedings of the Court Martial, op. cit.*, questioning of Cooke.
[9] *Ibid.*, orders from Secretary of War Marcy to Kearny, June 3, 1846.
[10] *Ibid.*, June 18, 1846.
[11] *Ibid.*, Kearny's testimony.

other messenger (Tom Fitzpatrick), and commandeered Kit to do an about-face and go back to California with him as guide.

On November 24, at the junction of the Gila and the Colorado, Kearny captured a Mexican bearing letters from California to General Castro in Mexico. These letters informed him that southern California had risen in revolt and that the Americans had been driven out of Santa Barbara and Los Angeles.[12] Fortunately the Kearny column had, the day before, captured 500 California horses being driven to Mexico,[13] and with these fresh mounts staged on with all speed for California.

In California, Stockton had left a garrison of about fifty men at Los Angeles and San Pedro, and still smaller garrison forces to hold Santa Barbara and San Diego, had named Frémont military commandant of California (September 2) and sent him up to the Sacramento Valley to recruit his battalion to full strength, and had then sailed away with his marines to make himself useful along the west coast of Mexico. Late in September the Californians had revolted in the south and driven out the garrisons from these four places. Stockton returned hastily at this news and by the first of December had reoccupied San Pedro and San Diego. He now heard of Kearny's approach, and sent a small escort out to meet him.

The Kearny column, together with this escort, came upon a band of native Californian troops at San Pascual, near San Diego, and in the following battle suffered heavy casualties and the loss of one of two howitzers Kearny was dragging along with him. Request for reinforcements was sent to Stockton at San Diego. Kearny's men were burning their baggage and preparing to cut their way through the enemy on a dash to San

[12] W. H. Emory, "Report of a Military Reconnaissance, 1846-7," in U. S. War Department, *Reports of Explorations and Surveys, etc.*, Vol. 2 (Washington: 1855).
[13] *Ibid.*

Diego when reinforcements, some 200 sailors and marines, appeared. The Californians vanished, and Kearny entered San Diego on December 12.

A month after this, Stockton moved on Los Angeles with the largest force he had been able to gather, 600 men more or less, including fifty-odd of Kearny's dragoons. Stockton held the title of commander-in-chief and General Kearny served as field commander under him, by courtesy of Stockton's invitation.[14]

At the same time Frémont was floundering down from the north—this was January 1847, and the rainy season was at hand along the Coast—with all the men he had been able to scrape together, more than 400. Los Angeles was retaken, with some noisy cannonading but little bloodshed, before Frémont arrived. The Californian commander then sought out Frémont, approaching north of town, and surrendered to him, and the California conquest was secure in all quarters for a second and final time.

This was the situation, after the recapture of Los Angeles, when Kearny showed his orders (". . . troops . . . such as may be organized in California will be under your command," and "Should you conquer and take possession of . . . Upper California . . . you will establish temporary civil governments therein. . . .") and demanded the place of command.

The Navy orders to Sloat, to which Stockton as his successor would fall heir (". . . take and hold possession of California. . . . This will bring with it the necessity of a civil administration. Such a government should be established, under your protection. . . ."), had been issued a month after Kearny's Army orders. However, Stockton had not yet received these orders. Nevertheless he indignantly rejected Kearny's assumption of authority. He sent word to Frémont "that he had full and

[14] *Proceedings of the Court Martial, op. cit.*

plenary instructions carried out by him sealed, not to be opened until he reached a given point; but he would not exhibit them like slaves did their papers; that he had no fear of his power being impaired by the instructions to General Kearny. . . ." [15]

The important stake in this quarrel was the title of Conqueror of California. Stockton may scarcely be blamed for feeling that Kearny had contributed nothing to either the conquest or reconquest, the help of his few dragoons at Los Angeles being more than offset by the nuisance of having to extricate him from San Pascual. But to the recognized commander in chief would go the claim of conquest, in the way of such things, regardless of the value of his direct participation. Kearny's bloodless conquest of New Mexico had also been temporarily upset by the Taos rebellion, with a greater loss of life, including the murder of the governor Kearny had named for the territory, than had occurred in the California revolt, and necessitating a bloody battle to put it down. But Kearny was still technically in command there and even though these events, entailing the only fighting met in New Mexico, took place in his absence, his position as conqueror of New Mexico remained unshaken.

While this quarrel stood at loggerheads, Kearny heard that Stockton had issued orders to Frémont concerning the reorganization of the California Battalion, and immediately issued orders of his own forbidding Frémont to obey. His purpose was to force Frémont to choose between his authority and Stockton's. He did not know the nature of the reorganization Stockton had ordered; he merely gave "orders to Lt. Col. Frémont against it." [16] (Stockton's orders had the object of naming a new battalion major in Frémont's place, thus freeing Frémont for appointment as civil governor of California.)

[15] *Ibid.*
[16] *Ibid.*, Kearny's testimony.

Frémont decided to obey Stockton. The battalion had been taken into the U.S. service by Stockton and had served under Stockton for almost six months before Kearny's sudden and unheralded appearance on the scene, and Stockton assured Frémont that he had sound authority for the chief command in California. Frémont feld bound to continue to recognize Stockton's claim to authority over the battalion.

Frémont then talked to Kearny, urging him to have a personal interview with Stockton, expressing his hope and belief that everything could be settled between them in such an interview. Kearny said he was willing to have such an interview, but would not ask for it. While Frémont was attempting to arrange this interview, Kearny left Los Angeles, on the morning of January 18, 1847. He departed without notice to Frémont, and without waiting for him to bring an answer from Stockton. Kearny said, "I sent no message to Commodore Stockton; and, therefore, could not expect an answer to be brought to me." [17]

During Frémont's conversation with Kearny, Kearny also offered him the governorship of California, affirming that it had been his intention all along to name Frémont governor.[18]

Kearny, when he left Los Angeles, sent a letter to Stockton saying he was remaining silent for the present "for the purpose of preventing collision between us, and, possibly, a civil war in consequence of it. . . ." [19] He wrote to the Secretary of

[17] *Ibid.*

[18] The sum of the evidence in the *Proceedings of the Court Martial* supports this conclusion and therefore supports the conclusion that Kearny, who gave a picture of Frémont cynically proposing to bargain for the governorship, was deliberately misrepresenting the facts. This accusation, weak though it was, outraged Frémont more than any other development of the trial. In his published *Defence* he made "the declaration upon responsibilities infinitely Higher than those of military honor or commission, that Brigadier General Kearny, in all that he has testified in relation to this governorship, has borne false witness against me."

[19] *Proceedings of the Court Martial, op. cit.,* Kearny to Stockton, January 17, 1847.

War at about the same time saying that when more troops arrived he would, ". . . agreeably to the instructions of the President, have the management of affairs in this country. . . ." [20] He stated definitely later that ". . . if I had troops under me, I would never permit a junior officer to disobey my orders." [21]

In the meantime, back in Washington, the War and Navy Departments had made an effort to head off this collision. Army orders were dispatched to Kearny on November 3, 1846, and Navy orders to Stockton on November 5. A new commodore, Shubrick, was already on his way, started early in September as a routine replacement for Sloat.

There was also a new Secretary of the Navy, Judge J. Y. Mason. He wrote to Stockton in the orders of November 5 that the naval commander was to relinquish to General Kearny or to Colonel Mason, his successor, then en route to California, "the direction of operations on land," and "control over the administrative functions of government," and to "turn over to him all papers necessary to the performance" of these duties. He added, "The President directs me to impress most earnestly on the naval officers, as it is impressed on those of the army, the importance of harmony in the performance of their delicate duties while cooperating. They are arms of one body, and will, I doubt not, vie with each other in showing which can render the most efficient aid to the other in the execution of common orders, and in sustaining the national honor, which is confided to both." [22]

Kearny received, together with his orders of November 3 sustaining his authority to organize a civil administration, an extract from the army regulations as to the relative rank between army and navy officers. These orders were from General Winfield Scott, who added, "I need scarcely enjoin defer-

[20] *Ibid.*, Kearny to Secretary of War, January 14, 1847.
[21] *Ibid.*, Kearny's testimony.
[22] *Ibid.*, Navy Department orders to Stockton, November 5, 1846.

ence, and the utmost cordiality on the part of our land forces, towards those of our navy in the joint service on the distant coast of California—reciprocity may be confidently expected; and towards that end, frequent conferences between commanders of the two arms are recommended. Harmony in cooperation and success cannot but follow." The orders included a paragraph dealing specifically with Frémont: "Should you find him there [in California], it is desired that you do not detain him, against his wishes, a moment longer than the necessities of the service may require." [23]

By the time these clarifying orders arrived in California (February 13, 1847), Frémont and Kearny were established as rival governors, Frémont at Los Angeles and Kearny at Monterey. The orders were never formally communicated to Frémont, but the decision they announced must have quickly become common knowledge. Perhaps rumor of the verdict even preceded the delivery of the orders, for three captains and five lieutenants resigned from Frémont's battalion on the same day the orders were received in Monterey.[24]

On this same day a letter went from Commodore Shubrick, who had now appeared and was at Monterey with Kearny, to Frémont, saying, "General Kearny, I am instructed, is the commanding military officer in California, and invested by the President with the administrative functions of government over the people and territory. . . ." [25]

On March 4 Kearny and Shubrick drew up a joint proclamation, dated March 1, asserting Kearny's authority over the civil government. This was printed and distributed in Monterey and a copy was sent to Frémont along with orders from Kearny,[26] the first communication Frémont had had from him since Kearny had left Los Angeles.

[23] *Ibid.*, Army Department orders to Kearny, November 3, 1846.
[24] *Proceedings of the Court Martial, op. cit.*
[25] *Ibid.*, Shubrick to Frémont, February 13, 1847.
[26] *Ibid.*, Order No. 2, 10th Military Department, March 1, 1847.

These orders instructed Frémont to discharge his battalion. Frémont, in reply, had a letter written by his "Secretary of State" to Lieutenant Colonel Cooke, commanding the district in which his battalion was serving, stating that "Governor Frémont" did not feel it safe at this time, rumors of another insurrection being rife, to discharge his force, "and will decline doing so. . . ." [27] Frémont then left Captain Dick Owens in charge of the battalion at Los Angeles, with orders to hold fast and obey no one but him, and rode to Monterey to see Kearny in person.

At Monterey Frémont asked Kearny if he would assume the government responsibilities accruing during the time Frémont was acting as governor. These amounted to some $20,000. Kearny said he would not assume one cent of those liabilities. Frémont offered his resignation, which Kearny would not accept. Kearny was only interested in knowing if Frémont was now prepared to obey his orders. Frémont, after some hesitation, said he would obey.

These were the events which gave rise to the court-martial. Frémont was tried on three charges: mutiny, eleven specifications; disobedience of the lawful command of his superior officer, seven specifications; and conduct to the prejudice of good order and military discipline, three specifications. All the specifications except two were based on incidents occurring before the dispute over authority was resolved by receipt of the new clarifying orders from Washington of November 3 and 5. Specifications No. 7 and No. 8 of the charge of mutiny dealt with the letter to Cooke refusing to discharge the battalion, and Frémont's instructions to Dick Owens to hold fast and obey no one but him while Frémont rode to Monterey, both occurring after the receipt of the clarifying orders.

Benton wrote to Frémont, ". . . in looking over the specifi-

[27] *Ibid.*, Wm. H. Russell to Cooke, March 16, 1847.

cations, I find all of them to be anterior to the settlement of the question of rank with Shubrick, and consequently all amounting to the same thing. I do not know when the question was militarily, or regularly, communicated to you, but, *if so communicated at all,* it must have been late in March, consequently all the specifications refer to acts done before Kearny had relieved you of the land command, and made that change known to you." [28]

As has been seen, this was not quite exact, specifications No. 7 and No. 8 of the charge of mutiny coming after the settlement of the question of rank.

However, the orders from Washington settling this question were never "militarily or regularly" communicated to Frémont, and his defense tried to make a point of this at the trial, implying that Kearny had deliberately withheld the orders to lure Frémont into further resistance. Kearny answered that he was not in the habit of showing junior officers his orders.

But even without formal display of pronouncement from Washington, Frémont could hardly have been in doubt that the game was up at the time he resisted Kearny's orders of March 1. It is worth noting that the letter to Cooke does not question Kearny's authority to issue the orders of March 1, but presents reasons against carrying them out "at this time." It seems clear that Frémont was only interested in a delay until he could ride to Monterey and see Kearny. He wanted to hold his pretense of governorship, also, until Kearny should relieve him of it in a manner formal enough to also relieve him of the $20,000 worth of liabilities he had contracted in the government's name. He wanted, in a word, a negotiated peace. But he was looking for noon at two o'clock.

It would seem then that specifications No. 7 and No. 8 of the first charge might hold some water. The other specifications,

[28] Benton to Frémont, Woodford County, Kentucky, October 8, 1847 (MS in the Southwest Museum).

based on acts occurring while Frémont was, as the president of the court put it, "placed between two officers of superior rank, each claiming to be commander-in-chief in California," would certainly seem to furnish an absurdly thin case for willful disobedience or prejudicial conduct, let alone mutiny.

But the court, in a divided opinion, found Frémont guilty on all eleven specifications of the first charge, mutiny; guilty on all seven specifications of the second charge, disobedience; guilty on all five specifications of the third charge, prejudicial conduct.

My own opinion, after spending some weeks in study of the hundreds of printed pages of the proceedings of the trial, is that Frémont received an astonishingly raw deal indeed from the time of his unconditional surrender to Kearny at Monterey. He was given a bad time at the hands of Kearny and his officers, particularly Cooke and Mason (a duel with Colonel Mason was challenged but never executed), and he was not warned of intended arrest until he was at Fort Leavenworth, far from California where were pertinent witnesses and records. In the course of the trial Kearny perjured himself too often for charitable interpretation, and this even though only written questioning was permitted. And in the end the decision was one that can only be considered, in the light of the evidence, unjust.

A NOTE ON THE TRAILS

At some time following the disaster of the fourth expedition someone sat down and wrote a letter, dated Don Fernando de Taos (presumably "San Fernando de Taos" was meant), New Mexico, 22d Aug., 1850. The letter began, "Dear Sir: Your letter requesting information from me of certain passes . . . has been received. . . ." It then discussed westward passes out of the San Luis Valley, saying there were only two "practical and travelled roads," one falling on the Bunkara and the other, farther west, falling on "the Cuchitope a branch of the compadre. . . ." The letter went on to speak of Bill Williams' knowledge of these passes: "His knowledge of that part of the country was perfect." It concluded, "The course which was taken by Col. Fremont was an impracticable one in winter—and no sensible mountaineer would ever for a moment have entertained the idea of taking it. As no road ever existed there known either to the trapper or the Indian." The letter was signed "Antoini Leroux." [1]

It is interesting to speculate on who may have written this letter. It almost certainly was not Antoine Leroux.

The letter turned up in the extremely valuable collection of Kern letters and documents, long believed irretrievably lost, that was suddenly brought to light in 1921. Called the Fort Sutter Papers, the collection contains many important manuscript items relating to the California conquest, the fourth expedition, and some later activities of the Kern brothers. The circumstances of the collection's discovery, after so long a time, were not revealed.[2]

[1] Letter from Antoine Leroux to unknown addressee, Taos, August 22, 1850 (Fort Sutter Papers, Huntington Library).

[2] The *Huntington Library Bulletin* speaking of the Fort Sutter Papers says the collection "was purchased at the sale of 28 November 1921 in the Anderson Galleries, New York, through the agency of Dr. Rosenbach (owner Edward Eberstadt, who bought from Forrest Sweet, who purchased from Gunther of Chicago). (Mr. Sweet says, 'No further information.')" It has been suggested that this collection may include papers lost by Ned Kern on the fourth expedition, but that seems pretty fanciful. Letters from Kern as late as 1853, four years after the papers were abandoned in the snow, reveal that he has not yet recovered them, and indicate no hope of now doing so. (E. M. Kern to Gillespie, March 11, 1853, and R. H. Kern to Bartlett, ca.1851, Huntington Library.) The California papers in the collection are probably made up of copies and allied papers left in Philadelphia.

The Leroux letter has caused considerable mischief. It has been regarded as a weighty piece of evidence, maybe the weightiest, supporting the theory that Frémont overruled Old Bill and plunged into a false pass of his own choosing.

But it is impossible to reconcile the geography in the letter with the actual features of the country described. The letter says of one of the two passes that it "falls on the Bunkara." The Bunkara or the Blue were names given by the trappers to the north fork of Grand River—what is now the Colorado River above Grand Junction. The nearest point of the Bunkara or any of its forks is far removed from the San Luis Valley. It is necessary to travel some sixty miles from the edge of the San Luis Valley to reach the first beginnings of the waters of the Bunkara—and to travel in a direction not westerly but north. Obviously such a pass could not be. This asserted pass is called in the letter "Rubidoux road." The other of the two passes was, the letter states, "discovered and first travelled by myself." This pass is described as crossing the mountain considerably to the west of "Rubidoux road." It "commences at the del Norte near where it takes its final western turn, and although the ascent of the mountain is somewhat steep, the summit is soon arrived at, and the descent practicable at all seasons of the year. This road falls on the Cuchitope a branch of the compadre—it is well known to most of the hunters and trappers—and Bill Williams has himself travelled it several times in company with me." This is a fairly accurate description of an actual pass, except that the "Cuchitope" (Cochetopa) is not a branch of the "Compadre" (Uncompahgre). They are separated from each other by some fifty mountain miles.

Errors of this sort are unaccountable, coming from the famous guide Antoine Leroux. They would be understandable, with their threads of accuracy mixed with strands of fallacy, coming from someone describing the passes by hearsay and with the help of an incorrect map.

Further, a number of points in the letter are contradicted in other statements made by Leroux himself.

In 1853 Senator Benton wrote a *Letter to the People of Missouri* arguing for the advantages of a central railroad route to the Pacific.[3] He included in this letter a statement from "Mr. Antoine Leroux, the best qualified man in the world to speak on the subject." The authenticity of this Leroux statement is apparently unquestionable.[4] It is at odds with the Leroux letter on nearly every point. The same man could scarcely have authored both.

The statement is squarely opposed to the letter on the issue of who lost the way on the fourth expedition. The letter tends to exonerate Old Bill and throw the blame on Frémont. The statement says, "Col. Frémont was looking for the Coo-cha-tope Pass in the winter of 1848-9, and was near enough to have seen it, if it had not been hid by the lapping of the mountains, when his guide led him off into the mountains. . . ."

The letter speaks of a pass "discovered and first travelled by myself." The statement makes no such claim but says that on

[3] *Letter from Col. Benton to the People of Missouri* (Washington: March 4, 1853). This letter is dated the day following the passage by Congress of a bill authorizing the Pacific railroad surveys, to be carried out under the direction of Jefferson Davis, then Secretary of War. Jeff Davis, with his Southern sympathies, could be expected to favor a southern route. Benton, stating that the southern (Memphis) route "has monopolized attention and acquired an engrossing prominence," anticipates that view and attacks it with this letter.

[4] The Benton letter says, "It has so happened that Mr. Antoine Leroux . . . has arrived here also [in Washington]; and from him I have received the information, embodied in a formal statement. . . ." The statement formally begins: "At the request of Col. Benton, I, Antoine Leroux, native of St. Louis of Missouri, and now an inhabitant of Taos, in New Mexico, do make the following statement in relation to the Pass at the head of the valley of the del Norte . . ." and formally concludes: "Antoine Leroux, Washington City, March 1, 1853." The Benton letter, including Leroux's statement, was given as much publicity as Benton could get for it, a reasonably sound indication in itself of the statement's legitimacy.

the map "made by Lieut. Parke and Mr. R. H. Kern," Cochetopa Pass "is there named after me, because I gave Lieut.
Parke information about it." [5] But this pass "has been known
to the Spaniards ever since they settled in New Mexico, and
by the Indians always."

The statement differs from the letter in mentioning that
in the mountains along the upper Rio Grande, a little south
of the Cochetopa, "there is also a summer Pass, but none for
the winter on account of the snow in it."

The statement describes Cochetopa Pass and the country
roundabout with considerable over-all accuracy, with only one
slip of memory, in saying Cochetopa Creek when Saguache
Creek, its opposite number over the Divide, was meant.

The pass falling "on the Cuchitope" of the letter, with its
"somewhat steep" ascent of the mountain, could not very
credibly be the broad and level Cochetopa Pass, "eight miles
wide," of the statement.

And one very minor but significant point of disagreement
between the statement and the letter should be noticed. In
the letter Leroux says that for "twenty or twenty-two years" he
has been familiar with the mountains in question. In the statement he relates that he first went to the Rockies with "Gen.
Ashley and Major Henry" in 1820, and that two years later
he went to Taos, and "from that place I carried on the business
of a beaver trapper for about fifteen years, generally on the

[5] Map of the Territory of New Mexico, 1851, compiled by Lt. John
G. Parke, drawn by R. H. Kern. A portion of this map is reproduced
in the end papers of this book. The pass there named after Leroux does
not in the least coincide with Cochetopa Pass. The pass there named after
Robidoux would be a more likely candidate. The statement, which fits so
well the real topography of the country, cannot be made to fit the
nomenclature of the passes on the map, in spite of the fact that Leroux,
in the course of the statement, praises the map as "the best one I have
seen of that part of the country," and does not remark the confusion
of names. Clearly, the map played no part in providing the information
in the statement.

waters of the Great Colorado of the West; and have trapped
the whole country, every river, creek, and branch from the
Gila to the head of the Grand River fork of the Upper Colorado, and out to the Great Salt Lake, and on the waters of
the Wah-Satch Mountain, and out to the Virgen River, and
have been four times to California, and guide to a great many
American officers employed in Mexico, and know the country
from New Mexico to California." This means he had been
familiar with the mountains in question since 1822, or, by 1850,
the date of the letter, for twenty-eight years, not twenty or
twenty-two. Whatever their other faults, mountain men were
never in the habit of understating the time they had been in
the mountains.

The statement ends, "And everything that I tell I can show,
and would undertake to guide a party safe through with wagons now."

A few months later he got a chance to prove it. The expedition sent out to explore "the route near the thirty-eighth and
thirty-ninth parallels," as part of the Pacific railroad surveys
just authorized by Congress, arrived in the San Luis Valley
in August 1853.[6] It was a wagon expedition, under the command of Captain John W. Gunnison, and including among its
people Dick Kern and Frederick Creutzfeldt of the fourth
expedition. Leroux was hired to come up from Taos and guide
the Gunnison party westward over the mountains from the
San Luis Valley.

He took them over Cochetopa Pass but evidently described
as well Carnero Pass, "equal if not superior to that of our
route," in the words of the report of the expedition, a pass
crossing the Continental Divide from the extreme headwaters
of Saguache Creek.

6 U.S. War Department, *Reports of Explorations and Surveys to ascertain the most practicable and economical route for a railroad from the
Mississippi River to the Pacific Ocean*, Vol. 2 (Washington: 1855).

Carnero Pass was in fact pointed out while the expedition traversed the Cochetopa: ". . . its summit does not appear more elevated than that of the Coochetopa, and its western descent much more favorable for a road. Our guide, Leroux, represented its approach from the east, however, as more abrupt than that of the Coochetopa Pass, and did not think it practicable for our wagons to pass through the rocks and timber which obstruct it, without more labor than our limited time and the season of the year would warrant. . . ."

But this Carnero Pass, with which Leroux is thus shown to be familiar, is not included in the Leroux letter of 1850. Combining the information in the statement and the Gunnison report, Leroux testifies to his knowledge of three western passes out of the San Luis Valley: Cochetopa, Carnero, and the "summer Pass" crossing the mountains from the upper Rio Grande. These passes do not agree in number or in description with the two passes named in the Leroux letter.

A little more, and we'll be done with the letter and can have a closer look at these three passes.

The letter is in manuscript, and presumably in Leroux's handwriting. Various words are stricken out or corrected, eliminating the possibility that it is a copy. On the contrary, it appears to be a first draft. But the handwriting, practiced and flowing, has no look of the fist of a mountain man.

A witnessed signature of Leroux's was located and compared with the signature on the letter.[7] The two are entirely different.

[7] Bond for license for trading with Comanches to Antoine Leroux et al., Abiquiu, New Mexico, December 29, 1849 (Ritch Collection, Huntington Library). This bond is signed by Leroux and one cosigner. A third cosigner signs with his mark. It is signed by two witnesses. It is dated within a few months of the date of the Leroux letter. The signature on the bond exhibits the labored look of a mountaineer's hand. It differs radically from the signature on the letter not only in the general features of the handwriting but in the formation of various specific characters, for example, using a printed capital A where the letter uses script.

Why was this letter composed? It states, to the unnamed addressee: "Your letter requesting information from me of certain passes through the Cha-ouach mountains has been received and in reply I have to state as follows. . . ." The reply is not only brief and, as we have seen, erroneous, but more than one fourth of it is taken up with a defense of Old Bill and an indictment of Frémont. The letter emphasizes this note and concludes on this note, and this note is apparently its reason for being.

The fourth expedition became a minor issue in the Presidential campaign of 1856, when Frémont was the Republican candidate. A letter defending Frémont on this issue was published over Godey's signature.[8] This letter fumbles facts, transposing the position of Cochetopa and Carnero Passes, and in general displays the embroidered look of campaign literature.[9] The Godey letter specifically refutes a "statement made by the Messrs Kerns," and maybe the Leroux letter played some part in these or similar charges.[10]

[8] Letter from Alexis Godey, September 12, 1856, published in the New York *Evening Post*, October 30, 1856. Quoted in Nevins, *Frémont, Pathmarker of the West* (New York: 1939).

[9] Alpheus Favour, in *Old Bill Williams* (Chapel Hill, N. C.: 1936), outlines the case against the reliability of the Godey letter.

[10] J. H. Simpson, an officer of the Topographical Corps with whose expeditions both Ned and Dick Kern had served, and who was active in the opposition to Frémont's candidacy, wrote in August 1856 to Ned Kern, then in Philadelphia: "Yours of the 12th inst was handed to me yesterday afternoon at Washington just as I was setting off for this place. I regret exceedingly that I could not have met you, particularly now that I have given to the public the letter your brother Richard left with me. [Richard had died three years before.] I have often thought that it was in your power to give expression to facts as they occurred in respect to Frémont's disaster above Taos, that would be of the greatest interest to the public, particularly now that Frémont is up for the Presidency. . . . Should you agree with me in this and feel so disposed, I would be glad to receive a letter from you, corroborating, and making more complete, if possible, the facts in relation to the disaster referred to." Letter from J. H. Simpson to Edward M. Kern, Annapolis, August 14, 1856 (Huntington Library).

Whoever wrote the Leroux letter had some bits of genuine information at hand. The pass described as the one discovered and first traveled by Leroux, and as falling on Cochetopa Creek, is a fairly good picture, not of the Cochetopa Pass as has usually been assumed, but of the Pass of the Rio del Norte, the pass mentioned in the Leroux statement as a "summer Pass."

The writer of the letter also consulted, evidently, the map drawn by Charles Preuss that accompanied Frémont's *Geographical Memoir* of 1848. This map shows the Bunkara far south of its correct heading. An identical error is committed by the author of the letter.

The letter also bears more than an incidental relationship to the Parke-Kern map of 1851, although going astray from the map in a number of instances. But the Parke-Kern map was published a year after the date of the letter. Since Leroux is credited on that map as one of the sources of the information on which the map was based it is possible the author of the letter had access to that information and based the letter on a fragmentary reading or recollection. Curiously enough, some of the extraordinary errors of the letter do appear on a map, one published at Philadelphia about 1856.[11]

One last and obvious point about the Leroux letter: its author was bitter enough, or aroused enough by some emotion, to take pen in hand and fabricate it.

An informal expedition headed by Edward Fitzgerald Beale preceded the Gunnison expedition through the San Luis Valley and westward by a couple of months. A Taos hunter and trader named Felipe Archilete (Archuleta), called Pegleg because

[11] "A New Map of the State of California, the Territories of Oregon, Washington, Utah, and New Mexico," Charles Desilver, publisher (Philadelphia: *ca.*1856). This map shows "Lareau Pass" approximately at Poncha Pass (the northern gateway of the San Luis Valley) and "Coochatope Pass" approximately fifty miles still farther north—and falling on the Bunkara.

he carried a wooden leg strapped to his belt to do occasional service for a foot that had been crippled in an Indian fight, was engaged as guide. The three western passes described in the report of this expedition [12] tally very well with the three passes named by Leroux in the statement and the Gunnison report.

They were, according to Harris Heap, the writer of the report, Cochetopa Pass; Carnero Pass, roughly parallel with the Cochetopa but considerably south of it; and the Pass of the Rio del Norte, crossing the Divide directly from the cañon of the upper Rio Grande.

Cochetopa Pass had two principal entrances, one via Saguache Creek from the top of the San Luis Valley, and one angling into it via Carnero Creek from lower down in the valley. Heap traveled this Carnero Creek entrance. He said it was the nearest for travelers coming up from the center of the valley. It was "called by the Spaniards El Rincon del Sahwatch (the corner of the Sahwatch), as it forms a cutoff into Sahwatch valley proper. The main entrance is a few miles farther on. . . ."

Heap also traveled part of Carnero Pass itself, which he called "Puerto del Carnero (Mt. Sheep Pass)," and affirmed that it was a shorter route than the Cochetopa and "proved to be, in many respects, superior even to the Coochetope."

Forty-some miles on beyond the Cochetopa they reached the spot where the trail "through the Carnero Pass joins that through the Coochetope. Traders from Abiquiu come by it into these mountains to barter for peltries with the Utahs."

Of the Pass of the Rio del Norte, Heap wrote, "Americans called it Williams' Pass, in honor of Old Bill Williams, who discovered it." It was the "shortest road to Grand River, one

[12] Gwinn Harris Heap, *Central Route to the Pacific, etc.*, with map compiled and drawn by Heap (Philadelphia, 1854).

day shorter than the Carnero and two days shorter than the Coochatope."

Leroux Pass, as shown on the Dick Kern map of 1851, taking off as it does from far up the cañon of the Rio Grande, is a very likely representation of the Pass of the Rio del Norte. In its description of the same pass the Leroux letter is also accurate, even more so than the map, in fact, in this one instance. The letter speaks of Leroux Pass commencing "at the del Norte near where it takes its final western turn." which would be near what is now Creede, Colorado, while the map shows the pass at the very head of the river.

The Pass of the Rio del Norte has been forgotten today, but a recent letter from Ambrose Burkhart, formerly Senior Clerk in the Rio Grande office of the U.S. Forest Service, has this to say: "Leroux's Pass as shown on Kern's map may not be as far off as one might imagine. This creek that turns off to the north at about the present site of Creede is Willow Creek. It is very rugged and stccp near the bottom or just above Creede and then tapers off to a gradual climb until the Continental Divide is reached. Opposite it on the other side of the Divide is Cochetopa Creek! . . . The descent down the Cochetopa Creek during the winter would be more practical than most any other drainage on that side of the Divide. Therefore, in my belief, it is not out of the question that Kern's map may be quite accurate on this point. . . . As to whether a wagon road ever went up Willow Creek and over the Divide, I don't know. . . . I do know, however, that it is possible to travel from Creede to the top of the Divide in a jeep." [13]

A later letter from Mark Ratliff, District Ranger, adds something more: "I had a chance of talking to Mr. S. B. Collins, about the last of the old timers that knew the Creede country. He came to Creede in 1898 as a mining engineer and surveyor.

---

[13] Letter from Ambrose Burkhart, Deadwood, South Dakota, March 26, 1952.

One of his first jobs was to go over, by snowshoes, onto the head of the Cochetopa Creek to survey a mining claim. He went via West Willow Creek. He said that there was then a well used wagon road over the pass at the head of this creek. He could not say whether it had been an Indian or traders' trail earlier or not. Since it is the first pass crossing the Continental Divide directly from the Rio Grande it would seem likely this was a used Indian and trader trail and could easily be the one referred to by Leroux." [14]

Carnero Pass, though, has entirely faded from the knowledge of men, so far as I can find out. These passes, Carnero and the Pass of the Rio del Norte, well known to traders and trappers a hundred years ago, fell into disuse when the mining boom in early Colorado brought a change in objective to the roads travelers followed.

The Hayden Surveys [15] in this area overlooked these two passes altogether, although one road mapped did touch on part of Carnero Pass, apparently by accident. The search then was not for a railroad pass leading to distant California but for a reasonably passable wagon-freight road to Howardsville and Silverton, locked across the Continental just beyond the extreme headwaters of the Rio Grande. Cochetopa Pass alone remained in use and is still in use today, so it was probably the best of them after all.

Frémont and Old Bill, leading the fourth expedition, did not have the unhampered freedom of selection among these passes that we have in studying them on a map. The problem for them was enormously complicated by the ferocity of the winter and the condition of the animals and the prospect of feed and protection for the animals. This point needs emphasizing for a proper understanding of the situation.

[14] Letter from Mark R. Ratliff, Del Norte, Colorado, April 28, 1952.
[15] F. V. Hayden, *Annual Reports of the Geological and Geographical Survey for the Years 1873, 74, and 75* (Washington: 1876, 77, 78).

After the first camp out in the open plain, the miserable and perilous sagebrush camp, the expedition swung over to the shelter of the timber along the Rio Grande. Once made, this forced detour, if such it was, may well have played a part in subsequent decisions.

When the cañon of the Rio Grande was reached the expedition, having turned to the river, was a day's march (up the open plain) below Carnero Creek, the entrance to either Carnero or Cochetopa Pass.

And there was, after all, another pass on up the cañon of the river, the Pass of the Rio del Norte or Williams Pass, called after Old Bill himself.

It is very hard to believe that Frémont would have preferred to investigate this steep and rugged pass as a site for a railroad route rather than the broad and level Cochetopa or the Carnero, unless he was swayed by important other factors. Some such factors may be suggested: the Pass of the Rio del Norte was shorter than either the Cochetopa or the Carnero, the approach to it up the river furnished the best chance at game, which they seriously needed, and the best protection and forage for the animals, and they were then closer to it.

There remains the remote possibility that Old Bill described an approach to the Carnero leading up from the cañon of the river and that it was this approach the expedition tried to find, a very unlikely possibility indeed.

The exact route of the expedition after turning off the Rio Grande probably led up the narrow cañon of West Alder Creek, past the present Round Park, on across the area of a feeder stream now known revealingly as Difficult Creek, and swung to the right up Long's Gulch, which brought them up against the flat-topped summit of Pool Table Mountain. They went around this and followed the extreme headwaters of Trujillo Creek (the highest fork of East Bellows Creek) to the ridge above its rincons and crossed this ridge to the head of

Wannamaker Creek. Wannamaker Creek would eventually have led into Carnero Pass.

There may conceivably have been a route up Alder Creek and across to Carnero Pass that was sometimes used by early traders. A crossing at this point above the Rio Grande is entirely feasible in summer and even in a mild winter not impossible. In the winter of 1950-51 a logging company taking out timber kept its operations going all winter, trucks running regularly all the way up to Pool Table Mountain, in the exact region where the fourth expedition struggled to the limit of its strength and skill to make two miles a day.

Another and easier approach to the same place on the dividing ridge would have been by way of a little creek east of Alder, passed when traveling up the Rio Grande five miles before Alder is reached, a creek named the Agua Ramon (pronounced Ah Ramon by the people who live around it today).

But there is slightly stronger reason still to suppose there may have been an occasional traders' crossing entering the mountains up Embargo Creek (today called Myers Creek), reached three miles before the Agua Ramon, and following up its eastern fork, now called Baughman Creek.

Oral tradition asserts this approach was used by early New Mexican traders and that Embargo Creek received its name as the result of a writ of attachment (embargo) served on a traveling Taos trader there in 1819.[16] Sheepherders today drive over the mountain from Embargo Creek to Carnero Creek in pickups or jeeps.

However, the ridge separating these two creeks is higher and more formidable than anything to be met in the actual passes of the Carnero or the Cochetopa, and the distance it would save as a short cut to either of those passes is unimpressive.

[16] From Antonio J. N. Valdez, Del Norte, Colorado.

But the strongest objection to any of these routes as a pass approach is not the crossing of the first ridge but the long and difficult mountain travel remaining after that crossing before any pass is reached.

In my own opinion, the expedition headed for the Pass of the Rio del Norte and Old Bill missed the way.

The fact remains, as pointed out in the text, that Frémont gave Old Bill an insurmountable assignment, insisting, over Old Bill's objections, on trying to cross the high mountains against this unusually severe winter rather than detouring south to skirt them.

Antoine Leroux appeared to believe otherwise, and told Senator Benton that if Frémont had kept up the "dry valley" it "would have taken him through easy." [17] Leroux was out for a time in the same winter guiding dragoons on an Indian foray from Taos; some stolen horses recovered by them from the Apaches were among the animals later turned over to Godey for his hurried relief expedition up the Rio Grande.[18]

On the way back to Taos Leroux took the small war party— fifty men—through the Sangre de Cristo Pass against heavy snow, which apparently prompted him to report to Benton: "It was the worst winter for snow, but we could travel all the time in the valleys and passes."

However, the troops in Leroux's charge were operating close to their base, with all the differences this would imply as to condition of animals, amount of necessary baggage, and concern for the future. Taos and home waited not far beyond their passage of the Sangre de Cristo, while the fourth expedition was midway in the vast distance from Westport to California.

Not only travel but survival itself was difficult for people

[17] Leroux statement in Benton letter, *op. cit.*
[18] Washington *National Intelligencer*, April 7, 1849, quoting an item from the Santa Fe *Republican*.

remote from towns or secure shelter in the winter of that year. Word from the Platte River in the spring said of the plight of the Plains Indians: "The snow is said to have been deeper, and the cold more intense, than it has ever been known by the oldest Indians in that quarter. The condition of many of the tribes is represented as miserable in the extreme. Many of them are subsisting entirely upon their horses, and numbers of them have perished from famine. . . . The winter has been so severe that all communication with the settlements was cut off." [19]

Old Bill's warning to swing south around the mountains indicates that he would have disagreed with Leroux's opinion.

Perhaps, too, Leroux slanted his opinion a trifle to oblige Senator Benton, who was pleading the safety and ease of these passes; his mention of the "dry valley," which was not dry, hints at that.

Finally, Frémont's fifth expedition in the winter of 1853-54, which went through the Cochetopa the quickest way and met a winter as mild as the other winter had been savage and still only got through at the cost of great loss and hardship, seems to clinch the point.

The fourth expedition could not have made it through the country ahead, no matter what the route.

Controversy about the blame for the fourth expedition disaster has developed two general theories, exactly opposed. One, resting principally on the Leroux letter and a story from John Scott, who reportedly told it to the old mountain man, Tom Biggs, who told it to the Army explorer J. H. Simpson (who had no love for Frémont), from whose journal Ned Kern extracted it, holds that Old Bill wanted to aim for the Cochetopa but that Frémont rejected it as bearing too far north and was lured instead by the apparent passage of the Rio Grande

[19] *Missouri Republican*, March 30, 1849.

gap, in spite of Old Bill's objection that "he could not by any possibility" go through there.[20]

This theory sees evidence that Old Bill was sent to the rear and replaced as guide by Godey in the incident of Godey going to the head of the column to lead the way over the sand hills— while Old Bill was gone with Frémont to examine Williams Pass in the Sangres.

To support the notion of a sudden change of guides, the theory assumes the expedition was heading straight for the gap of the Cochetopa before it turned suddenly to the river, and consequent failure.

The theory concludes with the notion that Frémont, when he found his way blocked in the cañon of the Rio Grande, attempted to cut blindly over the mountains on his right to Cochetopa Pass, rather than go back and around by way of the valley.

But in the first place Cochetopa Pass did not carry the expedition as far north as it had already been at the Pueblo and Hardscrabble. In any case Frémont, wanting a railroad pass, had no reason to rule out the Cochetopa because it was farther away across the valley. A railroad, as the Gunnison report stated, could run any direction in the valley with ease; a few miles farther up the valley could make no difference. It was the nature of the pass in the mountains that was important; there lay the real difficulties of railroad building. Frémont, together with Old Bill, could only have decided against the Cochetopa for urgent reasons similar to those suggested previously.

However, presuming Frémont totally disregarded the famous guide he had labored so persuasively to secure, this does not take into account the effect of such dictatorial behavior on Old Bill. Old Bill was the most independent man in the

[20] Extract from the Journal of Lt. J. H. Simpson, July 23, 1849 (Fort Sutter Papers, Huntington Library).

mountains. According to Ruxton it was his habit to pack up abruptly and leave a party for very little reason or none at all. His answer, if Frémont had sent him to the rear, would certainly have been to keep on going to the rear until he was back at the Pueblo.

It is opposite to everything we have been told of the man and his character to assume he would have continued to tag along with the expedition after being disgraced and put out of office.

He already considered their chances against the winter desperately small; he would assuredly not have kept on with the certain knowledge that Frémont was taking the wrong route and "could not by any possibility" go through.

To clear up a minor point: the expedition did not head straight for the Cochetopa after leaving the sand hills. According to Doc Kern's on-the-spot account, the Rio Grande was about seven miles south of them when they suddenly turned to it. By Doc Kern's and Dick Kern's estimates they had then traveled at least thirty miles across the valley, and thirty miles straight toward the Cochetopa from the region of the sand hills would have taken them clear up on Saguache Creek, at least four times as far north of the Rio Grande as they were. Their position when they turned to the river establishes that from the sand hills they had traveled rather directly for either the Rio Grande gap or Carnero Creek, some ten miles north of it.

As for Frémont trying a short cut across the mountains after finding the way ahead blocked in the Rio Grande cañon, he was not blocked at the point where he turned off. The cañon ahead appears easy, as far as can be seen from there. There was no reason to turn off the cañon at that point because of its difficulty, nor for a number of miles ahead.

Finally, the essence of this theory is demolished by the letter from Ned Kern written immediately after the event, stating that Old Bill said he was leading the way into a known pass; [21] by Old Bill's efforts to find a way ahead from the top of the snow-swept ridge; and by the choice of Old Bill as pilot of the relief party, all confirming that he remained the guide of the expedition to the last.

This theory, built on misunderstood hearsay and political elaboration, has achieved long and vigorous life because of the apparently strong evidence of the Leroux letter and because most of the investigation of the incident has been carried out without a sufficient knowledge of the geography of the country, many authorities presuming there was indeed only one pass westward, the Cochetopa.

The opposing theory has been based mainly on assertions by Senator Benton, bulwarked by the Godey letter previously cited and, ironically enough, by a remark in Leroux's statement to Senator Benton.

According to this theory, Frémont wanted to go to the gap of the Cochetopa but old Bill obstinately led him into the Rio Grande cañon instead.

This picture is too ridiculous for discussion.

The origin of this theory is clear enough. It is only an extension of Frémont's own emphatic statement that the guide lost his way.

But Frémont's statement omitted any mention of his own insistence on the general direction of the route, over Old Bill's warning, or his own participation in the decisions that must have preceded the final turning, when the guide did lose his way.

Robert Louis Stevenson remarked that "the cruelest lies are often told in silence."

[21] Letter from Kern to Antoine Robidoux, February 11, 1849, quoted in Nevins, *op. cit.*

Credit Notes

The titles of references are given in full in the case of those items not listed in the following bibliography.

CHAPTER 1

The Frémont quotations are from his Memoirs and Reports.

p. 6: The California emigrants of 1837 are named by Antoine Leroux in his statement included in Benton's Letter to the People of Missouri, 1853. Joel Walker and his family, traveling for Oregon three years later, are more often cited as the first genuine overland emigrants to the far West—as in W. J. Ghent, *The Early Far West*, New York: 1931; and Bernard De Voto, *Across the Wide Missouri*, Boston: 1947.

CHAPTER 2

pp. 15-16: Correspondence between Benton and Col. J. J. Abert, Chief of the Bureau of Topographical Engineers, concerning the objectives of the first expedition, is in the Frémont Collection, the Southwest Museum, Los Angeles. Also see an article by Jessie Benton Frémont entitled "The Origin of the Frémont Explorations," in *Century Magazine*, Vol. XLI, 1890-91.

p. 18 ff.: Colonel Waugh's journal, edited by John Francis Mc-Dermott, is published in the Missouri Historical Society Bulletin, Vol. 6, 1949-50.

p. 20 ff.: The quotation from the Washington *Daily Union* is reprinted in Phillips, *Jessie Benton Frémont*.

p. 22: The George Bancroft statement rests on the authority of a letter from Bancroft to Frémont, September 3, 1886, now in the Bancroft Library, Berkeley, quoted in Nevins, *Frémont, Pathmarker of the West*; and in Phillips, *op. cit.*

p. 23: The nickname "Gassy Bob" is found (spelled "Gasey Bob") in letters from William Rich Hutton, published by the Huntington

Library under the title of *Glances at California 1847-1853,* San Marino, California: 1942.

p. 23: For a description of the California Battalion and Frémont in camp: William D. Phelps, *Fore and Aft, or Leaves from the Life of an Old Sailor,* by "Webfoot," Boston: 1871.

p. 23: Stockton's remark about seizing the crown is from an undated newspaper clipping in a collection catalogued as the Mexican War from *Contemporary Newspapers,* Huntington Library.

p. 23 ff.: Jessie's letter of congratulations is quoted in Phillips and Nevins, *op. cit.* The letter is now among the Frémont papers in the Bancroft Library.

p. 25 ff.: Events concerned with the court-martial are discussed and documented in some detail in the separate Note on the Trial. *The Proceedings of the Court Martial* in conjunction with *Frémont's Defence* provide some of the best source material extant on Frémont's part in the California Conquest. Also see John Bidwell, "Frémont in the Conquest of California," *Century Magazine,* and J. C. Frémont, "The Conquest of California," *Century Magazine,* both Vol. XLI, 1890-91; and Edwin Bryant, *What I Saw in California,* Philadelphia: 1848 (republished Santa Ana, California: 1936).

p. 28: Frémont's note on Kearny's behavior is in the Frémont Collection, the Southwest Museum.

pp. 29-30: The newspaper interview with Stockton is from the miscellaneous collection of Mexican War newspaper clippings, *op. cit.,* in the Huntington Library. The item, from the Washington correspondent of the Charleston *Evening News,* is undated.

CHAPTER 3

p. 32 ff.: The quotations are from the Appendix of *Proceedings of the Court Martial,* Washington: 1848.

pp. 33-34: Congressional tributes: *Colonel Frémont's California Operations,* Pamphlet, ca. 1856.

pp. 34-35: Jessie's remark is found in the Frémont MS Miscellany, the Bancroft Library.

p. 36 ff.: Frémont description of Preuss is from his Memoirs. Jessie's remarks on Mrs. Preuss are quoted in Phillips, *op. cit.* Preuss' own quotations are from his journal, included in the report of the first expedition, published as part of *The Exploring Expedition to the Rocky Mountains, etc.,* New York: 1855.

p. 39: Benton's reference to Frémont's "children of the mountains" is made in his "Speech in the Senate," February 7, 1849.

p. 40: Godey's statement that he could work his way where there was grass enough to cover a snake is from William D. Phelps, *op. cit.*

p. 40: Frémont's description of him is from the Memoirs. A good sketch of Godey's character appears in H. A. Spindt, Notes on the *Life of Edward M. Kern,* Kern County Historical Society, Bakersfield, California: 1939.

p. 45: The best authority for the personnel of the California Battalion is now an article by Fred B. Rogers entitled "Roster of California Volunteers in the Service of the U. S., 1846-47," in the annual publication for 1950 of the Society of California Pioneers. Corrections and additions appear in the annual publication for 1951. In this roster Vincenthaler is listed as a sergeant.

p. 46: Ferguson and Marion Wise appear in Rogers, *op. cit.;* in H. H. Bancroft, *History of California,* Vol. V; in the records of Fort Sutter (*New Helvetia Diary,* San Francisco: 1939); and in the *Proceedings of the Court Martial.* They were two of three Frémont men to volunteer for the attack on Sonoma. Ferguson then joined the fourth expedition and a Wise also appears as a member of the fourth expedition, but his name in all accounts is Henry J. Wise. Bancroft assumed this Wise and the Marion Wise of the previous expedition were the same man. It is possible, but the difference in names appears to be explicit and well attested. The St. Louis *Reveille* couples Henry J. Wise with the young gentleman Andrews, as "well known citizens of this place" (in an item reprinted in the Georgetown (D. C.) *Advocate,* May 8, 1849).

p. 46: The *Missouri Republican,* March 25, 1849, speaks of Preuss' assistant, undoubtedly meaning Creutzfeldt.

pp. 46-47: Facts on King and Rohrer are from the Georgetown *Advocate,* April 19 and May 8, 1849. The further adventures of James King of William are found in Bancroft, *op. cit.*

pp. 49-50: For Benton's views on a transcontinental road see his *Letter to the People of Missouri,* 1853; "Discourse before the Maryland Institute," 1854; and "Speech in the Senate," February 7, 1849. The quotations here are from the latter.

pp. 50-51: The stirring Benton remarks here are from his "Speech in the House of Representatives," January 16, 1855, quoted in C. W. Dana, *The Great West or the Garden of the World,* Boston: 1861; and from the *Letter to the People of Missouri, op. cit.*

p. 52: For early discussion of a transcontinental railroad, see Dellenbaugh, *Frémont and '49;* and Dorothy Jennings, *The Pacific Railroad Company,* Missouri Historical Society Collections, Vol. VI, 1928-31.

p. 53: Jessie writes of her decision in notes in the Frémont MS Miscellany, Bancroft Library.

CHAPTER 4

p. 54: Identification of Ned Kern in the Leutze painting is established in Helen Wolfe, Notes on the Kern family, Huntington Library. Information on the Kern family is chiefly from the same source.
Ned Kern's biography has been rather briefly written by Spindt, *op. cit.;* and by W. J. Heffernan in *Edward M. Kern,* fifteenth annual publication of the Kern County Historical Society, Bakersfield, California: 1953.

p. 55: The remark attributed to Godey is from a letter purportedly signed by him, published in the New York *Evening Post,* October 30, 1856; quoted in Nevins.

p. 55: Ned's remark on the family luck is from his Letter to Mary, Taos, February 1849, Huntington Library.

p. 56: Dick Kern's discussion of business is from a letter to Ned, February 10, 1847, Huntington Library.

p. 57: A copy of Frémont's letter to Ned authorizing his appointment as artist for the third expedition, dated Washington, May 1, 1845, is in the Huntington Library. The letter established Ned's rate of pay as three dollars per diem.

p. 58: Ned's selection from among forty-two artist applicants is mentioned in a letter from Dick to J. R. Bartlett, March 14, 1851, Fort Sutter Papers.

p. 58: The Edward Fitzgerald Beale story is quoted in Frémont's Memoirs.

p. 60: The sociable and various other items of the third expedition are drawn from Thomas S. Martin, "Narrative," Bancroft Library.

p. 60: The example of California horsemanship is described in *Los Gringos,* New York: 1850, by Lt. Wise, USN.

p. 61: The California Battalion was described by Wise, *op. cit.;* by Lt. the Hon. Fred. Walpole, RN, in *Four Years in the Pacific,* London: 1849; and by Rev. Walter Colton, USN, in *Deck and Port,* New York: 1850.

p. 61: Frémont's orders to Ned: from a letter of July 12, 1846, Huntington Library.

pp. 61-62: Ned's letter to Dick: July 27, 1846, Huntington Library.

pp. 62-63: McKinstry letter to Ned: December 23, 1851; Sutter letter to Dick Kern: January 10, 1852; Ned's judgment of Hastings in his letter to Dick of July 27, 1846; Ned's letter on the Donner disaster, to an unknown addressee, 1847; all in Huntington Library.

p. 63: McKinstry's jokes were in a letter to Ned of March 4, 1847, now in the Fort Sutter Papers. Ned discussed the revolutionists in his letter to Dick, July 27, 1846, *op. cit.*

p. 68: Sutter's evaluation of California is from his letter to Dick Kern, January 10, 1852, *op. cit.*

p. 69: The quoted statement on pay is from the Thomas S. Martin "Narrative." A notion of the going wage scale for packers is drawn from Frémont's contract with Honoré Ayot, an engagé on the first expedition. The contract is in the Frémont Collection, Southwest Museum. Kit Carson's salary is to be found in his biography, *Kit Carson Days*, by Edwin L. Sabin, Chicago: 1914.

p. 70: Benton, "Speech," February 7, 1849, *op. cit.* Benton, letter to Frémont, October 8, 1847, Frémont Collection, Southwest Museum.

p. 70: The three backers are identified in the Frémont MS Miscellany, Bancroft Library; and in Dellenbaugh, *op. cit.*

p. 71: The Grimsley advertisement is from Vol. I of the *Western Journal*, a magazine, St. Louis: 1848.

p. 72: Carson statement on Frémont: Kit Carson, *Autobiography* (edited by Milo M. Quaife), Chicago: 1935.

p. 74: The Benton letter to the people of California is quoted at length in Wm. M. Meigs, *Life of Thomas Hart Benton*, Philadelphia: 1904.

p. 75: The President's remarks are from *James K. Polk, Diaries* (Vols. 3 and 4) (edited by Milo M. Quaife), Chicago: 1910. The letter discussing Frémont's popularity in California is from Wm. Rich Hutton, *Glances at California, op. cit.*

p. 76: Ducatel is identified in the Georgetown *Advocate*, April 19, 1849. The obituary of Henry King in the same newspaper is the source for the information on his marriage.

CHAPTER 5

p. 77: The Hawken pedigree is given in Charles Winthrop Sawyer, *Our Rifles*, Boston: 1941. Henry Hawkins (pronounced Hawken, and by his sons so spelled), formerly in the Harpers Ferry Armory, began business in St. Louis in 1808. Samuel T. Hawken, a son, worked in St. Louis from 1822 to 1860, and later worked in Independence, Iowa, and Denver, Colorado. The most celebrated son, Jacob Hawken, worked in St. Louis from 1820 until his death May 9, 1849, at the age of sixty-four.

p. 78: Thomas S. Martin, in his "Narrative," *op. cit.*, says that thirty-seven "of the company" returned across the plains with Frémont after the third expedition, but Kearny's order of August 22, 1847, at Fort Leavenworth, given in *Proceedings of the Court Martial,* gives the number as nineteen,

p. 79: Rogers, *op. cit.*, lists a Joseph Bacon in the California Battalion; the "Billy Bacon" of the Thomas S. Martin "Narrative" may have been an alliterative nickname, although it is also given as Wm. Bacon in the *Missouri Republican.*

p. 79: Bancroft names a Hubbard as a member of the third expedition, but the name is not on the Rogers California Battalion roster. There is no complete list of the personnel of the third expedition, and Bancroft tended to take too literally the remark in the Thomas S. Martin "Narrative" that the fourth expedition "was composed almost entirely of our old men." Thus Bancroft deduced that Preuss was along on the third expedition, which was not the case. However, the Rogers list of the California Battalion personnel is not complete either.

The St. Louis newspapers name Beadle or "Bedell" and Bacon as residents of St. Louis County, and place Hubbard from Milwaukee and Carver from Chicago. The Thomas S. Martin "Narrative" mentions that Hubbard is from Iowa. The generally western border region these men came from, coupled with the Martin remark about the preponderance of old men, can at least be taken as hints that they had previous experience, probably with the third expedition.

p. 79: The California Conquest activities of Stepp, doubtlessly for Stepperfeldt (the first names are the same, also), are drawn from Frémont's Memoirs.

p. 79: John Scott is on the Rogers California Battalion roster; Bancroft speaks of him being a "hunter in Copay County," California, before the third expedition arrived. The *Missouri Republican,* March 25, 1849, says he is a native of England.

p. 80: Frémont, writing to Jessie from Taos, February 6, 1849 (published in the *Missouri Republican* April 24, 1849), states that Jessie knew Manuel, the Cosumne Indian, but implies that she did not know his two countrymen, Joaquin and Gregorio. Otherwise it might be supposed these were the two California Indian boys of the same name who returned with Frémont from the second expedition. In the letter above, Frémont identifies Joaquin and Gregorio as Cosumne Indians, but in his manuscript notes (among the Frémont MS Miscellany in the Bancroft Library) he lists them as Tulare Indians.

p. 80: Saunders' problem is mentioned by Jessie in the Frémont MS Miscellany, Brancroft Library.

p. 81: François des Montaignes, "The Plains . . . Memoranda . . . taken during the Expedition of Exploration in the year 1845 . . ." published in *Western Journal and Civilian*, Vols. VIII and IX, 1852-53: St. Louis. Henry R. Wagner, in the bibliography of *The Plains and the Rockies*, identifies François des Montaignes as Isaac Cooper.

p. 83: Information on Captain Cathcart is from Porter and Hafen, *Ruxton of the Rockies*, Norman, Oklahoma: 1950; from the War Office, England; from Sir James Ferguson, Bart., Keeper of the Records of Scotland; and from David Cathcart-Walker-Heneage, Killochan, Ayrshire. The 11th Hussars, during Cathcart's service with the regiment, was under the command of the fantastic marti-net Lord Cardigan. An excellent picture of the regiment and the epoch is given in Cecil Woodham-Smith, *The Reason Why*, London: 1953.

p. 83: Dick Kern's sketch of Cathcart is in his Diary.

p. 84: The Frémont note on the roster of the party is among the papers in the Frémont MS Miscellany, Bancroft Library.

p. 84: St. Louis *Reveille*, September 29, 1848.

p. 85: Jessie's remarks on the death of the baby are from the MS Miscellany, Bancroft Library.

p. 86: The location of Westport is from Darrel Garwood, *Crossroads of America, The Story of Kansas City*, New York: 1948.

p. 86: Francis Parkman, *The California and Oregon Trail*, New York: 1849.

p. 92: Jessie relates Frémont's farewell in the MS Miscellany, Bancroft Library.

CHAPTER 6

Accounts of the expedition are, in approximate order of useful-ness and dependability, the Kern Diaries; letters and newspaper accounts; the McGehee "Narrative"; the Frémont MS Miscellany, Bancroft Library; the Thomas S. Martin "Narrative"; the Breckenridge "Narrative."

The R. H. Kern Diary has been published in *When Old Trails Were New*, by Blanche C. Grant, New York: 1934.

p. 96: Frémont's ride through a forest fire is mentioned in the story of the fifth expedition: S. N. Carvalho, *Incidents of Travel and Adventure in the Far West*, New York: 1860.

pp. 98-99: Frémont describes the route to the mountains and details of the march in a letter written from Bent's Fort, November 17, 1848, published in the *Missouri Republican*, March 7, 1849.

p. 102: Clark Wissler, in *The American Indian*, New York: 1922, notes that among some buffalo-Indian tribes a taboo was observed against edible fish.

p. 109 ff.: Fitzpatrick the Indian agent is drawn in excellent proportion and perspective in his biography, *Broken Hand*, by LeRoy R. Hafen and W. J. Ghent, Denver: 1931.

p. 111: Old Bill Williams on the Kiowa language: Albert Pike, *Prose Sketches and Poems*, Boston: 1834.

p. 112: Carvalho, *op. cit.*, testifies to cottonwoods eighteen feet in circumference at Big Timbers.

pp. 113-114: The Fitzpatrick letter is published in the *Missouri Republican*, March 7, 1849.

p. 114: Railroad distance to Bent's Fort is from N. H. Darton, et al., *Guidebook of the Western United States*, "Part C, the Santa Fe Route," U. S. Geological Survey, Department of the Interior, Washington: 1915. One of the many useful surveys of the Santa Fe Trail is Kenyon Riddle, *Records and Maps of the Old Santa Fe Trail*, Raton, New Mexico: 1949.

p. 115: Frémont's quotation is from his letter from Bent's Fort, November 17, 1848, *op. cit.*

CHAPTER 7

pp. 117-118: The Frémont quotations are from his letter from Bent's Fort, November 17, 1848, *op. cit.*

p. 119: The same letter above is published in a more complete version in John Bigelow, *Memoir of the Life and Public Services of John Charles Frémont*, New York: 1856, the source of Frémont's remark about never crossing the continent again.

p. 121: Hatcher's warning is in an Extract from the Journal of J. H. Simpson, July 23, 1849, in the hand of Ned Kern, Fort Sutter Papers.

p. 122: Extracts of L. P. Lupton's letter, dated Pueblo, November 28, 1848, were published in the *Missouri Republican*, March 7, 1849.

p. 123: The journal keepers were: Frémont himself, who of course always did so; Doc and Dick Kern—Ned Kern had let his slide; Old Bill, whose notebook is later mentioned by McGehee; King, whose journal is mentioned in a newspaper account of his death; and Cathcart, whose journal may have been the best of all—

Dick Kern later wrote him asking for additional facts from it. Of these only the two Kern brothers' Diaries exist today.

Also, Preuss was in the custom of keeping a journal, and probably McGehee at least made notes for use later on in his "Narrative." It would be surprising if among the other "gentlemen" such as Ducatel and Andrews journals or notes were not kept. Creutzfeldt, a scientific man, would have kept notes, and possibly a journal.

Leaders frequently discouraged formal journalizing; at the start of the third expedition, according to François des Montaignes, Frémont told his men to leave that occupation solely up to him.

CHAPTER 8

The best biography of Old Bill Williams so far is Alpheus H. Favour's. Ruxton remains a most important source. The mountain men of the Southwest are discussed in *This Reckless Breed of Men,* by Robert Glass Cleland, New York: 1950.

p. 133: Jim Higgins' killing of Big Jim Lawrence is described in Sabin, *op. cit.*

p. 133: Walker's plunge is from Thomas J. Beall, "Recollections of Wm Craig," Lewiston, Idaho, *Tribune,* March 3, 1919, quoted in Favour.

p. 134: Sir William George Drummond Stewart, *Altowan,* 2 vols., New York: 1846.

p. 135: David Brown's description of Old Bill is from "Colorado Mountain Men," by LeRoy R. Hafen, *Colorado Magazine,* Vol. XXX, No. 1, 1953.

p. 136: The story of the lone elk is told in *"Uncle Dick" Wootton,* by Howard Louis Conard, Chicago: 1890. Jessie's remarks are from the MS Miscellany, Bancroft Library.

p. 141: The quotation is Wootton's, from Conard, *op. cit.*

p. 143: Old Bill's hesitating consent is noted in McGehee.

p. 143: The oral tradition in the country is from Antonio J. N. Valdez, Del Norte, Colorado.

CHAPTER 9

p. 147: Horses are mentioned in the Lupton letter, *op. cit.,* and in the highly inaccurate reminiscences of Wootton, in Conard, *op. cit.*

p. 149: The Beale-Heap expedition, made up principally of Washington greenhorns, made the summer crossing in five days, while the Gunnison expedition made a leisurely and exploratory crossing with wagons in some three weeks. See A Note on the Trails.

p. 151: The Fitzpatrick letter from the *Missouri Republican,* March 7, 1849, says he has talked to these two men who wished to go along with the expedition but were not accepted. One of these men may have been the mountain man Dick Wootton. Breckenridge reports that Wootton joined the expedition briefly but had the good sense to drop out when he saw the wintered-in country ahead from the top of the Wets. But both the Fitzpatrick and Lupton letters, written at the time, say the two would-be volunteers were not accepted and left the expedition while it was five or six miles short of the summit of the Wets.

p. 165: The description of making a winter astronomical observation is from Carvalho, *op. cit.*

p. 168: Carvalho alleges deliberate attempts by packers to lose technical equipment.

p. 171: The emotional follower is Carvalho.

CHAPTER 10

p. 175 ff.: The Collins letter is from Benjamin M. Read, "Perils of the Santa Fe Trail in its Early Days," published in *El Palacio,* Vol. XIX, Santa Fe, New Mexico, November 15, 1925; also printed in E. W. Gilbert, *The Exploration of Western America, 1800-1850,* Cambridge University: 1930.

p. 176: The Benton quotation is from his letter to the *National Intelligencer,* September 6, 1853, quoted in Nevins.

p. 180: The Benjamin D. Wilson reminiscence is from his "Narrative," published as an Appendix in Robert Glass Cleland, *Pathfinders,* Los Angeles: 1929.

p. 185: Ned Kern letter to Robidoux, Taos, February 11, 1849; quoted from Nevins.

CHAPTER 11

p. 187: Horace Kephart, *Camping and Woodcraft,* New York: 1921.

pp. 187-188: The tale of the wagered hat concerns Kit Carson, and is from Sabin, *op. cit.*

p. 188 ff.: The problem of trails is discussed and documented with more detail in A Note on the Trails.

CHAPTER 12

Frémont's story of the disaster, frequently referred to here, is contained in a letter to Jessie, written from Taos, January 27 to February 11, 1849. The letter was published in the *Missouri Republican*, April 22 and April 24, 1849, in large part, and further extracts were printed in Bigelow, *op. cit.*

p. 218: Leroux lost his way guiding Gunnison: see A Note on the Trails.

p. 220: Ned Beale's letter is from Stephen Bonsal, *Edward Fitzgerald Beale*, New York: 1912. The further record of Beale's trip is from a newspaper account quoted in Bonsal under a mistaken date.

p. 226: Relics of the expedition are described in U. S. Forest Service Memoranda, and by local report.

A trip to one of the campsites under the guidance of Albert Pfeiffer is described by Frank C. Spencer in *Colorado Magazine*, Vol. VI, No. 4, 1929. On this trip, some fifty years after he had first stumbled on one of the camps, Pfeiffer could not find the Christmas camp. Two years later a sheepherder, Epimenio Romero, led the District Forest Ranger to the place of the Christmas camp.

There has been some local debate over the mule bones at the Wannamaker Camp, exponents of a skeptical school maintaining that bones could not have lasted there that long—for more than a hundred years. A jawbone was taken to paleontologist William Otto, of the California Institute of Technology, who identified it as from a mule or small horse and estimated its age as very considerable—quite easily a hundred years or more.

CHAPTER 13

p. 242: The quotation from King's journal was published in the Georgetown *Advocate*, May 8, 1849, reprinted from the St. Louis *Reveille*.

p. 246: Ned Kern's letter to Mary, February 10, 1849, "We all arrived on the River on the 14th glad to get there with our bedding and arms."

The Kern party's equipment and scientific collections and papers must have been cached at either the Seven Mile Camp or the Cottonwoods, one mile below. There is probably no connection, but three rock cairns are at the site of the Seven Mile Camp at the present time. However, doubtless everything cached was soon found and removed by the Indians. It is quite possible that Old Bill Williams and Doc Kern are buried near the site of the cache.

p. 246: Important testimony for the Kern side of the quarrel with Vincenthaler is the behavior of Taplin in choosing to travel down the river with the Kerns. Later, although singled out, with Godey and King, for exceptional praise by Frémont, Taplin did not go on with the expedition to California, but returned to St. Louis. Georgetown *Advocate,* May 8, 1849, *op. cit.*

p. 248: Jessie's story about the Ute chief is from the Frémont MS Miscellany, Bancroft Library.

p. 249: The Ute verses about "the American general lost in the snow" were once heard by Antonio J. N. Valdez, Del Norte, Colorado.

p. 251: Frémont's libel of the courage of his men is from his letter to Jessie, January-February 1849, *op. cit.,* but this statement is not included in the extracts published in the *Missouri Republican.* There, this statement appears as, "The courage of some of the men began to fail." The fuller statement is included in the letter as published in Bigelow's campaign biography.

p. 252: Frémont's summing up of the achievement of the fourth expedition is from a letter to Jacob R. Snyder, December 11, 1849, printed in Bigelow.

p. 254: The first reports of the disaster were: the *Missouri Republican,* March 25, 1849, reprinting the news from the Independence *Expositor,* March 20, 1849, which in turn reprinted the item from the Santa Fe *Republican* of February 2, 1849. Cannibalism is also mentioned in the interview with Taplin reprinted in the Georgetown *Advocate* of May 8, 1849. Benton's version of the cannibalism story is in his *Thirty Years' View.*

p. 256: The report that Frémont himself was leading the relief party is quoted from the *Missouri Republican* of March 25, 1849. The item states that Col. Frémont deserved "great credit in the whole affair . . ." for "his perseverance and humane gallantry in persisting to return in person to the succor of his companions in misery. . . ."

CHAPTER 14

p. 263: *The West of Alfred Jacob Miller,* Norman, Oklahoma: 1951, includes a story that Miller put down in 1837, about Joe Walker: an Indian war party, making peace after a losing fight, invited Joe to a feast, neglecting to tell him it had been wittingly prepared from some of his men killed in the foregoing hostilities. Miller felt it necessary to add the following note: "It must not be inferred from this that the American Indians are essentially cannibals. Their purpose was revenge, which they would have had at any cost."

p. 263: Emory is quoted from Lt. W. H. Emory, *Notes of a Military Reconnaissance, 1846,* House Exec. Doc. No. 41, Sen. Doc. No. 7, 30th Congress, 1st Session.

p. 268: Jessie's Italian-brigand thesis is expounded in the Frémont MS Miscellany, Bancroft Library.

p. 269: The five days in camp stated in Dick Kern's Diary fit with the timetable in Frémont's letter to Jessie, January-February 1849.

p. 269: Godey's discovery of the bodies of Morin and Tabeau, and other details of the rescue are from letters of the Kerns, Huntington Library.

POSTSCRIPT

p. 271: The Kerns' loan from Cathcart is mentioned in a letter from Dick Kern to Cathcart, Taos, September 30, 1849, Huntington Library.

p. 271: Stepperfeldt's temporary insanity: *ibid.*

p. 272: Investigation of the death of Doc Kern and Old Bill is recounted in letters to the Kerns from Army authorities in New Mexico; Fort Sutter Papers. Also see "The Journal of John Greiner," *Old Santa Fe,* No. 10, April 1916.

James S. Calhoun, in his *Official Correspondence while Indian Agent at Santa Fe,* says that "messages from the Utahs" state that the "Fremont property was parcelled out to those who found it, and that most of it has been consumed, and that the residue has changed hands so frequently that no human power can gather it into one parcel again—and that the murders, with which they are charged, was subsequent to the murders which *they* charge upon Lt. Whittlesey, and thus, they balance that account current." This has been taken to be a clear confession of guilt as to the murders; but reading it as a bit of diplomacy—the Ute messages were meant to preface peace talks—one is not so certain.

An article in *The Arizona Miner,* Prescott, Arizona, August 20, 1870, entitled "How Bill Williams was Killed," prominently cited by Favour, contains a number of points that seem to me questionable, particularly when compared with contemporary reports of the Army investigation of the deaths, referred to above.

p. 274: Frémont quote: letter to J. R. Snyder, *op. cit.* Jessie's remarks are from the MS Miscellany, Bancroft Library.

p. 275: The rumor of Frémont negotiating to buy the Rancho Santa Ana del Chino is also mentioned in Wm. Rich Hutton, *op. cit.*

p. 275: The fifth expedition: Carvalho, *op. cit.*

p. 276: Jessie's letter is in the Frémont Collection, Southwest Museum.

Bibliography

The following list specifies a few of the more important materials studied in the preparation of this book.

The standard bibliography covering the field in general is Henry R. Wagner, *The Plains and the Rockies* (San Francisco: 1921), revised by Charles L. Camp (San Francisco: 1937).

A useful survey dealing with exploration is found in Frederick S. Dellenbaugh, *Travellers and Explorers 1846-1900* (New York: 1921).

MANUSCRIPTS

Fort Sutter Papers

MSS numbering 161; 7 maps. 40 vols. Containing letters and papers chiefly pertaining to the activities of the Kern brothers in the West. Huntington Library, San Marino, California.

Frémont MS Miscellany

Including notes by Jessie Benton Frémont for the second (unpublished) volume of the Frémont Memoirs, and notes by Frémont on the fourth expedition. The Bancroft Library, Berkeley, California.

Frémont Collection

Containing letters, notes, and other material by Frémont, Jessie Benton Frémont, and Senator Benton. The Southwest Museum, Los Angeles.

Kern, Benjamin J. Diary, October 20, 1848, to January 6, 1849, of his trip with Frémont's fourth expedition. Huntington Library.

Kern, Benjamin J. Letter to Joe, February 20, 1849. Huntington Library.

Kern, Edward M. Diary, October 8, 1848, to November 11, 1848, of first part of Frémont's fourth expedition. In two copies. Huntington Library.

—— Letters. Huntington Library.

Kern, Richard H. Diary, October 20, 1848, to February 16, 1849, of his trip with Frémont's fourth expedition. Huntington Library.

—— Letters. Huntington Library.

Kern, John. Letter to Richard and Edward Kern, May 30-31, 1850. Huntington Library.

Martin, Thomas S. "Narrative of John C. Fremont's Expedn to California in 1845-6 and subsequent events in Cal. down to 1853 including Fremont's Exploring Expedition of 1848." Dictated to E. F. Murray for H. H. Bancroft, 1878. Bancroft Library.

Simpson, J. H. Letters. Huntington Library.

U.S. Forest Service. Memoranda, notes, and letters concerning the route of the fourth expedition. Copies in the possession of the author.

Wolfe, Helen. Notes on the Kern family prepared from data collected over a period of years. Huntington Library.

PERIODICALS

Breckenridge, Thomas E. "The Story of a Famous Expedition," as told to J. W. Freeman and Chas. W. Watson, *Cosmopolitan Magazine*, August, 1896.

Georgetown (D. C.) *Advocate*, April 19, 1849; May 8, 1849.

Missouri Republican, March 7, 25, and 30, 1849; April 19, 22, and 24, 1849; November 23, 1849.

St. Louis *Daily Reveille*, June 3, 1845; September 4 and 29, 1848; October 4, 1848.

McGehee, Micajah. "Rough Times in Rough Places," *Century Magazine,* Vol. XLI (March 1891).

—— "Frémont's Fourth Expedition," compiled from the Narrative of Micajah McGehee by James Stewart McGehee, *Outdoor Life,* May 1910.

PRINTED DOCUMENTS AND BOOKS

Bancroft, Hubert Howe. Works. 39 vols. San Francisco: 1882-91.

Benton, Thomas H. *Thirty Years' View.* 2 vols. New York: 1879.

—— *Letter to the People of Missouri.* Washington: 1853.

—— "Discourse before the Maryland Institute, on the physical geography of the country between Missouri and California, etc." Delivered at Baltimore, December 4, 1854.

—— "Speech in the Senate, on the introduction of a Bill to provide for the location and construction of a Central National Road from the Pacific Ocean to the Mississippi River, etc." February 7, 1849. *Congressional Globe,* 30th Congress, 2d Session.

Calhoun, James S. *Official Correspondence while Indian Agent at Santa Fe, etc.* With maps (including the Parke-Kern map of the Territory of New Mexico 1851). Annie Heloise Abel, ed. Washington: 1915.

Dearborn, William L. *Description of a Railroad Route from St. Louis to San Francisco; letters to P. P. F. Degrand from W. L. Dearborn, 1849.* With map. Compiled from the Notes and Profiles of Col. Frémont. Boston: 1850.

Dellenbaugh, Frederick S. *Frémont and '49.* New York: 1914.

Favour, Alpheus H. *Old Bill Williams.* Chapel Hill, N. C.: 1936.

Frémont, John Charles. *Memoirs of My Life,* Vol. 1. Chicago and New York: 1887.

Frémont, John Charles. *Geographical Memoir upon Upper California, etc.* With map. Washington: 1848.

—— *Geographical Memoir upon Upper California, etc. To Which are now added, extracts from Hakluyt's Collection of Voyages, etc. etc., Hasting's Guide, Farnham, Colton, President's Message of December 5, 1848, Larkin, etc. etc.* Philadelphia: William McCarty: 1849.

—— *Defence of Lieut. Col. J. C. Frémont before the Military Court Martial, Washington, January, 1848.*

—— *The Exploring Expedition to the Rocky Mountains, Oregon and California, etc.* New York: 1855.

—— *Col. Frémont's California Operations. Facts for the People. Opinions expressed by Senators and Representatives in Congress, etc.* Pamphlet, *ca.* 1856.

Garrard, Lewis H. *Wah-To-Yah and the Taos Trail or Prairie Travel and Scalp Dances, etc.* Cincinnati: 1850.

Heap, Gwinn Harris. *Central Route to the Pacific, etc.* Philadelphia: 1854.

Kern, Edward M. "Journal of an Exploration of the Mary's or Humboldt River, Carson Lake, and Owens River, in 1845." Appendix Q of J. H. Simpson's *Report of Explorations across the Great Basin, etc., in 1859.* Washington: 1876.

Macomb, Captain J. N. *Report of the Exploring Expedition from Santa Fe, New Mexico, to the Junction of the Grand and Green Rivers of the Great Colorado of the West, in 1859.* Accompanied by Map of New Mexico, and adjacent parts of Colorado, Utah, and Arizona. Washington: 1876.

Nevins, Allan. *Frémont, Pathmarker of the West* (New ed. of *Frémont, the West's Greatest Adventurer,* 2 vols., 1928). New York: 1939.

Phillips, Catherine Coffin. *Jessie Benton Frémont.* San Francisco: 1935.

Proceedings of the Court Martial in the Trial of Lt. Col. Fré-mont. Senate Exec. Doc. No. 33, 30th Congress, 1st Session. April 7, 1848.

Ruxton, George Frederick Augustus. *Adventures in Mexico and the Rocky Mountains.* London: 1847.

—— "Life in the Far West," *Blackwood's Magazine,* Edinburgh, 1848. Republished, LeRoy R. Hafen, ed. Norman, Okla.: 1951.

U.S. Engineer Department. *Annual Report upon Explorations and Surveys in the Department of Missouri.* Washington: 1878.

—— "Map of the Territory of the United States from the Mississipi River to the Pacific Ocean." Prepared for the Railroad Surveys. Drawn by Lt. G. K. Warren. 1868.

U.S. Superintendent of Documents. *Reports of Explorations Printed in the Documents of the United States Government.* Washington: 1899.

U.S. War Department. *Reports of Explorations and Surveys to ascertain the most practicable and economical route for a railroad between the Mississippi River and the Pacific, etc.* 12 vols. Washington: 1855-61.

Index